the
last
year
of my
life

the last year of my life

*Ten leadership tools that transformed
a deadly diagnosis
into a path of renewal*

By Eeki Elner and Joshua T. Adams

Micro Publishing Media
Stockbridge, Massachusetts, 01262

The Last Year of My Life
Copyright © 2023 by Eeki Elner

Printed in the United States of America

First Printing, 2023
ISBN 978-1-953321-23-7

Micro Publishing Media, Inc.
PO Box 1522
Stockbridge, MA 01262
www.micropublishingmedia.com

Dedicated to my parents, Jennie and Abraham Elner Z"L,
whose heroic survival of the Holocaust
inspired me to find life even where there's death.

"Circumstances don't make the man,
they only reveal him to himself."
— Epictetus

TABLE OF CONTENTS

FOREWORD

Facing an untimely death transformed the teacher into a student, and through the inspiring story of *The Last Year of My Life*, Eeki Elner is teaching leadership once again.

Rarely in life do you encounter someone who simply exudes confidence and leadership the way Eeki Elner does. For me it was on my first of what would become many trips to Israel, as a newly elected state senator. We were on an economic development mission and had taken some time to learn more about this complex, beautiful place and its people. Eeki took us to a hilltop outside of Sderot from where we could look out across rich farmlands into Gaza. As he told us about the very real danger of sniper and rocket fire, most members of the delegation instinctively began to crouch down. As an Army Green Beret with combat experience in Iraq and Kosovo, I started scanning the horizon to look for likely firing positions or the tell-tale shimmer of a sniper's scope. Eeki, a combat veteran himself, knew what I was doing and asked if I had military experience. So began a great friendship between us.

Eeki is an accomplished leader and a dynamic teacher of leaders. The son of holocaust survivors, resiliency and grit are in his DNA. He served in the Israel Defense Forces where he continued his journey of leadership development. As a member of an anti-aircraft artillery unit, he fought in Lebanon and was wounded in combat. Following his military service, he served as press secretary to the ministers of Education and Environmental

Protection. He was selected as Director of Constitution for Israel, advocating for an Israeli Constitution for more than seven years. Building on his life experience from the battlefield to the halls of the Knesset, Eeki had a vision in 2005 to create a leadership development program that would prepare young Israelis for roles in business, government, community, and non-profit organizations. From that vision, the Israel Leadership Institute (ILI) was born, and the inaugural class began studying in Sderot in 2008. ILI has since become Israel's most advanced leadership training institute, earning wide acclaim both in Israel and abroad.

In an instant, everything changed. When Eeki was diagnosed with cancer, four different doctors told him he had only about six months to live. As he began the last year of his life, the respected teacher would become the student, striving, fighting, self-examining, as well as setting goals and achieving them. What he learned were profound lessons, focused on mastering the practice of personal leadership to become a stronger leader of others. When my dear friend told me of his diagnosis, my wife Lauren and I started thinking through how we would get to Israel for the memorial we thought would be inevitable. I've now been to Israel numerous times since then but thank God not for that purpose. Thankfully that "last year" of Eeki's life has now become many years.

In a defining moment, one faces a very stark choice – give up or fight. Eeki has an insatiable hunger for life, so he chose to fight. The lessons he learned from this unique journey have shaped the leadership guide you now hold. It's an entertaining and inspiring story, full of his signature whit and classic Israeli humor, but it's more than mere entertainment and inspiration. It's also an instruction manual. Having dedicated his life to leadership development, Eeki chose to turn this encounter with fate into an opportunity to become a better leader and help you do the same. In many ways his existential struggle mirrors the very struggle the modern state of Israel has faced in its first 75 years. Just as Israel is stronger and more resilient for having battled to preserve its life as a nation, so has the resilience of Eeki Elner made him a better leader and a better teacher. In *The Last Year of My Life,* you'll learn the lessons of Eeki's experience without the mortal danger of facing it yourself.

Fortunately, Eeki decided that surviving is not enough. He chose to use his second chance to thrive and grow as a leader. He's been a leader virtually his entire life, but until he was shaken by confronting his own death, he hadn't learned to be his own leader. He learned only through personal leadership can you light the way and inspire others. His physical discomfort was profound, but he mastered the fact that leaders must become comfortable with failure to sustain success. Because he became intensely aware that each day could very realistically be his last, he learned what we all should remember: life is precious, and time is short. ILI has based its curriculum on teaching the values, language, and tools of leadership through a mix of experiential and classroom learning. In the years since his cancer diagnosis, Eeki has reshaped the curriculum based on his own story and consistent with the lessons and tools detailed in each chapter of this book. Whether you're an experienced leader or just beginning the journey, the lessons of *The Last Year of My Life* will leave you questioning, contemplating, and examining. They will make you a stronger leader.

Leadership is not an easy choice. It's a profoundly difficult process of continuous growth that demands a lifestyle of service to others. Leadership isn't a title, it's a behavior, and the Institute challenges its students to live by that principle every day. One of the simple traits that defines leaders is the simple willingness to lead. There's seldom someone telling you it's time to take charge. This book teaches that a leader must urge oneself into action and then the rest will follow. By picking this book up you're taking a positive step in your leadership journey. What many doctors called a hopeless case of terminal cancer caused a renowned teacher of leadership to become the student. In the pages of this book, Eeki Elner is the teacher once again, and all who read it will be better for having done so.

Frank LaRose
Ohio Secretary of State
US Army Green Beret

PREFACE

What if four different doctors told you that you had six months to live? Can you imagine this? I'll say for myself that each assertion felt like a hammer striking a nail into my skull. Mine sure was thick enough.

Cancer.

Death was the worst news of my life. I was just into my early fifties, which still felt like the youth of my twenties. There was so little time to process what my life and death meant; even my grieving process had a deadline. *This diagnosis couldn't be true.* How could I accept this?

The cards were dealt, but it wasn't a bad hand—I simply played it wrong. And as a bullheaded Israeli goofball, I had finally begun to see my own leadership program blossom—its bright students growing like a painstakingly tended garden. Even with all my political and public experience, my activism, and my work creating the Israel Leadership Institute (ILI), I realized as my body served itself a death warrant that, until now, my accomplishments had been all talk. I had received a fatal inscription in God's great Book of Life, but was my fate sealed?

But you didn't open this book for deathbed confessions. Especially those familiar with my work, you wouldn't expect me to catastrophize. This crazy story is my testament to personal leadership as a protocol for living through darkness, a beacon of light for yourself as much as for others. As you may have guessed, I am still alive beyond my expiration date. While my book is centered on the threat of death—and even more concerning, of not *truly* living—it also follows my personal revelations about living a good life, which were only possible through experiencing the terror of potentially losing it. Instead of dread, you'll find proclamations for living.

This book will serve as a call to action for living with confident intention, refusing to give up or settling for less. I want you to become a boundary breaker and understand you are worth more than you ever gave yourself credit. I believe the meaning of your life comes from within—and once ignited, it must be sustained by your efforts to stoke it. You must reach higher, burn brighter, and share your unique light with others spreading from one candle to the next.

This is not a philosophy book, though certain beliefs and perspectives drawn from philosophy form its core. To empower your unique journey—wherever you find yourself at this moment, with whatever problems that plague you—this *manual* seeks to set a concrete foundation with the tools of personal leadership to scaffold your approach to life. *You* are the architect. With the permits provided by your higher power (whether you believe in God, your highest self, or just chance) you can ascend to your infinite potential. This limitless, last frontier is only yours to conquer.

ACKNOWLEDGEMENTS

I have the privilege to thank—first and foremost—my coauthor, Joshua Adams. A true artist of words and master of writing, Joshua brought a unique partnership in making this book an accessible, clear, and inspiring story for everyone to learn from. I am and will always be grateful for every moment of work and creation that we shared.

I want to thank my only sister, Bracha, who committed herself to being there every moment through my journey of fighting cancer and for the long days and nights she has spent caring for me.

Thank you, Professor Amir Onn, for not only fighting together to save my life but also showing me the deepest trust that can exist between a doctor and a patient. You are an inspiration to all oncologists around the world.

Special thanks to my long-time friend Amnon Rahav, who agreed to share with me the first trip to Iceland at a moment in life when it seemed to be my last trip, and for being my charm at the many CT scans I went through in those years.

Thank you, Deborah Herman, my publisher, for revealing what was the essence of my message and guiding me so professionally through the process of bringing my story to be printed with such grace and support.

Thank you to my partners and team at The Israel Leadership Institute and the students and graduates of our leadership program for not giving up on our vision and dream even when at times, it seemed that I might not survive.

Thank you to all my training partners, who saw me struggling and witnessed my toughest moments at the gym and were always there to support and encourage me. Special thanks to my beloved and professional trainers: Amir Srouji, Aviv Sarit Cohen, and Anton and Valeria Kedik.

Thank you to my amazing dozens—if not more—friends, who volunteered to watch over me during my treatment period, every day and every hour for more than two long years. You are family to me.

Thank you, Todd Appelbaum, Larry Levine, and the late Wilma Jodan Smart, for such devotion and support given to me from the other side of the ocean.

Thank you Michael Yuen-Killick, for the cover design; Jane McWhorter, for the interior design; Belihun Alebachew, for the photography art, Sam Russek for copyediting, and Zack White for editorial consultation.

And thank you God, for allowing me to serve so many causes and be there for so many people in this life journey.

INTRODUCTION

I was very young when I committed to making the world a better place, learning all too early how challenging it can be to live here—never mind even prospering. It was either choosing life or becoming a victim to the troubles and traumas my life presented, something akin to death. It is one of the most fundamental choices a person can make: to lead your life or let it lead you—the latter enslaving you to what become meaningless circumstances.

The prescribed process in this book is rooted in the concept of personal leadership. My story demonstrates how I developed and used its practical tools for fighting not only for my life but for my way of living. The tools I am sharing with you must be personalized as much as your own leadership should be. There is a unique spark within you that only you can reveal, and the challenges you are given to champion are the tinder to help set you alight. *Challenges are the catalyst for growth.*

I have trained leadership for nearly two decades through the workshops of The Israel Leadership Institute, an international organization with the core mission of fostering a sense of leadership and accountability for community in its students. The ILI's core belief and motto is that leadership is not reserved for the elite and is found in anyone who wishes to bear its torch— but I must make an important distinction: personal leadership is precursor to leadership. By leading yourself along your life path, you become exponentially capable of lighting the way for others—all toward brighter horizons.

The tools you'll find within the book are open-ended directives that provide a strong basis for their use. I wrote them together with writer Joshua Adams to spark inspiration and urge you into practicing the process, so that you may become increasingly proficient in leading your life and fulfilling its potential. The examples of wielding the tools are found in the story itself, so I encourage you to draw what meaningful connections and insights they may afford you and put them to work in your own life. Tools are only an extension of yourself. It is up to you to derive the will to lead your life—you'll learn very soon how I did for mine.

PART I

Tool: The Reins

THE LAST YEAR OF MY LIFE

The Israelites wandered the desert for 40 years and—as if that wasn't enough—I was about to return home from a weekend trip to the Negev feeling like I had swallowed a sandstorm. My dear friend Judah, a worrywart Mr. Fixit with a heart of golden honey, was the first to point out my cough.

"Eeki, are you sick? You've had this since we got here, and it sounds worse." His face was smothered with worry while my eyes flicked from him to the dusty mountains on the horizon. We were such good friends, it was almost as if I could see a screen on his forehead with a picture of what he was thinking about: Me, sitting in a doctor's office, receiving bad news.

"It's nothing, Judah! Just a frog stuck in my throat. What's there to worry about?"

Judah was prone to hyperbolizing. Soon, he'd probably think I'd caught the plague. He insisted on driving me home, but I protested, believing he probably just didn't want to deal with my crazy driving. I tried to joke my way to the driver's seat. With enough bickering, I managed to quell his concerns, that is, until a wheezing fit had me choking on my words. There was no convincing him anymore. I relented and let him take the wheel.

We drove back to Sderot, a rocket-battered town where I founded the Israel Leadership Institute, an international organization training leadership to individuals seeking to better themselves and communities. I nearly suffocated holding in my coughs the whole ride there—each burst was like setting off a car alarm for Judah.

"I'm not going to croak in the middle of the night, I'm fine, really," I said. His frown didn't waver, not that I was surprised. "Alright, if it gets worse, I'll go to the doctor."

"See, that wasn't so hard now, was it?" Judah said. "I know it'd be harder for you to lie to me, Eeki."

We hugged, he left, and I went straight to bed, but not before posting my recent adventures on social media. I knew it was a terrible time-suck—what I planned to do for a few minutes could turn into an hour in just a blink. There was no doubt I'd die before my social media habit did.

A terrible night of sleep followed with what seemed like the cough's angry spirit possessing me. There was no medicine or method to exorcize it. I should've known Judah would come to check on me the next day. But I didn't hear him knocking on the door due to a raging coughing fit. My vision danced like it needed lessons. Rockets could have been descending on Sderot and I wouldn't have known. Eventually, I let him in, and he took me out. We went to the ER.

Five weeks later I would be officially diagnosed with stage-four lung cancer. And no, it didn't take that long because I had dragged my feet to the doctor's office. It's a crazy story... don't worry, I'll tell you soon. This diagnosis was a pivotal point where my previous leadership teachings at the ILI would get *really* personal and be put to the ultimate test. More than that, they'd have to undergo an evolution.

I would need to abide by my own protocols. How could I teach anyone to live a more fulfilling life through challenge and adversity if I failed to follow my own program? Life and death; sickness and health; passivity and action. Like many other aspects of living, they must be understood as contrasts.

You see, I hadn't lived my life as I should. I was living in oblivion until death showed me what life could not. I was aimless. I was a leader—but not of myself. In the months ahead, I would begin to see my truest self sprout and bloom. I would feel alive while I was dying.

Perhaps it was all too late to turn my life around? *How ironic.* I imagined my predicament was like sitting on a cliff overlooking the Dead Sea, a salt soup devoid of life, simmering under a vast, golden-blue sky of potential that I could never reach because my body was killing itself.

Still, I chose to reach for this higher me—it was painful, longing for what felt like a cosmic dream lightyears away. Would I reach it in time? And had

I really taken life's blessings and possibilities for granted? Throughout my journey, doubts like these would seek to throw me into a pit of despair.

My world was torn asunder. Oh, what I wouldn't give to see my students flourish, I thought, their impossibly bright futures shining through smiles that fill me with warmth. And mercifully, maybe my beloved ILI would continue to grow for yet more seasons, the shimmering garden of my life's work. There was only so much time for anguish; I was not going to spend my final days throwing a pity party.

To rebuild my life and find meaning in my plight, I knew this journey would need to become one of not just inspiration but *instruction*. As humans there are times when we need catharsis, so it feels appropriate and is effortless to conclude my life is over, I'm broken, or it is all my fault, but this instantaneously creates a self-made prison. I must share that at such an earth-rendering moment, natural, instinctual, knee-jerk declarations like *this is the end* can be catastrophic if they go unchallenged. Statements like these are akin to clasping on chains; we define our reality through perception. While facing the onslaught of negative thoughts swarming like killer bees, I recalled how thinking and speech can define reality. As I was ambushed, listening to their beratement and harping was enough proof. This all had been just an abstract concept to me before I was faced with imminent mortality. I would have my fill of catastrophizing and steer it into positive action.

I cannot pretend that controlling thoughts is easy. And for some, maybe it is nigh impossible. In the face of fear and pain, the mind can become a cage where the heart runs rampant like a terrorized animal. I have met some people with mental fortitude far greater than I could possibly fathom when it comes to physical and mental illnesses, disasters, and the worst of humanity. With all my logic, emotion, and inner, guiding spirit, I believe in the following as a mantra to mastering yourself as the basis of discovering your ever-expansive potential, to showing up at your best in any situation: the mind is the rider, the heart is the horse. No matter how difficult, we must take hold of the reins.

LIFE OR DEATH IS YOUR CHOICE

I *was not surprised by the news.* Rather, deep in the recesses of my gut, I had known all along that I had cancer—even worse, a violent and relentless breed. This diagnosis was my big slap in the face. *Eeki, you big stupid idiot, time to wake up and face the music!* But I refused to let my mental insides rot, becoming salty and bitter. What must be understood about the Dead Sea is that it cleanses. I'll say it again: all my life, I never understood, until now, that I had taken so much for granted. This might sound crazy at first: I had created this cancer—it is part of my body, manifested by my choices. Sure, smoking didn't help, but there's no time for pity or blame, no time for shame, what ifs, why "me"s, and victimhood that projects responsibility to the wind. Even if I considered my problems an "act of God," due to some kind of tragedy that seeks to turn me into a victim, my options would remain the same: yield or fight. It's a cleansing rebirth, a transformation, and it all takes place as a single, repeating thought and word: *Fight. You must speak your choice out loud. Use your voice.*

If there is anything you get from this chapter, it is the importance of acknowledging your inner worth and using the talents you've always had—actualizing your personhood. It truly can start with the snap of a finger, and believe me, you might be snapping until you start a fire—there will be setbacks. Success is based on perception—often fleeting and internally or externally defined. But failure—those little and big mistakes, those shortcomings—are where true growth occurs, depending on how you choose to respond. You must get comfortable with failure to sustain success.

So, here's my response to my trip to the emergency room:

A nurse sat me down in a tiny room. I had no real idea why I was in the ER, and there was no escape route! *Thanks, Judah...* Of course, there was a long wait, it was Friday—nearly the Sabbath, the Jewish day of rest, and the hospital was more short-staffed than usual because when God tells you to not work the weekend, how can you say no? Jokes aside, I did not want to be there. I had things to do!

After the nurse ran through typical diagnostics—no surprise my blood pressure was elevated—she had me take some x-rays.

"Should I smile?" I asked.

No laugh. She soon led me to a room where my results were to be put on display. "Wait here, Hollywood."

I grinned, but it disappeared as a tall, gaunt, Bedouin doctor entered the room, his emotion disguised under a desert-grown stoicism. He politely introduced himself and pulled up the x-rays. An ominous spot drew both our attention. A few moments of cool consideration filled the room. His long arm pointed to a ping pong ball shape in my lung. "You see this there? What is it? Are you familiar with that?"

Something stirred within me. "Yes."

He seemed to not expect such a suddenly certain response. "We need to run some tests. It could be many things—"

"I—I think I know what it is." There was a pause and the inevitable truth bubbled up from my gut: "It's cancer."

He scoffed, almost offended. "How can you tell it's cancer?"

"Because I knew this day was coming."

Exasperation cracked the dark, stolid landscape of his face. "It is not a medical thing what you are saying."

"I understand this—" I took a few moments to collect myself. It was like a sour belch—these words at last in the air, rancid with fear. The implications of this truth were uncertain. Undefined. We seemed to look at each other as if we were from different planets. "Look, it is what it is," I said. There wasn't anything smart to say. No jokes to tune the mood. In fact, it felt awkward.

And for an instant, his face turned impossibly pale. "I don't understand how you can be so calm—listen, we must run the tests first, and there's some paperwork we need to fill out. Just wait here."

He was out the door before I had a chance to refuse.

The moments before his return were replete with time-bending reflection. There was the psychological urge to dissociate as fear grew and spread throughout my body. My mind sought to foreshadow the dark days ahead. For many, the mind is an arena with the greatest of enemies. The times ahead would mostly depend on my mental state. Someone needed to take the helm of this sinking ship. Could I really do it?

My parents were holocaust survivors. I only saw the effect of the worst of humanity—not the cause. And I saw something else, surprisingly of the same cosmic magnitude: they persisted despite a phenomenon without comparison. What the human mind cannot fathom on its own but only witness—from the fires that cast an eternal shade of death, they led themselves beyond its smoldering reach. They had children; they *lived and gave life*.

But I don't think of myself as special or especially hardened by my roots, I really don't. My parents disliked how aloof I was in my youth. Many of my choices made their hair turn gray. As I grew into myself, particularly when the ILI was formed, this began to change. I was deeply accountable to other people, not just my students. Though I didn't have my own children, I would help others grow their lives. Until this change, I had wandered instead of led.

How did I bring this upon myself? How has this happened? You were born so lucky you ungrateful little… These were questions I often asked myself during this time fighting cancer. Living under stress was my poison, and I never did much of anything to change my relationship with it. Within this gaping maw of despair, I had to slap myself out of my stupor and make this choice. Roughing yourself up a little bit can be healthy if you understand it's all about taking accountability for the moment… Perhaps I had been running away from accountability, and the current that God was urging me toward. Stupid decisions, throwing opportunities to the wind, not truly thinking about tomorrow—I often made these mistakes. *Body and soul are connected.* There is a plethora of research that shows stress's impact on the body. This was my problem to own.

The doctor returned. "The plan is to send you upstairs to get a biopsy after you sign this paperwork," he said.

"Why go up? I'm feeling okay! I know I am sick, but not sick enough that I can't walk myself out of here. Who wants to stay in the hospital?"

"Not everything is cancer—you can't make assumptions for something like this. This is very serious."

I took a heavy breath. "Look, Doctor, there's a lot of work ahead of me. And there's no way to tell if it'll pay. I have it."

I suspect the look he gave me was that of belief. Still, he accompanied me to the door. "I truly hope you are wrong."

So, I couldn't go home. I had to go up to the diagnostic imaging department for a biopsy—*shouldn't take that long*, I thought. Judah was already following me and grabbed my shoulder.

I sighed. "They're sending me up for more tests. You've got a life to live, Judah, and it ain't here."

"Don't be ridiculous!" he said. "This is serious, Eeki." He wasn't going to put up with my antics, the sap! But I needed to go alone. And I couldn't tell him quite yet.

"Judah, please. I am putting both feet down. Please go home. I will call you as soon as I know something."

The look on his face melted. "I will be waiting to hear from you. No games."

What did I do to be blessed with such a friend?

There was another choice to make: the elevator or the stairs? I stared at a garbage can positioned between the two. I slipped out my pack of cigarettes and tore them up one by one. The first torn was symbolic of an echo; it was the same decision repeating until the dead weight was gone. I chose the stairs. Each step was a choice, not some autonomous shambling, but still, there was gravity pulling me down to wallow in my circumstances. They were moments to myself—moments to digest reality and let my stomach settle. If I were to survive this, I needed to take every step with intention. To make it a constant choice. When I fell short, I would make the decision to get back up and keep choosing—keep fighting.

Exiting the stairwell, I again became the hospital's hostage (how dramatic), but this time it was on a bed in a corridor that looked like it had been abandoned halfway through development. I recalled that today was the last day of Passover, you know, that holiday where the Jewish slaves are freed from pharaoh after ten plagues (he would have been a great contestant on that old show *Fear Factor*). I stared at the mind-searing fluorescent light above, like an interrogation room. A day would turn to ten as the biopsy machine failed and failed again, three times!

I felt my retinas burning from the lighting above as a figure eclipsed it. My thoughts dissipated, and I saw a doctor looking down at me.

"I was sent to check up on you," he said. This man's face must've never had to worry about smile lines. He was born, raised, and trained as a doctor in the former Soviet Union before immigrating to Israel. He had a "Soviet" approach to medicine and a professional attitude. And once you absorb the Soviet culture it affects your nature and behavior. Soviets? You don't argue with them because they're "never wrong"—well, most of the time. I repositioned myself on the bed as he gave me a once-over. "I am a specialist in lung cancer." He looked into my eyes to confirm I was paying attention. "As I understand it, the x-ray showed something in your left lung. Can you show me your hands?"

I looked at him as if he was crazy. "What? Why would I show you my hands?"

"Show me your hands and I'll tell you." I handed them over, and he padded and traced my fingers as if there was some diagram embedded in their outline. He turned them over with stern scrutiny in his eyes. Then flipped them again, concluding his inspection with an affirming grunt. "Yes, it looks very much like a serious situation—I am sorry to say."

"What do you mean a serious situation?! How can you say this? We don't even have the biopsy yet."

"I can tell the signs of the disease by the hands. Don't despair but do ready yourself for what the results may reveal."

I was shaken. But not from fear—it was anger. Anger that someone could suggest to me with such certainty that there wasn't room for hope, that I was going to die. It was between his words and unflinching eyes—Soviet severity—he wasn't wrong even though I wanted to argue *I would soon learn it was seriously bad.*

Ten days later, I walked out of the hospital with no biopsy. *Again, thank you Judah!* I was standing outside the emergency room under the high noon Israeli sky—cars whizzing down the main road, the ephemeral green landscape already yellowing. Now knowing what I knew, seeing life persist around me despite it—the single puff of white in the sky above and around a bustling hospital center and people going on with their lives—I saw what I never could. Time is of the essence. We have so little of what is most precious.

A dusty yellow sedan swerved into the emergency exit toward me, struggling to keep from crushing the curb. I could see Judah's face through the dust-free semi-circle his wipers had cleaned. His passenger window was cracked open.

"Judah, what are doing? You can't enter from there!"

He hopped out and gave me a suffocating hug. We rushed into the car. "Let's go!"

"Aren't you going to tell me what it is, Eeki? I haven't been able to breathe all week."

"I don't know yet. I still have to get a biopsy—so we'll see."

"What do you mean it is nothing? Why a biopsy?"

I didn't want to tell him. It was just my nature, and I couldn't upend his life—he had his own stress and I needed to get my footing before word got out. "They want to rule out everything. A doctor told me it's very serious. Judah… we'll wait and see, okay?"

A painful sound came from his throat. "Very serious? Are you dying?"

"I don't know yet."

"Eeki, stop this! How can you be so calm?!"

My heart screamed bloody murder as we nearly careened into oncoming traffic. "I might be dying and you're trying to kill me!?"

The car buzzed along for at least a mile. We were heading back to Sderot. His eyes were wet, and I could see his throat tightening like a blocked chimney. It felt like we were driving to my funeral. "Judah, this is how it is. We don't know yet and I need you to keep calm. Whatever the case, I am going to get through this."

A slew of questions ricocheted around the car's small cabin. I just wanted to get home. It was an exhaustion like no other. My survival instincts took over the driver's seat, but my inner voice—my inner truth that had long been squelched during years of oblivion keeping my head in the sand—whispered to me to stay awake.

That evening, I sat on my couch alone, my hands shaking. *How could he tell me not to despair?! My leadership program is going to burn to the ground!* I tried to bust the pity party, but in this moment I felt hopeless. Trust me, there was no doubt in my mind: to hope that the biopsy would indicate anything other than death was impossible to me. I just knew. This was the beginning of my battle preparations, but I was already attacking myself. Here's what I hope you understand: If you're distracted by whatever you might be feeling at the moment—maybe it is like the tide wavering from resolve to reluctance—you are defenseless to whatever the world throws at you. Your inner civil war makes you weaker.

I needed to rise to the occasion. My thoughts nearly blinded me, but I managed to focus on a framed picture on the wall, a vista of desert plains in full bloom. In one of the most desolate, unforgiving places, life was thriving—an ephemeral miracle moment. I stood up and soaked it in. How had I not seen this before? Never had this image evoked this feeling—this truth. Like a horse, I stamped my feet. This wasn't a situation to despair about. This was my defining moment, my inciting incident. I was the author of my own narrative: *all is foreseen, and freedom of choice is granted.* I would meet God halfway——this is what you must do. Meet your higher power, your higher self, with 100% of your share.

My fight would not be with fate; it would be with the current version of myself. I would not prophesize my future, but shape one instead, trusting my decisions would be my becoming. *We are what we do,* yet I was no misguided failure—my shortcomings were not who I was destined to be. Finally, I decided I would be defined by me.

I would be brave. While I may have trembled at the thunderclouds which had briefly masked the sun in my mind, I knew the sun was still there, right behind them, and this was no gesture of blind faith. Whatever lump lurked inside my lungs, spreading this disease throughout my body, would become my companion on this journey. *Sunshine,* I would call him: cancer personified, my inspiration who would help to illuminate the unexplored crevasses of my soul.

The mind and heart must work as a team with respect for one another. Both are a unique part of you, tools of the soul, but they can work against each other. To free myself, I would have to reframe the frenzy-ridden statements in my head, driven by raw emotion, into a logical question to better serve the outcome of my predicament. My mind took the reins. And at first this question was: H*ow will I ever get through this?* It invited opportunity but wasn't quite enough. No, I wouldn't settle for that. The question became more distilled and immediate: W*hat must I do right now?* I realized that I must fight. I would not be my own grim reaper, and I believe, as God would have it, *all is foreseen, and freedom of choice is granted.* I had a say in this, and I would choose to fight this war.

If you find yourself in a similar situation or with any of life's challenges, know that while you may not have the answers yet, you can make this life-saving choice by promising yourself you'll answer this call to arms. I was hopeless until I had the epiphany that what I had been teaching others for so many years had a greater importance—disseminating this realization was at least one answer to the question, *why fight?* After all, why would God have given me this challenge at such an auspicious time in my life and career if not to wake me up to something greater? I know the expression, "man plans, and God laughs," but I have never interpreted it as cruelty. It is always so we can be shown a new path to something we may not have anticipated.

So, I would unsheathe and wield the power of the question to find the right answers. Do we really know what's to become of us, good or bad? We can't really know what happens next, though we can predict as much as we'd like. Probability does matter, but tomorrow or the next day has not happened yet. Maybe a bus would get me before the cancer. Fate's hired hitmen were still closing in, but this just isn't how it works—this silly thought is simply a morbid falsehood—even if you do not believe in a higher power orchestrating the universe. I do believe in God's mercy, however, and that the universe is conducted with inherent benevolence and justice while impossible riddles are formed within His handiwork. Even Moses was denied the answer to why good things happen to bad people and the opposite.

This question, what *must I do right now?* is much like when God called out to Abraham to issue the auspicious orders for his life's mission, and Abraham responded, *Hineni,* or "I am here." And so, he pursued it! He answered this urgent call and decisively pursued his purpose, despite all he had to sacrifice. In this confusing, chaotic, and often cruel modern age, we are tasked with finding our own purposes. And I believe they're crying out from our cores.

The challenge at hand that you face, this test, this urge to start *leading* and not passively living your life, echoes this question and call, and we must respond, "I am here." I am present and not running away from this, and I will not go down without a fight. And not just fighting for the sake of it—

but intending to win, choosing life over death. Although what lies ahead may require courage that we fear we don't have, the turning point is now. There is a leader within all of us—our compass, our true north. We must trust in ourselves and keep faith. And get to work. *Take the reins and lead ahead.*

I should've been asking myself this question all my life—challenge or not—*what must I do right now to truly live my life?* My-oh-my, how retrospection is crystal clear.

As I have said, all the teachings in my leadership program had not yet reached their true, intended philosophical peak. What now seems like scattered puddles of maxims became holistic, oceanic truths (*geez—I'm boasting*). This newfound view on life was a deep, personal transformation, and the program is an extension of myself and the bedrock for *personal leadership.*

I understood leadership begins with the self. The message I believe God wished for me to impart is that, even in the most harrowing of circumstances, we can lead ourselves out of doom and into our empowered, higher selves. We can hold onto who we are, triumphing over our obstacles with humility and purpose. This is what our higher power wants for us, what our future selves want for us. They're cheering us on to success.

When you lead yourself, your will *will* lead you to live, but not like before. The universe is telling you it is time to grow, face your fears, and dare to live your life unhindered by your own limitations.

It really begins with a choice. It's your narrative to write—please, take it from me: this diagnosis spelled the last year of my life, and I chose to fight to the death.

I want to say to you: You are alive, and it is not over yet—unless you think and say it is. Perhaps you're reading this book because you have *the* problem, the kind that overshadows all others, threatens your status quo, strangulates you into paralysis, or you simply cannot cope with the pain and sorrow, and life's forecast is thunderstorms. Or maybe you *need* to threaten your comfortable complacency and discover there is more to living. Whatever the case, you are alive, and your choices count. Accept its significance—it means something to you, right now—accept that what you are going through is real, real enough to threaten your life.

It was during this tumultuous time that I experienced my greatest realization. I was the founder of a leadership institute, but I had not been my own leader. Maybe this was exactly what God had wanted for me. In my heart I was yearning to be of some service, to myself and to those around me—a higher purpose. I felt it was divine providence to bring together the ILI. There were so many exceptional people supporting the vision to better the world through training leadership. I felt truly blessed, but considering my past, on some level I may have felt it was too good to be true. Who was I to be the one at the helm? Or maybe I was too arrogant to even question myself. Now I had to look inside to survive this challenge. I had posed the challenge to God by asking for me to make a difference in this world.

I guess God answered me with the ultimate test. A proverb reverberating through time smacked straight into my thick head: *physician, heal thyself.* This was the journey I was given, but with my natural stubborn nature I would only act when facing the possibility of a life shortened before its time, with too much potential unrealized.

So, I urge you: *Act now.* Not tomorrow, not later—your chance is now. *And it starts with a single choice.* Take the reins and lead your life. Fight for it! This problem is your Dead Sea, your cleansing waters. First you must plunge before the sky's expanse and ready yourself for its embrace. For every descent is meant for a greater ascent. This is a crazy story and let me tell you: I'm a crazy person—crazy enough to deny care from four oncologists until I found one that would listen to *my* prognosis: I am going to live!

They all told me this was the last year of my life... *more than seven years ago.*

PART II
Tool: The Uniform

No, the Answer is Yes!

By the time you read this, you've hopefully made the decision to fight for your life. You're the judge and jury—the verdict is your own. I wish for you to get through this, but more than that, for you to be gracefully ready for all the opportunities your life has yet to give. But this choice is *your* first step. Whether you are reacting to strife or taking action against the inevitability of it—maybe you desire to take charge of your destiny—all of these begin with your commitment to do so. Ambivalence will have you teetering on a jagged fence, your energy fixed futilely on balancing to stay there. Urge yourself into motion, the rest will follow.

Perhaps you don't know what this decision looks like yet. Maybe it's a feeling without words, or maybe this all sounds like a bad joke, but I will insist on one fundamental point: personal leadership requires accountability for yourself. It's never too late to take charge of *you* and act accordingly. To achieve your destiny, you need to be in drive—not neutral, or even worse: reverse. Own your attitude and how it influences your direction and choices. Choose action over inaction. In some cases, choosing to let go of something, what seems to be choosing nothing, is an action in and of itself. Whatever choices are to be made, they're opportunities to expand your inner horizons—your growing capacity to traverse your path—no matter how dark the days ahead may seem. When we let externals dictate our feelings and attitude, our horizons shrink. We are not free.

I had to learn just this to live up to my own words on personal leadership. It was in my very own classroom a few days after I had learned I would soon die that this truth stared me in the eyes.

I had crossed the classroom threshold feeling as if some specter was stalking me. With a forced smile, I surveyed the modest-sized room, wondering how many more times I might see Matan, front-row and ready to go with all the rest of my students filling in to grab their seats. Matan had stood out to me as someone who had his fair share of troubles; I was privy to some, due to the intensive nature of the initial recruiting interviews for the workshops. He was somewhat forthcoming with his story, but inherent within his words was a fiery desire for change. The path he was on was not leading where he wished to go. Looking at him now, I would never have guessed there was much in his past to work through.

Similarly, I thought my demeanor was the same as any other day—nothing to suggest I might be dying. But there is much to see in someone's eyes that they cannot conceal. I imagined I could see through Matan's eyes and into his soul. Perhaps I would find a whole galaxy of sadness there. But on my own, I felt a blackhole swallowing any light around me, crushing my reality.

The workshop was a momentary refuge I got lost in, and one I was most proud of. It presented a whole new attitude toward entrepreneurship through a unique, leadership lens. I saw Matan smiling amongst his teammates while they role played and processed case studies using the laboratory method I developed for the ILI—learning the mental tools that would build successful initiatives.

I just knew he would be successful along with the others. It felt more than a gut feeling, like a premonition, but I struggled to see myself in this future. Doubt is a powerful distraction—fortunately, I was able to keep focused on the present.

Then it struck me that this day was like any other. We were here to make the most of our futures, however much was left, and suddenly there were only five minutes left of class. I felt like the wall clock was grabbing me by the shoulders and shaking me. Are you going to just walk out of here with such a secret?

I cannot tell them. I just can't. In some way, my students were the children I never had. I couldn't let my illness threaten their journeys and take away what they'd worked so hard to accomplish here. Would I see their futures? We were here to make the most of our futures, however much was left, and there were five minutes left of class. I felt like the wall clock was grabbing me by the shoulders and shaking me. *Are you going to just walk out of here with such a secret?*

I cannot tell them. I just can't. In some way, my students were the children I never had. I couldn't let my illness threaten their journeys and take away what they'd worked so hard to accomplish here. *Would I see their futures?*

"Everyone, please give me a moment before you go partying the weekend away." I caught a few smiles and tried to ride the mood's momentum. "I'm going to be out for at least a couple of weeks for a medical reason. But don't worry, I'll be back before you all forget about me."

I didn't see any smiles. Just troubled expressions. I struggled to keep my composure and glanced at the clock that now seemed to pause, waiting curiously for me to elaborate.

A few students pressed for more details, but I dodged and bent the truth until it nearly broke. I should've known they'd want answers, but I couldn't relent. They lined up barraging me with questions and offers to help. Assuaging their concerns was like trying to shake a swarm of bees after kicking the hive, but these stings were my own doing. After convincing them to go start their weekends without taking on my troubles, I found Matan digging in his heels. *You stubborn cherub, I thought.* He was as kind a soul as he was keen. Had my eyes betrayed me? Did he know the truth?

"Eeki, listen to me. Please let me help. My father is a nurse and can get you in with the right people."

"Thank you, but please don't stress yourself. I just stubbed my toe really badly." The joke didn't work to lighten the mood. I strained a smile, feeling my cheekbones crunch against my eyes. "I'll let you know, Matan. It's very kind of you. Thank you." We embraced. "Go relax and enjoy your blessed weekend already. It's your God given right, right?"

He nodded, smiling faintly.

I put my hands on the desk in the empty classroom, peering out the window at nothing. I'm not sure I ever felt so exhausted in my life. Despite this, I noticed anger simmering underneath it all. It was like a fire I could not put out. It would burn me unless I managed to channel it. I wasn't going to let my students down; I would see myself through this. I walked out of the room running hot.

During the drive home, the windshield was colored by the emotions painted by my heart like on a canvas. The more I tried to *think* about how I felt, the more I found my heart sharing the creative space with my mind. They spoke.

It was through their conversation that I came to understand you cannot deny or erase your feelings. You must confront them, and *then* decisions can be made. Strangely, when I tried evading my feelings, they would always bring me back into their orbit, confused and even more frustrated than before.

At the workshop, I thought I was trying to protect my students, but I was really avoiding my own discomfort. I grew up with this kind of attitude, but there was more to it. Maybe withholding the news was actually a reasonable sentiment, but I was infuriated with how I felt like I couldn't control anything, including how the news would impact them.

Ironically, they were learning how to manage crisis situations in a roleplaying simulation class as part of the program, but I dismissed their capabilities, concerns, and involvement while this anger roiled in my gut. I reasoned that my cancer was going to destroy every aspect of my life and others before it would put me down for good. What I needed was to get a hold of myself. I thought hiding my diagnosis from them was for the best— it wasn't the first time I'd hidden something from them, you'll surely see. I was avoiding exposure and the risk of imposing myself on others. Perhaps it was from my childhood—whatever the reason, it was not serving me now. *I will see myself through this, alone,* I thought. It was a compelling declaration, but hollow in its expression, and I would not discover why quite yet.

During troubling times, we need clarity, not confusion. Judgment is lost in your emotions' cloudy smoke. Sometimes you must stop and ask yourself, what is happening here? *Here, within me.*

I could at least see that I was not in the best mental shape. It was an important insight as I began to assess the communication between my heart and mind. I had been cold-shouldering myself, not just then, but long before I had ever considered my mortality so fragile as it was now. My feelings were shunned, my thoughts unheeded. At times, those thoughts were weaponized against me with words I'd never say even to my enemies. It was the first time I really *thought* about my thoughts, known as metacognition, and how what I said to myself—this inner monologue—shaped everything I experienced. An analogy I was once given was to imagine yourself in a lab coat, like a scientist, observing, measuring, and hypothesizing your thoughts and feelings.

Intriguing… why did I suddenly feel angry? It seems I was trying to control the outcomes of others. Is that my right?

Am I really a black hole? What convinces me of this?

Observing my thoughts without judgment was hard to put into practice, but over time, I found myself telling a different narrative about who I am and what I'm capable of.

As I reckoned with the unraveling truths I had told myself about my life, I was uncomfortably relaxed. The anger fueled confidence. This was good, but the need to control my situation had my pulse racing like I had all my money on it. Frenzied Eeki—perhaps not the best racehorse to place your bets on. I wanted the big fix, the giant step forward, but sometimes small minutiae are all we have until it's time for such strides.

And I still needed the biopsy. This was a true test of patience, let me tell you. Ten days in the hospital to walk out with a failed test? I followed up with another doctor, and the day of that biopsy I was told another patient had bitten through the wire! *Are you kidding me? This isn't a joking matter!* But they weren't lying. The wait was at least two weeks with other hospitals. Maybe a mouse would eat it this time. I could barely keep my composure on the phone with the administrators. Was I some kind of *schlemazel*? A foolish harbinger of bad luck? I really don't believe in luck, jokes aside. At last, I called Matan.

"I need your help. I've been trying to get a biopsy but everywhere is unavailable. You had mentioned your father works at the hospital—"

"Yes, I will call him, and he'll get you in. A *biopsy*? I wish you had come to me sooner."

He was right. I felt a dull thud in my chest. Reaching out like this was going against my inner nature. My hands shook. But I overpowered this behavior with a conscious thought and directive—a tactical action to wrest control over my fight. It is worth exploring your own conditioning, but this takes time. We all have them—some more, some less; some useful, some useless. It's sobering to learn how much they can get in your own way.

I heard that afternoon from Matan's father. He scheduled my appointment for the very next day. All that trouble for nothing. It really felt like a lesson. I had to take accountability for myself and acknowledge my weak points.

Address them earnestly. Those brittle parts break and become stronger.

I needed not just to be proactive, but self-aware and adaptable. I knew that my inclination to evade others' help and avoid sharing anything that might warrant concern would hinder my battle against cancer.

Not everyone is so fortunate to have a Matan, but personal leadership does not mean you should journey alone. When you rise to the occasion, show up for yourself, and you'll be surprised that others might find their way to your side—or at least you'll see who your allies really are. Don't be afraid to use what you have. Don't be afraid to seek more for your cause. This is *your* life. *Your* fight. While no one else will live and fight for it as you should—they can aid you along the way. By way of what many have called "manifestation," our energy does produce results. Our attitudes cast light or shade into the environment. A positive attitude can be as contagious as a negative one, but you'll quickly find yourself basking in miserable company with the latter.

The day of my (successful) biopsy, I felt like I was on death row. I had barely slept and couldn't eat or drink. *No last meal*, I supposed. I just shuffled around my apartment like it was my prison cell. But I had to cut the dramatics because my dear friend and neighbor, Garik, had offered to drive me to my appointment and would be here soon.

I sat outside in the garden, so I could see him coming through the gate when he arrived. We embraced with a pat on the shoulders. "Enough gas in the car, Eeki? Did you eat? We've got to go." He was a rough, steel-skinned man who immigrated from the Soviet Union to Israel at least thirty years ago, and those thirty years later he proudly still looks like an immigrant behind his thick Fu Manchu mustache. I could never breach his stoic exterior no matter how hard I tried, but he was one of the kindest men you could meet. For him, there was honor in suffering, a culture borne of asceticism. I could somewhat relate to this, especially because my own parents had escaped the Nazis through the Soviet Union.

The drive to the hospital was quiet except for the grumble of the engine. I was strangely aware of the road under the car. Garik had driven in the mountains for the Soviet army, so here he might as well have been riding atop a cloud. I had thought to turn on the radio, but Garik was such a Flintstone that he never used it and preferred the quiet. I kept thinking about how I already knew what the test results would be, and I just wanted to know what was next—what I must do to fight. I was tired of waiting for people to tell me what ailed me—and I wasn't looking forward to being told what time I had left.

"It's going to be okay. All will be well," Garik said in an authoritative, 'comforting' voice. "Don't worry, okay? No need." I was more concerned about what he might do if I *did* worry. It didn't seem he expected a response, and it was impossible to tell what he was thinking, but I wonder if he had said that more for himself than for me.

"I know I have it," I said. "I just need to know how bad it is." I didn't want to argue about whether I had it or not. Refreshingly, he didn't go there, but suddenly we were going faster—and faster. He passed a car and wedged in front of another—cutting through traffic with scary precision.

"It won't be that bad. Trust me. You'll be okay." It sounded more like a command. We swerved onto the off ramp.

"I'd like to make it there alive!"

He took a puffed breath, shifting in his seat uncomfortably, his face covered in a glint of red. Garik's heart could really melt his stoicism.

"We're almost there," he said suddenly. His energy seemed much calmer.

"Thanks, though I could've enjoyed the ride a little while longer, my friend." I think he may have briefly smiled, but it was gone just as fast. We pulled into the hospital entrance.

"Call me if you need anything. I will be in the lobby waiting. Yes?"

I gave him a pat on the shoulder. "Thank you, Garik. Try and relax, I am not so sure how long this will take. Hopefully not another ten days, right?"

I couldn't tell if he was amused. Likely not.

A nurse led me to the testing room where they'd perform the biopsy. Unfortunately, I wouldn't get to see Matan's father, but he'd hear my thanks again later. The nurse had me put on one of those gowns that I can never tie correctly—I can't be the only one. She told me that a Dr. Hartman and his colleague, Dr. Cohen, would perform the biopsy after I underwent anesthesia.

As she left, the doctors came in to introduce themselves. "We didn't want you to be put under before we met you." Dr. Hartman quipped.

Dr. Cohen explained the procedure, but I think he was just trying to gauge my sense of what was happening. He seemed to want to reassure me of some positive outcome, but he withheld the urge. I was grateful for this act of realism, but I also didn't want to deny a dose of hope.

Then came the anesthesiologist. She gave me the rundown.

"Let's get started," I said, "but doctor, I'm going to need a double dose."

She chuckled as if I was joking.

"No really, I'm not kidding. I know how you determine the dose, bodyweight, calculations and what not—it doesn't work that way for me! I don't fall asleep easily."

As she administered the injection, the side of her mouth curled into a crooked smile. "I gave you a little more."

"Thank you, but give me a little more. Just a little extra, please. I'm not making this up!"

"I know, I know. I believe you. I'll give you a little, little extra."

I don't think she did.

Time melted. I stared at the monitor in front of me with a camera cable projecting an unflattering close-up of my face. *Funny, wish I could be awake to...*a soft, fuzzy fog filled my head. Everything was suddenly unfamiliar: was this what the French call *jamais vu*? Whispering murmurs of voices or thoughts tickled my ears. I'm not sure I ever noticed the doctors come back inside—only a faint millisecond memory, like trying to remember everything you saw from a midnight lightning bolt.

Somewhere, a door opened. A chair rolled. Or maybe two? Words ping-ponged between someone and someone else. Was it already over? Consciousness. Presence. Plastic keys clacking. A computer. *Hmmm...* A dismayed decrescendo from someone. "Hartman, you're thinking it too?" It sounded like I was underwater.

"Yes." A molasses-smothered moment passed by before he spoke again. "This looks like a lost case... just look at the spread. It must be stage four."

I lay there with my hands cuffed by some phantom force. All I could do was listen and think. At some point, the door closed, and I was alone.

...Looks like a lost case... I fell back asleep.

I didn't tell Garik about my waking dream—*nightmare—no, reality?* What good would it do? He certainly pressed me for answers, and I just told him we'll find out when we find out. The doctors never would've imagined I would still be awake to hear them—obviously oblivious. And I'm not sure what another ten days or so of omitting my diagnosis from any concerned person would have really benefited except prolonging the inevitable—just ten days until it was "official." I wished I could keep it all a secret. I wasn't disillusioned. I wasn't in denial. I just wanted to live as if nothing was wrong for a few more moments—like how those ten minutes of sleep after hitting the snooze button a couple of times really matter (maybe a little). It is what it is, so the saying goes.

But I absolutely knew better. Ten days; my own little Passover vacation in the hospital. Although this holiday commemorates when the Israelites were freed from Egyptian bondage by Moses, in their own minds, they were still slaves. It was a mentality.

You see, when problems are our masters, we are being told what to do, we relinquish responsibility, and we become dangerously compliant. Often, it's because we predict all the potential negative consequences that influence our sense of self and power.

The ancient Israelites and their sense of reality and its laws were shattered with impossible miracles that brought them out and redeemed them from slavery. They were taken out of their suffering and rescued by God—and *still* they would wander the desert for 40 years questioning their lives with what wonders their eyes beheld, catastrophizing that they would perish, and asking if such a grand redemption was all for nothing. They were repeatedly reassured by God and Moses and provided for—their daily food literally grew overnight! Wouldn't that be nice? Yet they were so used to the years of slavery, of *unbeing,* that they pined for the predictable days of discomfort where hope would not burden them. Hope can be like holding a hot coal: it'll burn you if you don't put it to use.

So, if the path to liberation was miraculously revealed by the splitting of the sea, you'd think faith would follow the rest of your life. But all too often, doubt casts such long shadows, chasing you into the future. Must it be this way? Is this simply part of the human condition?

I was scared, but still I made the choice to break my chains and fight cancer. Yet I learned very quickly that this fight was also with myself. I didn't have Moses to lead me out, or mighty miracles to convince me I would find salvation, and I had to go to the grocery store for my own food. But the Passover story persists all these thousands of years later to this day for a reason. We as people still war with uncertainty, and all too often, we become trapped in servitude to it. But I had breath despite my plagued lungs, divinely given breath which allowed me to live another moment and take action. I would not let doubt, despair, or complacency become my tyrannical pharaoh. I would garb myself in the royal vestments necessary to take accountability for my life. This was personal leadership's uniform. And I would deny only one thing: *this looks like a lost case.* Because I would not be enslaved by these words. And neither should you.

As soon as I arrived home, I paced around my apartment racking my brain for solutions. How to prepare for the days ahead—how to get ready for battle. I could not become my own worst enemy. Accountability of self recognizes that we have the potential to defeat ourselves more than anyone or anything else. We must be vigilant. And next to whoever or whatever you hold as your higher power—you, yourself, must be your greatest ally.

Ten long days. At least I was able to sleep in my own bed. The secretary from the hospital called at last. "Would you be able to come in today or this week to receive them?

"Can Dr. Hartman tell me the results over the phone? I'd rather save the gasoline."

"The protocol is that we must have you come in—I can't change this."

"Look, I know I have cancer. I am not driving all that way to hear this. I just need to know the extent of it and who to see next."

She paused. "I'll speak with the doctor and have him call you back."

It was as simple as that. That drive would just be another waste of precious time.

I instantly recognized Dr. Hartman's voice. "Eeki Elner?"

"Yes, this is him. Thank you for calling me back, doctor."

"Look, I think it would be a really good idea if you came in so we can discuss your test results." There was heaviness in his voice.

"Please, just tell me how bad my cancer is, doctor, and who I should plan to see next."

"I'm sorry, but it isn't good—"

"You sound sorrier than I am, doctor."

"Sorry?" He seemed to collect himself for a different approach. "Look, you sound like a bright guy. I am sorry to say, but it is a serious case and—"

"That's okay, because I heard what you said."

"What do you mean?"

"When you came into the biopsy room, you thought I was asleep, but I wasn't." He was quiet. A 'serious case,' he said—I wish it was just a serious case! At least that had a little room for optimism, but he had said it was a lost cause. I could almost hear him holding his head in his hands. "That's okay, doctor, because I did fall asleep afterward. Both of you said it, but it's good. I will prove you wrong."

A long pause. "For that, I *am* deeply sorry." He took a breath. "And I hope you do, but you must know the chances are against you. The statistics show ninety percent die within the first year. What I am trying to say is, my claim was not unfounded."

I felt like I was sinking underwater. Before I completely tuned out, we discussed setting up an oncologist visit with a couple of referrals, and then we hung up.

I slumped onto my couch, which seemed to become the go-to place for my sadness ever since Judah had taken me to the E.R. A place where I could sink and wait. It would be a slow but certain powering down into paralysis. I had finally broken ground in the U.S. for the ILI, a hard-won expansion that had people's livelihoods tied to it, such as my close friend, Todd, who served as the president of the Israel Leadership Institute North America. How could I tell him that the ILI may soon collapse on top of us? Could he handle it himself?

I proudly broke that intercontinental wall, but now another barrier, sky-high, stood in my way. Flashbacks dragged me further down. *Why did I waste so much time?*

There is one perspective that resonates with me the most by Tzvi Freeman, a prolific writer and editor on Jewish mysticism:

"Solomon the wise said, 'from every sadness there will be an advantage.' Meaning that sadness itself has no advantage—but an advantage comes out of it—when it's over and done with. But is there any advantage that comes out of depression? Yes, one thing: A depressed person feels very small. That's good. Smallness is good. Especially when breaking out of your cell. Because once small enough, you can fit between the bars of any prison cell and escape. Especially the prison cells in which we lock up our own selves." He goes on to say that a small person believes they do not deserve anything, but if they were big—the small things would be insignificant.

Ah, *humility.* I took a breath and realized that despite my lungs carrying the poison determined to destroy my body, they still gave me breath. My body was listening to my mind—there needed to be a healthy, positive dialogue between them. *I'll show you the way out. Follow my lead.* It was a drawn-out moment, but I felt my heart calm my restless mind—*we can't stay stuck here. Let's go.*

In this moment, I managed to slip through the bars. I would not spend any more time fighting with myself. Sure, we could bicker, but what would come of it?

Get up.

I embraced discomfort as an alternative fuel source and sprung off the couch.

It was time to make a difficult call.

The first person I told was none other than Eyal Arad, otherwise known as the kingmaker of Israel. He had led the campaign teams that got three prime ministers elected. He is an expert in leadership and a seasoned strategist. With an unassuming persona, he was the kind of person you could philosophize with and walk away carrying near-tangible treasures of wisdom. I always enjoyed a hard drink with the man when I really needed one. He was one of the closest friends I had.

I asked him if I could come by the next day to go over "something important."

He didn't press for what it was.

I would do some reading on my diagnosis before I came by the next afternoon.

I squeezed my car into a nearby side street and made my way toward his apartment. Tel Aviv was bustling, packed to the brim with life. I hadn't lived there for a few years now, but it wasn't just this span of time that made me feel disconnected. It felt very different now, or maybe I felt very different about myself.

I walked up the stairs to Eyal's apartment and knocked on the door.

"Eeki, come in. Coffee? Tea? Vodka?"

I hefted a laugh. "Huh, you know I almost drove home when I couldn't find parking. It's why I don't come here more often."

"And that's why I live here."

Eyal grinned as he went to his ceiling-high liquor cabinet and grabbed a couple of glasses and a bottle of whiskey. His apartment was pristine. On his couch, I looked through his picture window with a view of a sunset soaked street. A nearby bookshelf and desk glowed with books on theology and philosophy amongst other classics; they were well kept but had seen use.

As he handed me a glass, I spotted a cluster of his grandkids' toys shuffled into the corner of the apartment's impressively broad living room. He noticed what I had seen and shrugged. "Sometimes you have to pick your battles."

"I didn't say anything!" The clear liquid swirled in my glass as I leaned back into the couch.

"Your eyes did," he said, raising his glass. "L'chaim."

"L'chaim!" I downed the shot, feeling the warm liquid in my chest. "Eyal, you know that one workshop, Leadership in Times of Emergency, where all the students are put through mock-crisis and stressful situations?"

"Of course, what about it?"

"I'm going through it right now, but it's real." My eyes hovered over my empty glass for a moment while I collected myself. "I have stage-four lung cancer."

Eyal looked at the floor, quietly considering what I had told him. He threw back another shot and met my eyes. "Have you spoken with an oncologist yet?"

"No, but I have one I'll be seeing in a few days."

He was unsurprisingly calm, but sadness radiated throughout the room like an electric current. "What can I do to help? I'm sure there's a lot going through your head right now. The ILI?"

His stoic composure was an incredible relief. I was doing all I could to not break down.

"Look, I'm not sure how things are going to go. I've chosen to fight, you know me, but there's got to be some kind of plan to keep the organization from falling apart. Once I see the oncologist, I could use your advice. I'm sure there will be some big decisions to make.

"The biggest one has already been made, my friend. I'll help you with whatever I can."

We spoke for some time after as I sobered up—but not so much mentally. I felt like I would slip into the sewer on my walk back to my car. A couple with a baby stroller was crossing the street and greeted me, *shalom*. I walked past them without even realizing it, though I still swiveled around awkwardly returning their greeting. We exchanged brief smiles, but as I turned toward my car, mine melted. I felt like I wore the brazen visage of a dying man.

In the next couple of days, I found an oncologist and Garik chaperoned me to my appointment. I told him I had cancer the moment he arrived. I felt like I didn't really have a choice, but it was a much easier one to make. I wish he would have let me turn on the damn radio. On the drive over, he broke the quiet again and said, "It's going to be okay. All will be well." This time it was more like an affirmative chant.

The first three oncologist visits were like a string of heartbreaks—I felt like I walked out with my tail between my legs. Each one looked me in the eyes and told me I had, at most, six months. They simply stacked me against the statistics, the odds obviously not in my favor, and their outlooks the same. I went ferociously for a fourth round, but I was feeling like I had already struck out. I was going a little crazy by this point. I felt bloody and bruised, but at least the fourth oncologist had given me the same life sentence with a pretty bow on top.

I had gone alone this time. I was sitting down in the fourth oncologist's office a few weeks into my search. I imagine he saw my weariness—notably, his brow rose with a strained smile.

"Six months is what the statistics say, and there's approximately a ten-percent survival rate after the first year." There he was scapegoating the number sheet, though, he genuinely seemed sad and almost as if he didn't believe it.

He gently rotated side to side in front of his computer like the pendulum on a grandfather clock, each turn a solemn second counting down the approximately sixteen million seconds I had left.

"You know doctor, no one has been telling me how to fight this. Sure, chemo, drink water, get sleep—" I took a breath. It was no use dispersing my anger on him. He considered my words.

"Is there anything you wanted to do in your life that you never got around to? Seriously, something you always wished to do?"

"Sure, I always wanted to hike a glacier in Iceland. Maybe even climb a mountain."

"Really?"

"Yes, that wasn't a punch line to a joke."

He smiled. "Go. Make the most of this time, however much is left. Really, who knows how much any of us have—but at least there is some urgency to really live on your end."

At least he didn't tell me to go to Disney World, but I certainly could've used a little more urgency earlier in my life. It wasn't bad advice, he had good intentions, but it certainly was not the answer I was looking for. Four oncologists—four—had come to the same determination. Week after week. It's not that I hoped the numbers would magically change. I wanted an ally. Someone to be on *my* side.

I took the scenic route home. Israel constantly shimmers in golden sunshine, but it seemed artificial that day—or perhaps I was looking through dirt-tinted glasses. I was in some kind of trance, the car humming down the road and my mind juggling the voices of the past few weeks like some crazy clown—all of them telling me how sad it was, or that I'm going to die soon. I slammed my fists on the steering wheel and held back tears. My old wipers groaned across the dry windshield—something about it hit my funny bone. *Wipe your eyes, you silly fool. You look ridiculous. Just breathe.*

The sun vanished, now filtered through a dense forest, light flickering between trunks. Like a flip book, my life flashed by, now disintegrating into dust. I told myself to squash this thought—this senseless analogy. We make sense of things through stories, from vantage points that are but one possible perspective. I watched birds fly into the forest, lost between the trees as they vanished into the piercing light.

I felt small and shackled—these trees were a barrier to the light like the bars of my cell. I thought of looking down to see if I was wearing prison garb.

Sunshine, what are you trying to show me? What good are you hiding in my lungs?

In this void, my lowest moment, I prayed to God to help me make sense of it all. I felt like I was doing my fair share, but it never seemed to be enough. My life was still ending. I took a good look through the forest and saw the setting sun, the galaxy's heart still beating through a wooden ribcage.

Life still courses through my veins. Fight this. I kept saying it until I heard it—until I wanted to tell myself to shut the hell up.

In my mind's eye, I saw myself leading myself. I realized that, at all times, my life is dependent on my own leadership to weather the universe's calculated chaos. *This was the uniform tool at work.* To be a leader is to choose the persona and attitude of a leader and come to believe in and comport our lives as such.

I was not going to let anyone else tell me how my life would be any longer. I would walk the talk and wear my insides out proudly. I would keep searching until I found someone who would tell me yes! I would have to fight for my throne. When I got home, I sat on that couch like a king, ready to reign over my future.

PART III

Tool: The Library

SPEEDING DOWN MEMORY LANE

People often forget when they have survived. All the times you've overcome challenges can become dusty trophies left on your mental mantle to rust. In my own life, I fought to forget *what had* scarred me because I was so severely wounded by my past. I knew well when the beginning of my ill-advised survival mentality was born.

This was not some sort of amnesia or repressed collection of memories, though I had often wished it was. I was a track star in high school, but I could not run away from my past. I was often running despite my successes, which inevitably curtailed my potential for growth. During my battle with cancer, I had to adopt another method in order to fight.

I had always admired my parents for the unfathomable hardship they faced. *They were survivors.* The Holocaust did not keep them from their potential—a feat of epic scale.

I survived my mistakes, blindsides, and an assortment of challenges, including cancer. It's no boast, truly; I would opt out of such a terrible competition if I ever had the choice. I'm not just surviving anymore, and my sense of fulfillment could not be based on survival. Instead, it had to be sourced from my spiritual core, my essence, and consist of everything I was, am, and am meant to be, without a survivor's mentality. I couldn't keep running away. *Easier said than done.*

I had long lacked proper gratitude for my life and potential and had mostly lived each day as if to further distance myself from my past. My decisions were often built on whims instead of wisdom. I was living less because I didn't want to think about the bigger things in life. It all was just a bunch of white noise.

Cancer's call was a concussive grenade in my head, and while my ears were ringing, I was frantically grasping for solid ground when all around me was sand.

This is not an attempt to self-deprecate but to show the impact of an attitude on one's life. *Living care-free costs.* My survivor's mentality was some kind of maladaptation shaped from an early age by my environment. My means of survival was to not care as much about the outcome of my life.

I would like to say that I had accomplished a lot: I helped shape Israeli politics, supported various causes, and fostered intimate friendships throughout my life. I invested a great deal of heart into revealing and developing leadership in others, but something amiss had long simmered within my soul. I overlooked many opportunities, missed connections, and pleasant possibilities because I was hiding behind my career. Before I had ever been diagnosed with cancer, a cancerous attitude kept me from myself and who I was meant to become.

Experiences felt too fleeting. I couldn't get excited about what was to come because I was preoccupied with avoiding the wreckage of what once was.

What had I survived exactly? I had long kept these memories to myself. And for now, from you too. It wouldn't be until I developed a stronghold of self like a *fortress,* built on my personal leadership, that my mentality could truly transform.

And there was something else that had me struggling with the sense of squandered opportunity. I had been intimately involved in developing what could have been the constitution of Israel—if you didn't know—it doesn't have one.

The day I was appointed general director of the Constitution for Israel, one of the most influential public organizations in the history of our country, was one of the proudest of my life. I was chosen from 70-plus candidates. I saw the opportunity to shape the future of my country forever. And as a son of Holocaust survivors, who had no homeland from which to escape Nazi persecution, it was a moral mission for me to secure a constitution for my country. Thrilling a journey as it was, the legislative body of Israel known as the Knesset was still not ready to ratify a complete constitution. Personally, I came out of this period of my life with great advantages and learnings that have been my strength for years to come. For this, I am eternally grateful.

I began to use gratitude to challenge my survivalist way of thinking. When wielded as a tool, and especially when you might not feel very much of it, gratitude is most effective. Gratitude is a present-oriented way of thinking that allows us to also look at the past and future and accept what we have with serenity. Ultimately, without gratitude, and I mean, the truest of gratitude—living each day as if we have been blessed with one more breath to fulfill our purpose—we may not truly live. This is idealistic, but is it really that far out of reach?

In the absence of gratitude, there is a void in its place. You will fixate on what you don't have; there's room for envy, a lack of this and that. It must be said there is nothing wrong with wanting more or moving on to circumstances that fit your path at its due time, but if you do not cherish what you already have, and that you, yourself, are invaluable *at this finite point in time*, no change in circumstances will satiate that hunger in your heart. What is enough for today is not enough for tomorrow if we don't believe in our potential.

I am growing. It was a lovely thought that aided me time and time again, especially when I felt empty, when purpose was nowhere in sight.

Perhaps you are feeling such a void. Rightfully so! Why should you be grateful when life just flushed you down the toilet? Your business, health, marriage, relationships, sense of life in the face of loss—whatever may be circling the drain to God knows where—is a form of grief. You are losing or missing something.

During my fight with cancer, I would lose both of my parents. There is no shortage of loss in life. There's plenty to go around. Large or small, you may still find yourself going through the stages of grief for countless things. Reaching acceptance has its own path and pace for everyone. As part of your grief process, you can reflect on how you got here. Perhaps it can help it all make sense, or at least, give you a place to rebuild from.

In the grand scheme of life, what are your "ground zeroes"? Do you need to bottom out? Is that what is happening to you? And for what?

I believe all people have a unique destiny always waiting for them, some innate sense of direction. And when you are lost, you feel it. Open your eyes, and you might realize you are not where you should be. This destiny doesn't have to be an epic, theatrical movie with a great, grand finale—it must be you, wherever you are, who climbs into tomorrow. As the American artist Paul Palnik once said, "life is not about the big things, it is made of all the little things."

I learned the greatest gratitude is that which sees each moment as an *opportunity*. The moment is all we truly have, and whatever you may be going through, there is still some kind of opportunity, however big or small, that you can take advantage of—because when there is *truly* nothing you can do, that is when hopelessness becomes your tyrant. Tomorrow is not promised and nothing on this earthly plane lasts forever—opportunity allows for change.

So, *how am I going to lead myself through this?* Remember this question?

But maybe you aren't ready to ask about what can be done right now— maybe you don't know where to start. What if I were to tell you that, perhaps, you've already started? The past is your library. It is time to study *what was* to appreciate *now*, and to imagine what can be. This isn't meant to be fancy talk. I only know my successes because of my shortcomings. If I am to competently lead myself, I must know where I came from. And I dare to say that all of us at some levels are guilty of this: I lived as if tomorrow were promised.

Was it too late for me to start living my life after the onset of this medical death sentence? No, it never is. But sometimes, let's face it, you may need a big slap in the face to finally appreciate what you've lost. I thought I believed nothing was too late, but all the doctors were telling me it was—and for a moment, I believed them. It was on my drive to the fifth oncologist that I found myself riding down memory lane—where I ask you to take the schlep with me. To live personal leadership, to lead your truth, you must know where you came from. I would see the past for what it was, and this would help me forge my future.

❖   ❖   ❖

The drive from Sderot to Tel Aviv was a long hour. My eyes strained to see through the blinding morning light as I left the comfort of my home for oncologist number five. *I am not driving all this way to hear him tell me no, I thought.* Moses was infinitely more patient than me! It felt like a projector was beaming through a dark theater. I smoothed my hair, which I realized might not be there much longer once I started chemo. Flustered, I recounted how I got here and why I was going to another hospital to possibly hear I was going to die again. I recalled the holiday of Passover, how the Israelites' sudden escape from Egypt represented their physical liberation, but their much longer journey afterward through the desert represented the fight to liberate their souls from slavery. Passover was a miraculous redemption of an entire people, not just from slavery, but from themselves.

My ingratitude for the ephemeral nature of life and my penchant to squelch my inner voice of truth would be my sacrificial offerings for redemption. I would pave new mental pathways. My old motto, *there's no use dredging up old dirt*, would become, *let me redeem this for a greater purpose*. The past is a resource, and there is nothing to regret or lament over because these difficulties are diamond opportunities to learn. And if need be, regret can be the energy to make necessary change, but you must expend the feeling until it's burnt out. Growth is life, and through pressure, even with a pristine past, there is always more expected of us because that's what destiny demands. If you do nothing and stagnate, you may feel like you're dead. My destiny demanded I return to the hospital for a different answer:

The heat inside my car put me into a trance-like haze (don't worry, both eyes were on the road!) Just a few blocks from my apartment, I noticed a couple strolling, hands interlocked. I had known them for a long time. Hard working and well-off, their kids almost out of high school, this couple had recognized their destiny, not because these accomplishments are necessarily the gold standard—but because they had built a legacy, something I feared I wouldn't leave behind. Their sanguine walk stirred something within me. I saw this couple as future-minded and self-determined, placing their emphasis on building tomorrow, today. It wasn't a matter they achieved what I could not—as Victor Frankl once said, "No man and no destiny can be compared with any other man or any other destiny." But still, they reminded me that I had not fully pursued my own.

There was an energy between them, a visible electrical current, as if they had just fallen in love. I smiled, but my mind sunk into love-scarred memories, recollections from what felt like another life—my younger self viewed as if he were my own child. *How did I get here?* Answers played before me the whole ride to Tel Aviv. *Giselle.*

RESEARCH YOUR PAST
FOR A BRIGHTER FUTURE

T he year was '85. I was living in Tel Aviv, hunkered down in a cramped apartment scouring law books with loose leaf paper spread across my desk. Right after I left the army at the ripe age of 21, I went to law school—not at the behest of my family, it was my idea, and they all thought it was a great one. I was hustling alongside my studies, selling paintings across the city and the next one over. I was a hard worker. But I didn't quite know what I was working so hard for. Then I met her.

It was just an ordinary evening out seeking some adventure. The night welcomed me with the unknown—Tel Aviv was awake in the dark, and a bar I had not noticed before beckoned me as I gazed around the bustling streets. As I crossed the threshold, loud disco music drew me in like a siren reeling me in. I ordered a drink from the busy bartender and eased into my stool chair, casing the row of people along the wood grain countertop. After my first drink, I realized I wasn't really here for anything other than blending into the ambience. It was pleasant to just float in the moment with the sense of direction of a bubble. A growing warmth encompassed me like a bath over the course of the next hour.

I spent some time on my second drink, gazing into it while I wondered where my life was going. Uncomfortable thoughts began to emerge, so I eyed the door, readying myself to leave. But then *she* walked in. Tall, thin-necked, with cascading light brown hair resting on a mink coat—she must've stepped out of a *Vogue* magazine straight into the bar. Museum-worthy jewels adorned her fingers and neck—they were nearly as bright as her green eyes. I realized I wasn't breathing. Was this some kind of lucid dream?

Her eyes embraced mine for a moment—I was already out of my seat—my thoughts were unintelligible, and I found myself goofily sitting back down. A rough translation of my brain's garbled words was, *I needed to know her.*

I waved the bartender over. "Hey, do me a favor please. Can you put whatever drink she orders on my tab?"

"Can do."

I noticed my foot was tapping. Despite having a couple of drinks, my nerves were still like livewires. Why are you nervous? I had looked away long enough to lose her, yet she found a seat next to me.

I glanced at her glass. "So, what did you end up getting?"

"A Kir Royale." She smiled.

Expensive. "I'll have to try one."

"Oh, you'll be staying? Seemed like you were about to leave."

I grinned. "It depends."

"On?" Her eyebrow raised.

"What your story is."

"Well, mine's still being written."

We spoke until the din of the bar mellowed and grew sleepy. She was significantly older than me—years more of lived experience—but I was not too concerned. We promised to meet again at another bar she recommended. And so, we would get drinks again and again. Any time I had away from studies, we'd be together. I was enamored, future-tripping dreamy scenes of laughter and storytelling, lavish parties, and traveling the world together. An all-consuming hurricane of my own making took form. There wasn't much room for anything else in my head.

I was high on love, but it wasn't just that. I am not trying to tell you a lovelorn story—there was something else underneath it all that I believe applies to everyone, at one point or another, especially in the face of adversity: I was avoiding big questions. The ones that have you explain yourself inside out. *I could answer them another day.* And so, the whirlwind spun, and my hot air balloon of a head continued to rise high aloft in dreams, above the tangible textures of reality.

A year in and I was still riding the wave. We were at the Sheraton this time—shoreside in Tel Aviv. This place felt majestic compared to where we first met. Inside the lounge, soft, amber light filled the room amongst the sound of European dance music. It was quite a sensory cocktail. We sat catty-corner, basking in each other's presence while other patrons dotted the room, notably twice my age, though it never occurred to me for more than a moment.

"We've talked and talked about travel, my prince. Let's go to Paris. I'll take you down Champs-Élysées—there're so many shops and cafes to see. And I know people there. You haven't been to parties like these. And the food, Eeki," she gushed, "there's nothing like it."

I scanned her face. We'd gone out on quite a few fancy get-togethers, and plenty of euphoric nights, but this was something else. Something about her proposition stirred me up like the moment I first saw her.

"Let's go. I'll figure out how to get my work done around it."

A classmate appeared in the hotel lounge. He approached me with a smile, yet his eyes looked confused, his brow raised.

"Eeki... what are you doing here?" I don't think he was just asking to be nice; there was genuine curiosity in his tone. I shifted in my seat, oddly avoiding Giselle's gaze. His eyes flicked to her and then to me again. "It's good to see you—"

I spoke up. "Uri, it's a special occasion with my girlfriend here, let me introduce you to Giselle." But it was just another ordinary day for us. I wasn't necessarily embarrassed, but I didn't want to explain myself. Answering his question meant explaining not just to him, but to myself, why I, a law school student, was lounging at one of the most expensive spots in town like it was any other night. Why wasn't I studying, or thinking about what I would do when I graduated?

I could make any number of excuses, but you see, Giselle had nearly twice as many years on me, and even though she had achieved such an alluring lifestyle that I wanted to emulate, she was wondering what the plot of her life's story was and wasting time with me. My story had yet to truly begin.

It's a wonder when a person's story begins. At birth? A memoir-worthy time like when I got cancer? Or is it whenever you decide it has? There doesn't need to be an inciting incident or fire starter for your personal character arc—though I surely needed one.

I was blind to my blessings bursting at the seams, particularly *time*—arguably the most precious of possessions. Family and friends told me I had looks, wit, and a way with people. I'd do great things. *Great things.* Whether that was true or not, I still went back to my own apartment that night to study with Paris on my mind and not much else.

There was only so much hot air my head could hold before exploding. Our first breakup wasn't long after the Paris proposal, though we got back together again a couple years later and married, then divorced and got back together again! A clumsy pattern of foibles, failures, and even triumphs. When investigating the past, you can't only search for your mistakes. You can consider what times you truly listened to that voice and *chose* to follow it.

Shortly before our first breakup, Giselle and I were at a café on the edge of the Mediterranean Sea. It was calm after a period of calamity. Our fights had been about the clash between my studies and our outings. Despite not thinking about much beyond graduation, I knew a crossroad was approaching. But there would be no inciting incident at this intersection. A light breeze wisped her hair.

"Giselle, I can't keep doing this. I need to be focusing on school, but we keep fighting over time that I can't spare anymore."

Her gaze shifted to the road, watching a few passersby. "Eeki, relax. You're doing well with your studies. You told me yourself. Nothing has changed."

"You're not taking me seriously. Look, I don't want to fight again, but this time it's really different."

She still didn't hear me. But I heard myself. In the weeks that followed we spoke less and less. I decided to use that time to work toward my degree. Eventually, the calls between us stopped. The end of us was a slow melt, yet the gravity of my decision hurled me toward the ground. I had mentioned this decision wasn't predicated on a reaction to a clear conflict. Personal leadership requires the will to fight for what you believe in, but sometimes these beliefs can be blurry or hidden behind our own limitations. My soul called out for me to stop wasting my life, but I wasn't going to fight for time if I felt like I had it all. It was a hard truth to hear. I had to act then. *And I had to act now.*

Our dream of Paris would remain a dream, that is, until we married. By then, it was nothing like I had imagined it to be—it was wonderful, but it felt more realistic. Maybe I had matured? Eventually, we broke up again. It wasn't so much later that she died of a heart attack. Life is so short. I had learned so much through her about *being me*.

◆ ◆ ◆

As I passed Ben Gurion airport on my drive to the oncologist in Tel Aviv, I considered how this bittersweet memory on the shores of the Mediterranean carried an echo of self-determination. *I had chosen to walk my own path.*

There was a void after Giselle, but I still wondered if it was a longing for love or purpose. Only until my diagnosis did I realize the latter was true.

Brace yourselves—it wasn't too long before I fell in love again with someone else. She was a friend of a friend, and her name was Orit. We can often make the same mistakes more than once, or worse ones. The nagging voice inside me was patiently waiting to see what I would do next. Orit and I dated for a bit. She was a student too, and my age, and better understood where I was in life. But she didn't really consider where I was going—never mind herself. Orit was a salt-of-the-earth hippy whose thoughts went where the wind blew. I can't remember a time when she wasn't wearing a baggy band shirt with some obscure album art that was beginning to fade. She always wore a threaded headband with her hair messily cascading over it like an overgrown flowerpot.

Giselle and Orit were from two different planets, and I simply lived in their orbits. I don't quite remember the moment we fell in love. But near graduation, it happened. We bonded—perhaps only because we knew our romance was destined to end.

She just cut it off one day. It was worse than with Giselle because I had no part in directing my future; I was simply an actor in it. But it was a blessing in disguise. At this pivotal point, it became a choice between law or Orit. Her parents had just divorced, her brothers would stay with their mother— and her father would move to Belgium. Orit couldn't let him be alone. *Law or Orit?*

Go ahead and guess which option I chose.

My parents had gifted me a ticket to LA to visit my sister. I hadn't seen her in quite some time, yet we wrote back and forth over the years—remember people did that back then? But this trip would never be. Without anyone's knowledge, I had the airline adjust the ticket. One way to Belgium. Goodbye law school, right before the finish line.

Again, you'd think I was chasing after love, but really, I was running away—trying to hide from my purpose. It never was about Giselle or Orit, though I do think I loved them. I believe there are many ways you can overlook, hide, and minimize your options without being aware of how you even do so or if these choices exist. Maybe you do know and it's just willful ignorance. At its worst, you are completely conscious of the wrong path you willingly trek.

Before my flight, I gave Orit a call. Our relationship was close to death.

"Orit, you won't believe me, but I'm going to be stopping in Belgium." I told her I needed to see her. I dropped everything. I had slammed the door shut on law school, an opportunity that I had worked so hard for, and threw it away as if it was nothing.

She instantly began to cry. I couldn't help myself either. Those tears were like a salve for this gaping wound we shared. *So naïve!*

Yes, I was foolish enough to drop out to move in with her for a year, only to come back after we broke up with my tail between my legs. Never saw that coming, *sheesh*. There are lessons in life, universal yet unique to your soul. Maybe law wasn't for me, but that isn't the point.

Alas, as my car sputtered along to the doctor's, I passed Ariel Sharon Park, named for the late Israeli prime minister. I took another breath, one of acceptance. Then came another memory, the same exact mistake. I should've known better. *At least now I do, I thought, trying to console myself.*

There were literal phone calls beckoning me toward my calling that I denied. In '99 I received a call from the leader of the secular-liberal Shinui Party, Tommy Lapid, who offered me the third-highest position on their list of candidates for the upcoming Israeli parliamentary election. At the time, I was still leading Constitution for Israel. The Shinui Party's platform shared the basis of our mission—we had the same goals. Tommy gave me the pitch of the century.

How could I say no? I found plenty of reasons. I was already a growing public figure, yet I wanted to remain private. I didn't want my personal life under a microscope. I didn't have anything to hide—aside from maybe smoking a little pot and who I might've dated. There was so much to gain and not much to lose. This would've furthered my cause, but I had little consideration for the future, and I lacked appreciation for my capabilities. I was capable, but for what? I kept on the move—on the run—fleeing toward adventures that would take me further from what was inside myself.

In full hindsight, I can now see this path would not have renewed me or my sense of direction. The occasional negative voice would try to convince me otherwise, but this was the truth. I would have grown professionally but not personally, the way I was meant to. At the same time, I preferred fighting for the constitution from the position of a social activist, not from a political seat. I was not ready to pay the cost of a "political life" and all the exposure it required. Years later, when I retired from the movement with the job not yet finished, I was proud of my efforts. But the fact that achieving our goal—passing a constitution and ensuring rights for everyone—was no further in sight was a great source of frustration. I stuffed this feeling away not knowing that one day it would erupt again when I got cancer.

I had no doubts about how comfortable it may have been to work in the Knesset, to be a member with no primaries to struggle through, being paid generously and acquiring a high status in society. But I thought I could get along by making my own path.

It might sound rather bad just throwing this opportunity away. Six years later, the Israeli prime minister's son and personal messenger, Omri, called me with another offer I refused: a seat in parliament. Think of the influence I would have had, the possibility of making a difference in the country I love with every atom of my being! I was in the same position as before, with the same vision, and yet I was still unable to accept. I would be tied down, tethered. Freedom to flee was a source of comfort for me, and comfort can cannibalize the good in your life.

I remember driving to capitol hill in Jerusalem—it was late and unusually dark, the area's large buildings sleepily resting like dozing giants. I went into the main building, worried I'd wake someone or something, and found my way to Omri's office. There was an austerity to the place, a bit materially majestic, sure, but *work* was done here. It was like that in his office—real spartan-like, the chairs built for discomfort. No plants to green the place. We had known each other for years, and I could see his eagerness to give his pitch.

He gave me his no B.S. look that I'd become accustomed to. "Look, we're forming a new party. And one of the main pillars of our platform is to finalize the constitution—something you're intimately familiar with. We need you here. I want you to become the chairman of the constitutional committee. I want you to lead. *Finalize it.* I can't think of anyone else. This is what you wanted, Eeki." A full, glorious orchestra of musicians might as well have been playing on his desk.

"You know me, I like to have fun, I like to party—I'm a little crazy and childish." I tuned myself to be more serious. "Look, there's a flexibility working more independently, and it works for me now. I won't have this as a member of Parliament. It's not going to work. You guys are going to be successful without me. The polls show it." I looked out the window searching for something but only seeing a void. I guess some part of me wanted to escape into the courtyard where I might get away from the good fight because of what it meant for me: I would have to revamp my lifestyle, and particularly my attitude toward it. This was quite a discomfort. I definitely wasn't a spartan.

He looked as if he had just stuck his hand in an electric socket. He hid neither his shock nor his frustration. Instead, he tried to convince me. "Yes, Eeki, but this position—this honor is especially for you. It *is* you."

I didn't take the offer seriously. It was another choice I took for granted. I declined. This wasn't a conscious decision, but one from my gut. Nonetheless, the choice was made. I may as well have started tooting a kazoo during that profound symphony. I must have been such a buzzkill. But I would come to understand this path would not have renewed me.

At times when I doubt myself now, these memories come back and hit me like vengeful boomerangs. *Let it go, I remind myself.* But it isn't that easy, is it? I had lied to myself and taken the easy route. Why? The truth is, I didn't think through the implications. It was an uninformed decision because I had not fully explored my past and what influence it had on my present. It formed a lens that had falsely colored much of life.

My survivor's attitude toward living meant that I clung to what worked well *now*. I wasn't going to dive into an ocean of possibilities if it meant risking my raft, but beneath the depths could be treasures and hidden wisdom. Beyond the island of my safety and comfort, there could be new lands I could settle and really build my life upon. I was grateful for what I could hold onto, but not for the opportunity. I learned some of this from my parents. As Holocaust survivors, they knew to hang onto what little you had to live. I had my own soul-wrenching experience that taught me the same.

In that meeting with Omri, a voice spoke from the depths of me. I needed to get away from it. There would be no third offer.

I was my own pharaoh. It was as if I believed more and more opportunities would come—there would eventually be the big one. Maybe I was feeling a little entitled at the time, but I think I was just so detached from the ephemeral nature of life—you don't have all that much time to fulfill your purpose here, and time goes on ticking for everyone else.

Battling cancer was not something I could turn down. It was as if God had grabbed me by the shoulders and pushed me to look at my life. It was a challenge to test my mettle, so I might teach people how to find their true purpose. I was rapidly running out of time—I would die—this was something I could not deny.

You don't have to go cutting back on sleep now to make it all up, of course not, but each day must be a step toward a greater goal—even if that begins with recovering from disaster. The road may be unpaved, rocky, and unstable, yet we can learn to rely on our abilities to traverse any terrain. Our pathways may take twists and turns, but we are meant to move forward, ever striving to ascend to our potential. *Change is good.* But sometimes we must plummet if we are ever to realize and appreciate our summits.

◆ ◆ ◆

There was one more memory that bubbled up in my brain. I was just out of school in the military during mandatory service in Israel. I was placed in the anti-aircraft unit somewhere in the mountains near Lebanon. I was nearly 19 years old and had just finished my training period as a fresh soldier. It just so happened that Tommy Lapid's son, Yair, who would later become a prime minister, was in the same training camp and even shared a tent with me.

Once, in the middle of the night, a heavy hand grabbed my shoulder and woke me up.

"Get up. We're going into Lebanon."

"What? What do you mean?"

"We're going to war. Let's go."

I quickly joined everyone scrambling to get ready. My backpack was already ready to go—something I would understand as a meaningful metaphor for mental tools later in life. As we were making our way out of the tents, I thought to myself, *once you step out that door, you're going to war.* I thought about how war makes you a hero, but I never intended to be one. I would need to fight for my life, my family and friends, and my country. I would need to be a leader of myself with the proper mentality. You can develop the mind of a soldier, but it must adhere to some higher state of mind—I thought about how I needed to speak to myself within my own head. What would this voice sound like? It needed to be strong, brave, and confident. I would consciously develop it over time.

I was soon wounded by some shrapnel and transferred into a non-combative unit. I struggled with this for a while, but I left with a new appreciation for the power of the mind, and that inner voice who knows your truth.

FINDING WINGS

M y trip down memory lane reached its end. As I finally pulled into the hospital, I noticed how the large glass panes that walled the exterior seemed to embrace the inquisitive light from outside, yet still obscure my view with its reflective shine. I sighed deeply. The repeated rejections had nearly crushed me. I felt hopeless. *What's going to be any different this time?*

Inside, there were a few bookshelves in a waiting area near the large windows. A few people were reading in cushioned seats. My eyes hovered over the scene for a beat—a man with wispy gray hair was nestled next to the broad windowsill peering through a paper tunnel into another world. He briefly glanced up at me, like a comforting acknowledgement from an old cat. *These books...*

All my road trip reminiscing suddenly made sense. *The past is a library,* a vault of precious knowledge, but you must know how to study it without getting drawn into the undertow.

What felt like ruminating was instead researching strategies and solutions for overcoming my plight. I never fully appreciated the usefulness of reviewing my past, particularly in an intentional and formal capacity. It was certainly painful admitting my shortcomings. I wasn't sure of how much I could learn from it while also overcoming some of the holes it burned in my soul. There was quite a lot of knowledge I didn't know. And this meant there might still be something that could save me.

As we know, there is the duality of contrasts that give meaning to our lives. Pleasure and pain, light and darkness, and so on. And without my past, I would be doomed to repeat the same mistakes—this would be like leaving an entire vault of knowledge behind, like burning my own library of Alexandria. *If I were to live, things would have to be very different.* I knew God was involving Himself in my life, and this renewal of hope was fueled by my willingness to do everything I could do to not only survive but thrive beyond the next six months.

And so, I forgave myself. *It is okay. Let go. You see now. You know better. Experience is wisdom earned.* I thanked the old me for showing what I must do now. I returned the books of my past, maybe some of them were well overdue, but I put them back on their rickety shelves. I was done thinking about them until it might benefit me to reexamine their lessons, but some books are only worth a single read. (Hopefully not this one!)

Whether you are stuck in a cycle denying yourself decisions, stuck in the pit of ever deepening sorrow, or perhaps you feel all options have been exhausted, and hope is a hot coal you cannot bear to hold any more. If you choose to believe there is nothing to live for, then you have led yourself to the ultimate dead end.

I didn't want my life to end like this. Although everyone told me it was a waste of time, I still went to the office of the fifth oncologist. I entered the doctor's office hoping for a change in the forecast.

The room was quaint, purposeful, and the energy felt entirely different. Was it me? The man before me, Dr. Amir Onn, was gracefully unassuming. As we transitioned from small-talk to the big elephant in the room—no, not me—I felt I had something to say that wasn't necessarily meant for only him.

"I know the statistics, doctor. I know what you are supposed to say, but I am going to fight this. I'm not going to live out my days blowing what money I have left on skydiving or trying to make it to the moon. I am going to fight, but not to the death."

He watched me intently. Mighty Eeki, a Maccabee warrior, a ferocious lion—a stubborn, bull-headed oaf who finally stepped out of Plato's dank dark cave and saw the light.

"What can you do to help me battle this? No, the real question is, are you willing to stick with me beyond six months? Because I'll still be here."

He seemed to process the data—new statistics—and flashed an approving smile. "I'm with you. Yes. Let's do this together."

I was ready to clap back with some sort of rebuttal, but it was as if I had stalled my old stick shift car. He folded his hands on his desk and said, "There are a few new treatment options we can look into. One in particular may be of interest: a new biological medicine that is part of a research study. I can't promise I'll be able to get you in, but let's explore it because at this point chemo alone will do nothing to save you. You'd have to take the new medication, and it would be a critical commitment. Along with this, we'll try to eliminate anything that might not be so good for your health."

A part of me wanted to ask him why he didn't balk at my bold request for him to join me in this fight. He signed on to my life plan without reading the terms of agreement. Why did I want this? Maybe this moment felt too easy, too calm. All the resistance I had already faced, and this was the climax? Really?

Well, it was but one turning point of the journey—the warpath beyond the dark horizon. Maybe God spared me five more no's knowing I couldn't tolerate them like Moses did to the Pharaoh when he was fighting to free the Israelites from slavery. Lord knows I hadn't the patience. *Let's go!*

There was a distinct difference in my attitude. I felt the first four oncologists saw me as a page to fill, and they had the pen. They wrote a predictable, tragic ending each time. With Dr. Onn, I filled out the page and handed it over for him to sign—not for an endorsement, but as an agreement. We were to be partners. I chose to fight, took accountability for my own destiny, and I would own the mistakes of my youth because my younger self told me what must be done now. These are but a few tools of the personal leadership trade. I was the steering mast and becoming the captain, leading myself through the storm. Cancer would be the storm of my half century—and now I had a chief mate, *Dr. Onn.*

My sister Bracha met me at a coffee shop shortly after I left the hospital. She got a small latte that seemed more like a prop and just sat there looking at me—seeing through me, right through my funny facade I'd used so often to deflect anyone's concern for me. It was strange seeing us all these years later like we washed up here on dry land by happenstance, evolved and crawling our way to get some espresso. I awoke in that moment with a bird's eye view of my entire life. I was sure glad it was her across the table. All of what we'd been through, the good and bad and crazy too. Distance never mattered to us—neither time nor place—though I'm still not sure she forgave me for skipping out on that visit to LA.

She glanced at my wrist. "Maybe I should get you a new watch."

"For what?"

"So, you find yourself watching it more closely. Guarding it. Savoring it." She finally took a sip of her drink.

"Bracha, you know that time I was supposed to come to see you in LA. Back when—"

"You're not trying to apologize again, are you? Look, all I want for you is to live your life at its best, to be healthy and happy, but most of all to not miss out on your true potential." It is the way she said it—that familial knowing beyond all the filters, partitions, and armor we equip; the love-loaded words that caress your cheek and carry you into the wind—that moved me the most. "God's telling you to wake the hell up."

I laughed. Personal leadership is an awakening and becoming. An increase in your awareness. All becomes trivial except *what you are really here for*. What this looks like for me may be different for you. All people have a unique light that is concealed by distractions, worries, and challenges. For me, God expected more. My story wasn't over. I still haven't fully reached that higher self, but I certainly feel a whole lot closer.

My sister and I embraced. My usual defenses were all disarmed and subverted. She was a master infiltrator, but with the best of intentions. It felt like a kismet how she was there for me just as I overcame this critical leg of the climb. I wasn't sure what was at the top or if I was meant to surmount it, but the culmination of my experiences would be on my back—not as a burden, but as wings.

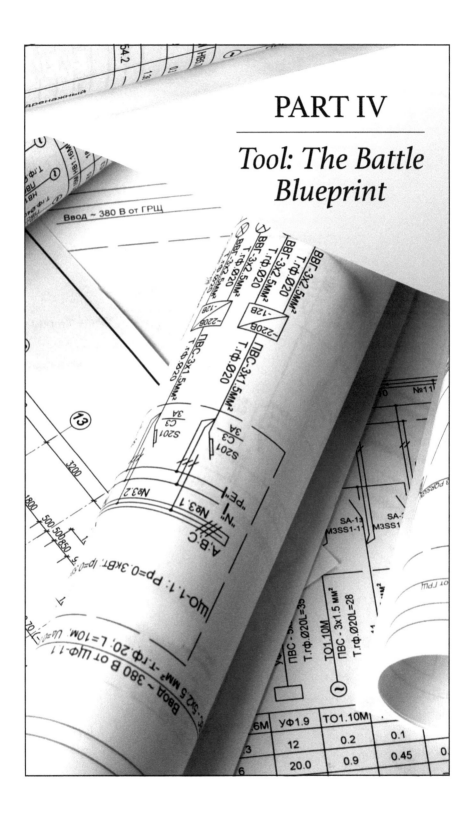

PART IV

Tool: The Battle Blueprint

CONQUERING THE UNKNOWN

I anxiously awaited Dr. Onn's call to see if I would be accepted into the treatment group. I couldn't sleep. One day to the next, what troubling thoughts I tried to filter and thwart in my waking hours now seemed to slip in at night.

You're just idling around slowly suffocating yourself while pretending it'll all be fine, aren't you, Eeki?

The little devil on my shoulder had a point. Despite all the willpower I had mustered, I was wasting energy without a guiding system to wage this war. I needed a term with a little punch to it—*battle blueprint* would suffice. It would provide momentum guided by strategy. I could not be my own opponent—not again. What I needed was a leader, and that could *only* be me. Perhaps my oncologist was my coach, training me to be the next champ. Dr. Onn's call came through like a bell. *Ding!*

"You're in, Eeki. I got you a spot on the research group. Still, I must tell you that there is a wait before you can begin. This could take as long as four to six weeks."

My thoughts clotted in my throat. "Oh, really? Then I'll probably die before it begins. You saw the tumors growing in my neck." A few nights before, while brushing my teeth, I had found two lumps forming below my ears that had since increased in size along with my fear. With this seemingly deadly delay, my expectations crashed.

So much for the bravado. I felt my temples throb as Dr. Onn on the other end of the phone placated, reassured, and even reprimanded me for being so quick to throw in the towel.

"Now, you aren't trying to fool me, are you? You are the same Eeki I first met?" I could almost hear his smile through the phone. "Now's not the time to quit. From what you've shared, it sounds to me like you've put yourself through enough stress in your life… You can start changing that now," he gave a pause. "It won't spread that quickly. Keep on your positive attitude."

Enough stress? I considered his words carefully and took a moment to survey my life… he was exactly right. I had always seen myself as quite formidable against adversity, but Dr. Onn put a magnifying glass over me.

Maybe my antiquated way could effectively deal with certain aspects of life, but it was equally corrosive to others. I thought I had a good handle on things, and when I won one battle, I would forget the toll it took on me. And I wasn't one to wallow in misery, but I kept every little thing close to my chest. It was an unnecessary weight that wore me down.

I considered how thoroughly impressed I was by Dr. Onn. Initially, I thought he was a *sabra*, a nickname for natural-born Israelis derived from a prickly yet sweet cactus in the Levant. But I quickly found he was one to wear his insides out. His heart pumped for his patients just as mine did for my students.

While his words were a salve, the end of the call left a cancerous lump of unresolved feelings in my chest. I just stood there, brain ticking—*what to do, what can I do?* I couldn't just wait around watching the clock. *Should I sleep more?* How could I sleep with my thoughts circling like this?! I couldn't see the tumor in my lungs, but these lumps on my neck brought a whole new dimension to my illness.

I rinsed my face in the sink and held onto the porcelain, my head hanging over it. I struggled to bring my face to meet the mirror. I didn't want to see my expression. If I looked into my eyes—my soul—would pity be staring back at me? I slammed my fists against the counter and locked eyes with mine.

What must I do right now? Plan. Create a battle blueprint.

My laptop rested atop the coffee table, set crookedly on a couple of art books that hadn't been read in years. If my computer had a mind of its own, it probably would have had a panic attack with how I pounced on it. I brought it to what I came to call the war table, a large glass top that helped host parties and fun get-togethers during times of peace.

This war with cancer came with no notice and barely any training at all, like my experience in the first war with Lebanon. But this time, I wasn't following any commander or even a plan that the military had for me. This time I needed to slip into the commander's seat and prepare a plan myself.

The war table would become layered in notes and printouts as I began searching all the various treatments, methods, and even home remedies for fighting cancer. I came across endless ideas, alkalinizing my body, foods to eat—this and that—whatever I could verify that wouldn't interfere with what Dr. Onn had in mind and the eventual treatments I would get. And there would be many people close to me who were ready to rally for the cause, but I did not know how to fully accept their kindnesses because I always questioned them—well, more so I questioned myself. It was easier to accept that I had cancer, but for those who would fight for my cause I still asked, *why me?*

Support is a two-way street that allows one to give kindness and receive gratification. I knew personally it was much easier to help others than to accept help from them. And unfortunately, when someone important to you doesn't help, it can blind you to everyone else that would.

This old way of thinking needed to die. Someone once told me it is not God, I should be angry with, but my perspective of Him. He had given me everything: the good, the bad, and all the bad that I eventually understood was for the greater good. I would need to sacrifice the old Eeki for the sake of a renewed one. Along with this, my relationship with my higher power needed a reboot too.

Soon after the call with Dr. Onn, Garik texted me that he would stop by to check in, but I told him it wasn't a good time—I just didn't want anyone to see me so broken down.

There was a rap on the door that sounded like some secret code I wasn't privy to, but I knew right away who it was.

"Garik? Come on in." I had given him a key for the times he helped me with my dog, but he still insisted on being let inside.

I opened the door and saw his weary expression, as if his stone face had been eroded. I felt disarmed. He found a seat, and I prepared some coffee.

Garik and I had grown especially close in the days since our first ride to the hospital. There was something about exposing my personal life to him that better allowed for this.

"Eeki, remember, everything is going to work out." He spoke as if this was some kind of enchantment. "Remember that tonic I told you about a few years back?"

"The garlic one?"

"Yes, the drops. The ones that you can take only once in five years, because they have a strong influence on the immune system. I checked with other people who took it in the past and believe it may be helpful for fighting cancer."

Why not? I thought. This was my initial reaction, but I had already committed myself to a work in progress plan that insisted I vet all prospective treatments with scrutiny. I needed to become an expert on my cancer. I would welcome ideas, but I needed to be meticulous with the details. While it may sound like a silly home remedy, I wasn't about to guzzle anything that would possibly detract from my other efforts. I am about taking risks, but I had only one shot at this, and my plan needed to be as close to perfect as possible. I was the leader of this battle blueprint, so I needed to know everything about the battle and the weapons being wielded. Learning is—as I always taught my students—essential to leadership.

It seemed there was little time to clean any of my mess ups "Maybe I should've taken it back then, but now, I have to be extra careful, Garik."

"What harm can it do? I have never heard of any problems with it. I'll prepare it for you, don't worry."

"I am not worrying. Do I look worried? You look worried, my friend. Besides, there's some snake oil in my cupboard I need to try first." His brow furrowed, and his expression looked like it could cause an earthquake. Israelis are known to be strong-minded and adamant about getting our friends to accept our ideas. "Garik, just let me do my research first," I said. "I'll let you know what I come up with. You're my holy devil's advocate, and I certainly appreciate it."

"So stubborn, but alright." He took a big swig from his mug. "Should you be drinking coffee?"

"Ah, well, probably not." I watched his eyes flick to the sink. "If it makes you feel better."

Some habits are meant for the drain while others must be adopted. I spent a lot of time reexamining what led me here to this very day and decided what habits were worth *abstaining, maintaining, or obtaining* for my fight.

Lemongrass tea! It is known to help ease symptoms from chemo treatments, which are brutally harsh on the body. I would need to find a plant before they commenced. The little details counted too.

I needed to call my deputy director, Rumi, at the ILI, who had also graduated from the leadership program. Fiercely loyal and earnest, she always saw the person in everyone and was an exceptional leader. I especially admired her contagious optimism. My anxieties about the ILI were absolutely mitigated by her presence on the team.

A new cohort of students was about to attend our soon-to-commence classes, and I needed someone to step in when my treatments began. I glanced at my phone on the table. This call had been chasing me while I was procrastinating and there was no outrunning it. She needed to know what was going on, but I couldn't imagine stepping away from the ILI knowing I may never return. It was time to face the threat and resolve it.

As the phone rang, I thought about how it might be better to break the news in person, but it would be much easier this way.

"Rumi, do you happen to know where I can get a lemongrass plant?"

"A what?"

"A lemongrass plant to make tea."

"I am sure I could find one, but is this why you are calling?"

Rumi knew I was a goof, but there are very few who are astute as her.

"No, and I meant to call sooner. There's something very important I need to discuss with you."

She waited for me to continue.

"I have cancer." I was unsure I'd ever get used to saying this. There was a hushed sound on the phone. Static? Exasperation? I continued: "There are some upcoming treatments that will potentially, well, most likely keep me from running some of the leadership workshops. I need you to help cover my absence while I am away. Can you do this for me?"

"Of course, Eeki." Her voice sounded choked. "I'm sorry, I am not taking this news so well…" There was a pause. Silence always made me uncomfortable. If there wasn't *something else* to focus on, the silent space was effectively a vacuum trying to suck out answers and inner angst. My parents didn't like sharing the details of their harrowing past, so maybe it was just a tradition I carried. Rumi managed to mentally unmute before I did. "You don't have to worry about the ILI. Anything you need, I'll take care of it."

"Even the lemongrass?"

She laughed and released the tension. "Yes, of course. But let's get serious for a second. There are leadership classes currently running and if I need to step in your shoes for a while, I'll need your contacts list. How soon can you send me this? But first, Eeki…"

"Yes?"

"Why couldn't you tell me this in person? Such news…"

I didn't have an answer for her. Well, a decent one that is. It was a risk of vulnerability. I had been trying to keep a tight lid on my troubles and control their spread. "It has been hectic with all the appointments and planning, but I should have."

"It's okay, I understand. I'll take care of things here. Send me the list when you can."

"That's too much Rumi. Thank you. Thank you so much. Ah, someone else is calling. We'll talk soon, okay?"

"Bye Eeki. All will be well."

There really was another call coming through, my sister Bracha. You didn't think I was fibbing, did you?

As I answered, I noticed a strange but pleasant residual feeling from my call with Rumi. It wasn't like me to beat around the bush, or, in this case, lemongrass plant. While it was not such a big deal to meet in person for such a thing, it was a symptom of a larger issue.

I breathe leadership principles; they are part of my daily life. I believe these skills lay dormant in everyone. But focused as I was on these principles, it was becoming painfully obvious that my fight with cancer was exposing the contradictions in my own practice. Leaders must be open and present a challenge to others with confidence. *These leadership values must all be part of the battle blueprint.* Is that how I had just conducted myself with Rumi?

Here I could see the benefit of these principles reflected in another person. Rumi had learned and embraced personal leadership. She instantly chose to stand up to the challenge. She had answered *what must I do right now? for herself almost immediately.* It wasn't just about me. She had much at stake as well. I would hear later about how much the news tore her up, but her composure and attitude held strong in the face of it. It evoked within me a mirror moment. Personal leadership has an impact on others. Leaders have a gravitational pull drawing others toward light and inspiration. I knew I could either shine personal leadership as a form of gracious *giving* or become a black hole that swallows energy—a terribly powerful and negative form of only *taking*. Instead, I would take her example and give my own version of personal leadership. In this introspective moment I wondered, *was Sunshine giving or taking something from me?*

Rumi gave me a mental boost but also reminded me of my own capacity. It wasn't just her practical support—it was her attitude and authenticity, the choice she made. You often can play tug-o-war while deciding your attitude, but a positive one is not like a light switch. This energy must come from within, which takes determined effort, especially if you have become accustomed to the dark.

I took a breath before greeting Bracha over the phone. She sounded so weary ever since I told her about my cancer. We always looked at each other as if the other was so much stronger. We called each other fighters. As children, we were competitive with one another—like cyclists, we often drafted off one another's success in a wheel-like pattern. But that was a long time ago. I think it was hard to feel a crack in the foundation of what we had. Rumi gave me a sneaky blessing. I needed to maintain myself and keep my focus on the moment—future-tripping into dystopian daydreams was not in the plan—I double checked this developing battle blueprint, and it wasn't there.

Bracha must've stayed up all night researching potential doctors and treatments.

"There is also this doctor in the states. I really researched this one, Eeki. We should speak with him. He's one of the best. I'll call him right now to see if we can get in."

"I have a doctor, and there's already a treatment protocol planned. Bracha, look, you said so yourself, I am not going to waste any more time. There is no magic fix. I need to change my life, my behavior, and my mindset. The rest is covered for now."

"You can be so stubborn," she fumed.

I smiled, thinking of all the times I stubbornly disagreed with her, even when I knew she was right. But in this heavy situation, I was not being stubborn. I made a proactive choice. Perhaps it was to cling to any measure of control I might still have. I had an opportunity, and I recognized it. Unlike times in the past, I wanted to give it my all and see it through. "The treatments are going to be starting in a few weeks. I'll need your help then." I paused and considered her kindness. "I feel good right now—I really do." Saying it made me more aware of my feelings. It had been a roller coaster from one hour to the next, but I wouldn't let this positive peak go unnoticed. It was nearly imperceptible, but I think she also found her mood lifting, and it seemed she would be climbing up the tracks with me. But a climb could lead to a drop.

I planned for downturns and failure while at the same time maintaining an attitude that drives through the low, dark fulcrums of life toward higher and brighter places. It is like cracking the code and transforming bad things into good. And I believe everything is meant for the good. Because I would continue to discover how my diagnosis brought me to live my personal leadership, and *to finally live.*

"You're going to fight this, you hear me?" She was demanding and pleading at the same time.

"This time I do," I said solemnly. The call ended. It was suddenly hard to breathe as I sat at the war table with research printouts and a handful of possible remedies sprawled about. My shoulders slumped as I scanned the materials before me. My sister's voice echoed within my heart. I sighed as silent tears dripped down my cheeks. It felt good to let them escape, something I would never do in front of other people. *I'm going to break my family. If I die, they won't recover.* A web of fears strung together like some cursed harp playing a sickly song to poison me.

Would they ever see this coming? My parents… Dear God.

I leaned into my elbows and finally allowed the tears to open into sobbing. I wept as if mourning my death as I knew my family would do. *They can't afford another loss in the family…* My closest cousin, Moshe, was my age and died just a year ago from cancer. *Now me? No, this can't happen.*

It would be one of the darkest nights of my life. I didn't want to sleep knowing soon I may never wake up again. But I must have drifted off eventually because I found myself stirring to rays of sunlight caressing my face. I went out to my balcony for some fresh air to refresh my mind. The battle that day would be to get back on the horse. My proverbial horse would be the rare and endangered Akhal-Teke. With their rare golden coat, most humans will never see this thousands-of-years-old breed in their lifetime. These coveted horses are considered heavenly and like me were born in the desert, adapting to challenging conditions.

Yes, I would ride the golden Akhal-Teke to victory. I knew in my heart, Hashem, my God, would never give me more than I could handle. I had the tools inside me. There was a purpose to this battle, and I would ride to victory.

I got busy right away. When I fail, I find that I'm doubly productive in response. This was a detailed tactic within my plan. But what I realized is that as much as the battle plan consisted of all the assets, values, ideas, and tactics to employ, there was an entire other side of the tool: *I needed to behave as a leader.* What personal leadership begets is a life model for not only yourself but others. It inspires and offers opportunities for others to emulate. My friend Eyal Arad, a top Israeli political strategist who was an adviser to three Israeli prime ministers, had reminded me, as a leader, *you become a lighthouse, a beacon of light for others.* I resolved to follow my plan, but also lead it, acting it out to make it my own.

The morning was a blur until a text came through from Yoram, a fresh graduate of ILI that I was friendly with. He was an older guy in his 40s who I admired for his choice to develop himself at his age despite already being a lawyer and businessman. He wanted more in life, but he was also incredibly humble, always so down to earth in our workshops. And maybe he also made me feel a little younger compared to many of my other students.

And compared to the average fresh-faced leadership students, all so full of future promise, Yoram was already well-established in life, but there was unexplored potential within him that he still wished to see. That was like me. It's never too late for this.

"Are you home?" he asked.

"Yes, why?"

"I am in the area. Can I drop in for a moment?"

"I'll be around, When?"

"Soon."

"Cool"

It was rather odd he'd want to randomly stop by, which instantly led me to consider if we were going to talk about *it*.

No. I couldn't. I needed to make sure I looked okay, so he couldn't tell something was wrong. It wasn't long before I heard a knock on the door.

He carried a potted plant with leaves sprouting outward like a fountain. A line of dirt trailed behind him that looked like it came from his shoes.

"What the heck is this?" I was more curious about the dirt trail than the weird looking plant offering.

"Lemongrass from my garden. I know you could make good use of it."

"Oh, yeah. Did Rumi send you?"

"She said you were sick with a fever and needed one, so I volunteered."

"Please, come in."

Their kindness touched me and momentarily soothed the sense that I was riding into this battle alone, the tough warrior on his golden steed. A thought dawned on me that would slowly grow in brightness in the days to come. I still needed to welcome help. For the first time I truly saw kindness from the perspective of the giver. I wasn't burdening them. I was allowing them to do good deeds for someone they cared about. It had not fully occurred to me that people feel helpless when faced with the possibility of losing someone important to them. Perhaps this shift in point of view was also a part of personal leadership. Now I could see this as an opportunity I shouldn't pass up.

"Yoram, would you like anything to eat, drink? Tell me what you need?"

"I'm fine." His expression became grave. "I would rather know what *you* need." There was a peculiar tone in his voice.

He knew. Rumi must have told him. In a way I was relieved. He was nothing if not observant and he would have sensed something was wrong. Now we could get past the pretenses. "Thank you for the plant. It should help me with chemotherapy, not a fever."

His expression also revealed that he knew the terrible truth; this was a deadly diagnosis and at least four of the doctors wanted me to ease off into the sunset. Always direct, Yoram asked, "What are you going to do?"

"Well, we're preparing for a special treatment. I'm quite ready for this. There's a plan in place, and what I need is not everyone to fall apart on me."

"Eeki, we're not falling apart. You have taught us well. We're all behind you to help you fight. Whatever you need. We will follow your leadership."

I knew he meant that. My friends would be there for me as I had been there for them over the years. I was used to giving and would have to learn to receive. The biggest challenge was for me to connect with God. I had struggled with my understanding of his involvement in my life. I was fiercely faithful, but like a child whose concept of his parents developed over time, my understanding of His presence was limited. Truth be told, I had wrestled with my relationship with God and would often put play, politics, and business over Him, especially when my soul stirred about the past. God had smacked me silly with cancer to wake me up, as if a new dawn was welcoming me. *Sunshine*. It was time at last to get serious. He was assuring me I had free will, and it was time to choose if I wanted to grow up.

This realization was like being able to see the electrical current, which had been there all along. In your life, there is a golden thread of purpose that you can weave, but if not reflected in the right lighting, you may not even know it's there.

I would have to hold tightly to the thought that this was a blessing, and not only would I come out of it on the other side, but I would also survive and find a renewed sense of purpose.

"I'll go plant the lemongrass," Yoram said. I was glad he had broken the uncomfortable silence.

Due to old habits, I insisted, "Please, no, you don't have to do that. I'll take care of it."

He gave me a look that quickly changed my mind. I was being more childish by wanting to do everything myself. He took charge as any good friend would do, and I let him.

I watched him plant the lemongrass with such care that it almost made me weep. When he returned, he opened my refrigerator and noticed a container of soup. He checked my cabinet for a pot and heated it up. "You must eat something. I need you to." After some quiet slurping he asked, "Where did it come from? What stage?"

"Stage 4. It can happen to anyone, Yoram. People are not even aware it could be growing in their body like they live in *Lalaland*. Then, it hits them like a truck. But don't worry, I am going to beat it."

He thoughtfully gazed at me. "Yes, you will."

There could be many reasons for what causes cancer. Some are environmental, others merely happenstance, and more still are due to lifestyle. I believe it's true that you can become so accustomed to problematic habits that they become like a white noise. But there are always consequences. I smoked and my stress pressure gauge was always maxed out to the limit. But it could have been anything. Cancer is caused by changes to genes. I would need to combat it by addressing something as foundational to myself as that. My entire mentality needed to change on a similarly cellular level. I needed to understand my leadership DNA, so I would write down the various values and behaviors I understood as necessary for becoming one myself.

I decided not to angrily point fingers at what exactly caused this to happen to me—including my higher power. I knew my habits had played some part, but all my energy had to be resolutely focused on change. I could not change the past, but if I practiced the lessons it had taught me, I could redesign the path of my present and alter my future.

"Please, let us help you," Yoram said with tears in his eyes.

The "us" was an odd, accentuated detail. Perhaps he meant his graduated class.

It made me uncomfortable to think that my students, some of whom I considered my children, would now come to my aid. Vulnerability was never easy for me; I defined myself by how I thought they saw me. If they saw me as weak, I worried, would I become weak? But Yoram's sincerity softened me. He was being a good leader—and so were they. That was a good thing and something for which I could be proud (after all, I had taught him how!) "Of course," I answered, consoling him with a pat on the shoulder. "Thank you, from the deepest place in my heart." For the first time, I felt like I had allowed the disappointment and trauma from my distant past to dissipate. I truly trusted that he meant what he said. I embraced this, and it helped soothe what had been long left untreated. Still, I pushed the more painful memories out of my mind, saving them for another day.

CREATE A SACRED PLAN

Rumi and Yoram must've gotten right to work. I began to hear from people who wanted to help in any way they could. This would be another test of my strength and courage: they wanted me—no—*needed* me to be dedicated to my life and the good fight. This was leadership training in action, and it was time for me to proudly walk my talk, as a leader, no matter the outcome.

Aviya, another graduate, but also a brigade commander in the reserves, called me a week or so later. He was a real macho man who oversaw a large swath of the Gaza border. I remember him taking more training days than anyone else.

"Eeki? I heard the news." This 'news' started to seem like a plague. His voice broke and wavered. I felt like I'd been hit by a freight train. Did I actually hear him crying? My composure instantly crumbled. How many more calls like this could I take?

"I—I don't know what to do with it."

What? I thought. *This was for me to handle...*

"Don't use it to bring you down. You know, Aviya, the battle is just starting, and I don't have any plans on dying."

For him, this was ripping open his heart. He had lost his father to cancer five years ago. It was still a fresh wound, slow to heal. His father was a renowned educator and larger than life for Aviya.

"I can't lose someone like this again, I can't bear another loss to this."

I just couldn't keep it together.

Moments passed. It was too painful to be awkward. For him to break open like this, it shattered my heart along with his. Eventually he spoke.

"I have a friend who can help—he has developed a new treatment for cancer. I'll connect you. I will do anything I can."

"Aviya, I'm in line for a special treatment. What's important is that you called and care—"

"It is not enough, Eeki, please. At least call your doctor and see what they think of it." He wouldn't let me get off the call, as if my seeming complacency was some kind of insubordination. There was a plan, but he needed this battle to fight—honor bound as he was to come to my defense.

"First of all, there will be a lot you can do for me. For now, we go from strength to strength. We'll win this. I'll mention the treatment to him." I could almost hear his grip loosening on his phone. My body felt weak from emotional exhaustion. There would need to be some defenses put in place to shield me from all the turmoil—surprisingly not just my own.

The truth is, I hadn't heard from Aviya in quite a while, but the connection held strong and true. I was humbled by this. While I did keep in touch with my graduates, it still struck me. *You are cared for by so many people... you can't die.* It was a strange thought to be telling myself this, almost an out of body experience. More likely, I had achieved a greater vantage point and was finally seeing beyond myself. Perhaps there was more to it for others than helping me win; my plight also represented an opportunity to triumph over death—our enigmatic enemy who paradoxically offers meaning to our lives, its joys and sufferings. Was it this that people saw in me and this terrible turn of events? Were they reminded of their own ephemeral existence? What did it all mean? I hoped to have answers for everyone.

Even when you are surrounded by people, you can sometimes feel lonely. This bridge of weeks between diagnosis and treatment pressed me to learn how to allow others to embrace me and how I could embrace them—*how to truly give to others, staving off the loneliness.* I could give them my best self. My personal leadership would be the answer. It was how to give *and* receive in harmony. If someone like Aviya opened his heart to me like never before... if I had the opportunity to bring him healing—there was no question anymore. *I must fight.* There could be no other choice. It was always the right answer. And now with this realization, I understood its importance in my planning. This blueprint was a collaborative document;

it was not just on me to make.

Several days later, I was sitting in my garden watching the sunset with my new, friendly lemongrass frond. I had prepared some tea from its leaves to make sure the taste would not make me as sick as the chemo. It did not disappoint. A curious text appeared on my phone.

"Eeki, we were thinking of taking the first shift when the time comes. Is that okay?"

"What do you mean 'shift?'"

"You didn't see the messages?"

"What messages?"

"On the WhatsApp group. Are you not on there?"

A moment later, I received an invitation to a group called "Let Eeki Win."

There were at least a hundred people in it. My heart fluttered as I scrolled through the messages coordinating all sorts of help for me when the treatments would start. My thumb grew tired flipping through the message thread. I laughed. My body could barely process this swing from dread to delight. Rumi had organized an entire collective for one single goal: helping me in my time of need. And as hard as it was to admit, I needed the help—*I can't let them down.*

I could not forsake the people on my team—at my side—they were part of my battle blueprint. With respect to them and myself, I needed to be tactful. No, I needed to be military minded, and this meant keeping my emotions in check. It meant staying vigilant against desperation, doubt, and despair. While some ideas would appeal to my emotions, I needed to remain strategic and grounded within my own body and *mind my emotions.*

I believed the medications and treatments would work better for people who fought—who leapt into the unknown with an adaptive battle blueprint rather than clinging to the rails while imagining future failures. This was my adopted mentality. Lifestyle changes necessitate a shift in attitude as much as in your external environment. One of the greatest threats to my success would be unbuckled emotions. And I thought *I* was a crazy driver. Those emotions would grab the wheel and steer me off a cliff if I let them!

I would ask myself—*does this emotion serve my purpose?* For instance, I would be terrified if I did *not* feel fear with my diagnosis. I began to appreciate what a powerful source of fuel it offered. I needed to know my assets, allies, and arsenal to create a clear goal that I could fix in my sights.

Without it, my aim might stray from the target.

Fear was an unbroken mustang. Fear that the ILI would suffer because of my loss; that I would miss out on what I could've, should've, and would've done. That I would die alone in my apartment, and that what I left behind would not give enough to others—if only I had finished what I was here for. I feared it was too little too late. And so, I decided all of this gave immeasurable value to the moments I had left, however many, and that this fight would at least be one to be proud of in the world beyond.

With a blueprint, fear could be steered into action. The bucking bronco would respect me as I respected it. This would require focus, and there could be no procrastination. I was no Israeli cowboy, as cool as that sounded, but I needed to maintain a conscious effort to keep the course and brave the land ahead. But let's not be mistaken, it is okay to stop for breaks along the way—maybe you need to shift your priorities, make a pit stop to care for another, or drink a cup of tea to a somber sunset. Let's be realistic here—but you must also have a sense of urgency to reach your goals.

It was during these weeks that my mind was in a feeding frenzy. I couldn't waste any time—I had done that already. Sure, each day is one closer to death, but there would be much more to my story before the finale arrived. I needed to recreate my life while trying to save it.

I mapped out all my resources and allies in a diagram. I described a routine that kept me productive, and the healthy habits I needed to form. I even committed mantras to memory to inspire myself, and I habitually said a prayer every time I left my home for the day. I noted the routines I needed to break, and an incremental plan to lose them.

Mapping requires a correlation between the goals you set and the tools, skills, resources, and allies you have to achieve them.

After reviewing my diagram, I immediately asked myself, am *I really this blessed?* I felt empowered. Sure, there was still room for improvement, but given a chance you'll find people are willing to help you when you need it. All or nothing thinking often leaves you without anything because what you need is something in between.

Perhaps, whittled down to the barebones, all we have are our attitudes and our thoughts. This is all we reliably possess unless mind control is a real thing. Everything else is subject to the unknown. And the *unknown* is a force to be reckoned with. This was my contender in the ring. The reigning champion of the world against crazy, little old me.

The battle blueprint would be of no use if it just sat on my coffee table like some pretty, creative showpiece collecting dust. Those pages would feel worn if I kept to my strategies. I was already facing the greatest discomfort I had ever felt in my life. How much worse could it be to put effort toward possible resolution? The unknown had the answers, but I would only find them if I searched.

The essence of the unknown, which represents all possibility, is subject to two polarized vantage points, negative and positive. We can use statistics and probability to predict what we do not know, but if I had chosen to believe that I would be part of the 90% who met their demise instead of the 10% who lived. I would be fighting for nothing. I did not make it my mission to prove the stats wrong; instead, I wanted to prove that I could live as my best version of myself in the time with which God had blessed me—whatever remained. If I limited my goal to just a year, I would sizzle out. There is no future beyond the expectant year of death until there might be, so I set my sights further—I would be one of the survivors, but I needed to do more than survive. I needed to thrive.

Perhaps this sounds too easy. Writing this seven years later, have I really lived up to these words? Yes! And each time I crumbled—because I surely did—I reminded myself that *it was built into my blueprint to fail. By* design, I would experience failure but refuse to think of it as such—it only served as intel to adapt the blueprint.

The next time I saw Doctor Onn, he welcomed me back with a tight hug. The man really saw his patients as family.

"Where are they?" He ran two fingers along the side of my neck. "The tumors, I can barely feel them. What did you do?"

"I found a mysterious herb in the Odem Forest."

He responded with a snort. "Let's look at the blood tests."

He pulled up his computer and flicked through a few pages. The good doctor's forehead creased; the slight curl of his mouth suggested impressed surprise. "Where can I get my hands on these herbs you speak of?" His body jerked as he hefted a laugh. "Alright, tell me what you did."

I went on to explain my battle blueprint, all the various strategies and ideas that I put to work. Maybe it was the alkalinization of my body, maybe this or that, but nothing would've worked without my earnest effort. As strange as it sounds, seeing his disbelief was reassuring. Doctor Onn believed in me from the start. He saw my sense of accountability—my determination and no-nonsense gorilla grip on my own steering wheel of destiny when we met. I was my own crazy driver, and he was thrilled to join the ride. He was my partner in this venture.

He looked across his desk at me as a thick blade of sunlight from his windowsill cut into the room. "We'll be beginning the biological medicine and chemo soon. About two more weeks. Keep this up, Eeki. Keep this going. Maybe you'll be rid of it before the treatment"—he seemed to catch himself mid-joke— "I don't mean to give the wrong impression; it won't be easy. In fact, it will be very difficult, being sick, and the strain on your body. You'll need to consider getting help. Plan to not be able to meet your commitments as you normally would. But what you are doing will put you in a great position for success."

Two more weeks felt like two more years. I tried not to show my disappointment. Not now. This was good news.

"But you should know, it's Russian Roulette… one out of three participants in the study actually get it. The pharmaceutical company keeps it secret so there's no influence on the process. And even as your doctor, I wouldn't be told until after you died. You'll either get saline water or the actual medication. But I am optimistic."

My vision started spinning. I had placed so much faith in this treatment, *and now I may get a blank.* I might as well just gargle salt water for good measure.

"Why? Why are you optimistic?"

"Because I know you won't lose this battle. Look what you have already achieved. We have a soldier here. Nothing has changed, and that includes sticking to your plan. Treatment or no."

"You're right. You're right again and again. I should know this." I noticed my hands shaking. My heart was resisting my attempts to soothe myself.

"I'm only sharing my observations, and of course, my hopes. I do believe you can win this, but you can't let up."

It was impossible to not feel his optimism, though the horse in my chest rapidly beat, frightened and frantic. As the sunlight disappeared behind his curtains, the mood it had inspired remained. *Lead by planning and plan to lead.* I would conquer this, but I needed to model personal leadership to embrace my blessings. I am eternally grateful to have shared this voyage with Dr. Onn.

He gave me a considering look, his eyes flicking to my buzzcut—I thought I should get comfortable with my new look ahead of time. He leaned back in his chair. "The chemo treatments won't be easy on the body, as I am sure you're well aware. Your hair may fall out, there could be nausea, fatigue—these issues can accumulate over time. You'll need to push your body and face them with resistance. Eeki, you'll be dead tired, but you can fight tiredness by doing sports and exercise despite feeling exhausted—that's the best solution I have in mind for you. Feed yourself well despite the trouble to keep it down, you know what I mean?"

"Already solved that. Lemongrass."

"Ah, seems you thought about it already." His eyes returned to what was left of my hair.

"I'm going to feed myself well, don't worry. You should know I'm a good cook. You see how prepared I am—I didn't even lose my hair. I shaved it."

"Well, not everyone loses their hair…"

I scrubbed my head. "Really? Ah, well, I suppose my optimism might grow it instead, hopefully."

Dr. Onn led me out and we embraced. This was a bond beyond patient and doctor; at times, it felt like he was an older brother.

I must remind you and myself that it only takes one, and that one is *you*—others will be drawn to your light in the storm. Dr. Onn was like my north star. His leadership had the same effect on me, perhaps as mine did on him. This made for a true bond.

As I walked to my car, I had another choice to make. Do I worry like an untethered gambler with my life savings on the table, or do I forge my peace through processed planning and action? This blueprint would be my guiding tool as much as any compass. Plan your life's direction, but be prepared to adapt this living, breathing document to achieve your goals. Don't get lost at sea wishing you had one.

PART V

Tool: The Fortress

REVELATIONS AND RENOVATIONS

I was the happiest I've ever been during the most stressful time of my life. It wasn't an immediate realization, but one that grew as I did. Between my diagnosis and the first biological medication treatment, I felt like I was living my own movie, captivated by the fight, my life's rising action. I didn't know if this was a horror film, drama, or fantasy, but it was my own script—my own plan for how to lead myself through the worst and best of times. Despite the sorrow that threatened to drown me, I felt alive. This was the *real* me.

It became very clear to me that the challenge I was facing was *the* force for growth and fulfillment. Some challenges are imposed; others are chosen. While you might find yourself riddled with "problems," labeling them as such suggests they are circumstances to be squashed or pushed out of the way, whereas *challenges* should be welcomed as a fertilizer for your character development. Challenges are opportunities to make you a better person: You are born with potential, and without them, you may never reach it.

Consider again how there are two kinds of challenges: those you are *given* and those you *choose* in order to exceed your limits. They are two sides of the same coin. I discovered how important they were to my fight to stay alive. This attitude encouraged me to be more optimistic and was a crucial lesson that I had unknowingly long lived yet learned from one of my brightest students—so often I found myself learning from those I taught.

But what more had I learned about the antagonist of my story?

If you asked me who the real villain and opponent was, I'd say *complacency.*

While you can destroy yourself with despair and negativity, it still means you care. But to feel indifference, *to feel nothing*? Life erodes into a barren wasteland.

All my painful tears in the weeks prior to my treatment told me I was finally alive and cared enough to fight. I had showered this battlefield until it became fertile ground. Pain in my diagnosis's aftermath was necessary. To be honest, I don't know if this was a given or taken challenge—it feels like both—but it doesn't change the fact that, like a plant, I had broken the rocky ground and started stretching toward the sun. While the cancer in my lungs grew, so did I. *Is this some sort of race, Sunshine? I won't wait for you at the finish line.*

I didn't feel alone in the dark anymore. Over time, I found myself more willingly sharing my challenges with friends, family, and even strangers offering their sympathies, empathies, and support. I was still keeping a tight lid on my diagnosis, but the dam began to break. I became more active on social media describing the difficulties that were helping me become whole, and it wouldn't take long before reactions started pouring in.

The increasing exposure left me more vulnerable. The stakes seemed to increase, and I found myself more easily swept off in tides of emotions. Countless people stepped in to influence my plan. There were positive and negative forces that I would need to filter. And from the outset of this battle, I had already witnessed my mind's ability to shape or distort my goals and strategies. So, what was there to really protect my plans from being amended, nullified, or repurposed? I realized my plan needed to be fortified. I needed a *fortress*. Otherwise, I would be pulled in too many directions. I could hear advice and other people's concerns, but I needed to maintain a sturdy center protected by a barrier.

Raindrops streamed down the hospital window, some zigzagging and others strangely paused, caught in time and seemingly resistant to gravity. No, I wasn't tripping on medications, but it did seem symbolic. What keeps them, or me, from slipping? My sister, Bracha, had chaperoned me to my first appointment. She had briefly excused herself while I waited for the nurse to begin my treatments. I considered how the blueprint was now being put into action. I made it this far, but would the other shoe drop if I lost my footing?

"I am sorry if it hurts," the nurse said as she stuck the needle into my arm. I didn't feel anything.

"No, it's okay. I am accepting this process as a blessing—inviting it positively."

"Well, you sure should be." Her tone wasn't snarky. It was solemn. "I'd be grateful too." It would've been $8,000 per treatment. She was stating the obvious. "You should know that someone had to free a space for you to get in. I'm sure it was nerve-wracking to wait."

"What do you mean free a space?"

"There are only three hundred participants at a time, and in order for your battle to begin, someone else's needed to end."

I felt my throat tighten as my face flushed. There was a short silence only disturbed by the rain. Guilt coursed through my veins. "Who was it that passed away? I know you can't tell me…" I tried imagining the person's face: someone I didn't know yet strangely felt like family and who shared the same fight. It was as if I'd just learned of a relative who I'd never get to meet.

"I don't always have an account of who's not showing up anymore. I have been at this for a long time." She sounded tired. "I wouldn't be able to tell you anyhow, but I am sure they are pleased to see you with this opportunity."

"Thank you for letting me know. Really."

Afterward, as Bracha walked me to my car, I felt heavier, like gravity might pull me through the ground. Bracha would ask me every five minutes on the drive home how I was doing, but she must've eventually gotten the sense that I needed some time for reflection. My wipers rhythmically flicked rain aside, replaced again and again with each scythe-like swipe.

Are we this replaceable? Our lives, our tears, just swept away like flies? What of this, God?

Like the biblical city of Jericho, I felt my walls were being besieged on all sides all my woes and worries—and the pressure from my family and friends, who expressed their heartbreak and shock at my diagnosis conjoined their worries with my own. It was a great thing to have so many people care, but it also became an incredible responsibility. Now, I felt a greater pain knowing how they would all feel if I lost this fight. My *Sunshine* was creating such a sweltering heat, I feared we all might melt.

All the good, bad, light, and dark came rushing over the rubble toward me. I had no defenses, no filter to properly process the forces storming into my mental castle. Soon, they would reach my heart's keep, my most vulnerable place.

In times of turmoil, it can be exceptionally hard to keep grounded. My fortifications were falling, and I realized the weeks building up my defenses had also worn me down. Now, I felt like questioning the choices I had made all over again. My doubts had flanked me, and despair was marching toward my inner sanctum, home to my soul. *God, what am I made of? Help me see this. You've given me a foe too great.*

I needed to step up and lead the defensive. I would rebuild a fortress that would protect all that I had fought to create. As you go through life, you find ways to cope through defense mechanism processes, which can be adaptive or maladaptive. Often, what you learn in your formative years gets you by rather well, so well in fact that you may never think to inspect your *security systems* for blind spots and vulnerabilities. Your challenges persist, and resist being thwarted. I knew there was some deep dysfunction in the way I had learned to adapt to my circumstances. My coping mechanisms had served me well and had never really been tested, that is, until cancer.

I hated vulnerability. I kept control by not letting people enter my inner self, which was where my emotions hid. Avoidance was my brand of defense. I tried to deflect with my humor and speed away full throttle from to keep from opening up. This distance afforded me stronger footing to step into leadership roles, but this didn't carry over into my personal life. Leadership was my job, but once I realized I wasn't going to just clock out from work, *it became my life.*

This was, and is, my main weakness. Whenever someone got past my walls with good or bad intentions, I would often deflect and misdirect them back out. I still must consciously think about authentically opening up, keeping tabs on how I treat my relationships, even if it's uncomfortable to do so.

That process began with my cancer diagnosis. I consciously tried a kind of mental reprogramming, coding actions to override antiquated coping strategies. If I was going to continue to lead myself through this with all of those who supported me at my side, I would need to ensure the integrity of my entire ship was intact, or we'd all sink.

The hot summer weeks following my first treatment were strangely filled with days like any other despite feeling so down. *Too normal.* Life mostly looked like it once was before my diagnosis, which should have been a good thing. But I didn't want to forget for a minute that I was fighting for my life. I was different now—personal leadership had begun to rewire my brain. I had a stronger sense of presence within my body.

A part of my being, long buried, was exhumed, within which was an internal pressure ready to burst. I imagined my battle blueprint was contained deep within my chest like an arc for the Torah, a Jewish Bible scroll—not in my heart, but in my soul.

As my next dose of the treatment approached, Judah had an interesting request. He offered to go to the Western Wall in Jerusalem, the holiest place for the Jewish people where about a hundred thousand people go to visit every day for prayer or simply to behold such a glorious site. It had been a while since my last visit. Typically, I would have resisted. This time, I immediately agreed. It was time.

The pressure within me turned into anticipation. I knew something was going to happen, but what?

The car hummed along under a summer sun, and I could practically hear Judah's thinking over the drone. Before I could turn the radio on, he spoke. "I guess you've been preparing your home for when people come over, right? Is there any special food to get? Cooking? Anything I can help with?"

I looked at the signs for Jerusalem, surprised we were already so close. "Why, what for? Is it someone's birthday party?"

He stammered a mish-mosh of words. He wasn't in the mood for my deflection, but when was he ever? "—well, kind of, *Eeki,*" he took a breath. "It is your birthday."

"So, it's November already?"

"No, this is when you'll be born again. You've told me as much with what this has all meant to you. I hope you find the answers you're looking for while we are here."

I smiled. "You're right, but I had considered this during my first treatment. Why do you think I chose July fourth for it?"

"Something about America?"

"Yes, this was the birth of the American nation, a day to start just wars."

"Quite a patriot."

"Proudly!"

The hillsides were covered by buildings that seemed to have been artfully grown from sandstone. The way old and new buildings blended together reminded me of the movie *The Time Machine,* the same spot changing through time yet maintaining the same backdrop. A golden sheen of sunlight hovered over the city like a warm blanket—perhaps it was just my vision, but it sure appeared that way. We curled up the road to a parking lot next to the Old City gate, where we'd have to approach on foot. We passed several modern storefronts built into ancient walls. Delicious smells from bakeries and Mediterranean street food wafted by. We descended the steps toward the Western Wall, its magnificent stones with caper bushes thriving from its crevices.

As we neared the massive stones, I felt like I was shrinking.

It's customary to touch the wall while praying, and to place letters to God into the cracks between, but I stopped in the middle of the courtyard near a wooden podium with a book of Psalms planted on it. Judah patted me on the shoulder and proceeded ahead to an open section within my line of sight.

I stood there searching. Eyes soaking in the sight before me, and admittedly I felt nothing. *What was wrong with me?* I lamented. *Am I broken?*

I closed my eyes, and my insides began to brighten like the first light of dawn. I held my hands up, hip level and underhanded, welcoming anything, hoping whatever spark that had led me here would find me. What would I find? An answer? A feeling? Perhaps God's will detailed before me? But there was still nothing. *God, I know You know why I'm here.*

I grabbed the book of Psalms as if it were a manual left for me to piece my purpose together. This certainly wasn't like those instruction slips for furniture you ordered online that might as well be cryptic hieroglyphs. These were the soulful words of King David, timeless and penetrating. I grabbed a chair and began reading it as the words fluttered in front of my eyes. I lost connection with them, yet I kept reading, chasing their meaning.

I plucked a thought out of the buzzing jumble flying around my head.

Plunge. I would not sink, I would dive.

When you feel sorrow, there is a space in your chest, maybe your throat, your gut, somewhere it fills like a cavern. I plunged into that very place amid my turmoil—all my fears leading to this very moment—into a ruin of structures I imagined much like the lost city of Atlantis, eerily placid and silently still, obscured by the deep blue murk.

I wanted to find or be found. *God, I am here.*

I wanted to have some direction, some purpose, some meaning that was beyond myself. Something to give reason to this ephemeral blink of God's eye, this mote of God's breath. To give *me*.

I had resisted the One who was my only real hope. But now I had nowhere else to go.

I need your blessing. I need your support. I need you, God. I need you to fight with me. You are my reason.

The last words were like an echo at the bottom of a dark, desolate sea.

Like sunlight bursting through the clouds, I felt the cracks and crevices within my insides illuminated. Light shone on the darkest period of my life.

A flash of memories. I was just a kid enjoying childhood and school. Three older boys—no, men—they surrounded me. I was attacked but could not defend myself. I was more than molested. They violated me until I was a kid no more. They told me if I told anyone, they'd kill my family. When I got home in tears and ruin, my clothes were completely torn up. I tried to rush to my room, but my parents saw me. I did everything I could to convince them I had been playing too rough with some friends, and surprisingly they believed me. I wanted them to know the truth and to protect me, but I chose to bury my pain, and they had had enough trauma during the Holocaust to last their lifetime. I almost couldn't blame them for accepting my easier explanation rather than the truth of being sexually brutalized and beaten.

Three years of these three men dehumanizing me. I survived, but what was left? In that moment, sitting on a chair near the Western Wall, holding a book of Psalms, I became that little boy again. Deep inside my soul, I felt pain rise like bile. It was a spiritual heartburn. As I grew into manhood, I swore I would never feel as helpless as I had back then, but now I was alone and terrified again.

Then, an angelic embrace. Time stopped, and these scars and sorrows vanished from my body, dissipating to ash and drifting away, carried by God's easterly winds, which promised to destroy the wicked. Facing the wall, I started sobbing in the middle of the square, unaware of passersby and Judah, who walked toward me.

This was the first time in my life I truly felt like I knew who I was. God released me from the chains of my past, but only after I had chosen life despite all the darkness. Whatever force you may believe in, God, the universe, the collective energy of humanity, something beyond comprehension— some intangible thread wraps you up in the most complex tapestry ever imagined. I was but one piece of a greater whole, no longer on my own. My unique spark was separate but important.

I wanted to give myself back not to only others but to God. I had to be torn down to see who I really was and what I could be. While I kept letting things get to me, I really needed to *let go*. This was a restructuring of myself to its truest form. While Jews mourn the two destroyed temples of Israel, we longingly await the rebuilding of the prophesized third, what will be the most glorious of them all. We never lose hope, and neither would I.

I needed to rebuild a fortress to house my sacred plan for survival. It would never quite be a wall of stone. I wasn't protecting the innocent, broken child in me anymore. He had become a man. I could not live in a husk of materialistic ego either, like a kind of carapace—instead, my protective shell would be built by my soul. A great rabbi likened our existence as body and soul to a wick and candle. Would I choose to be weighed down by my material existence like the wick, or reach higher by the flame of who I am, what I was given? For personal leadership to be of any merit, the old me had to be broken down and cleansed.

These were the flooding tears of yesterday clearing a space for a new state of mind. This was my life's path, as ugly as it might be, but for none other than me and God to judge.

My desire to connect beyond myself was key. Personal leadership is not selfish; it is self-*full*. If what we do is full of our authentic humble self, we fulfill what we must give to the world. My new fortress would not wall out reality and those around me. It would serve as the structure that housed who I am as a vessel to be brought wherever I am meant to go. How strange it was that nothing quite so empirical had moved me like this before. This was all spirit, but it was as real as anything I had ever experienced. It was then that the seed of knowledge was planted: the spirit always has the transcendental capability to exceed the body's limitations and perceptions. In the challenges ahead, whenever I felt I had reached my limits, I would see this in full effect. What previously felt so emptied by doubt and despair was now refilled with high-octane faith in myself and God. I rose to my feet anew.

It was then that Judah joined me. There was a light in his eyes. It was nice to see him seemingly devoid of worry, considering how often he did. He must've found his own sense of peace.

As we ascended the steps, Judah took a deep breath. "How are you doing?

"I'm fine. Not too hungry."

"You know what I meant." A grin flickered on his face. "You don't want to go around the city?"

"We've got to get back, Judah. I can't spend the day walking around right now... what I received here—I need to make the most of it while it lasts." I flashed a smile. "Thank you for coming here with me. This was just what I needed, including a friend like you."

We hardly spoke on the drive home. A renewed vitality coursed through my veins. When you go to war against your problems, it's not just about your weapons; there's also your spiritual strength and fortitude. These can't just be bought in a store and taken like a pill. It is found within, though sometimes you need an ember to set your soul alight. I was reunited with my inner self—this reignited my will to fight. It was my miracle moment, nothing like the splitting of the sea, but awe inspiring, nonetheless.

GUARD YOUR KINGDOM

I brought that energy home with me from Jerusalem and realized I didn't know where to channel it. I regretted not taking that walk with Judah, but we'd surely make up for it later. I rifled through several ideas. I wished to accomplish something—to create some tangible product—rather than idle my fuel away. The house was already clean, it was getting too late to go to the gym, and an uncomfortable feeling emerged. *Todd. Dear Lord... he needs to know.*

Todd, my dear friend and partner in the ILI, the president of the North American branch, was blissfully ignorant of my plight. Of all the people with whom I hemmed and hawed about sharing the news, this was one of the most egregious examples. Never in my life had I ever considered how hard it would be to tell people I was dying.

I met Todd when I first came to the US—a quirky city, Columbus, Ohio—to expand the ILI. He was a bit of a kid inside like me, the kind of person that draws that out of you. Why Ohio you're probably thinking? I found it fascinating how such a state had so much sway in elections, a swing state that seemed to blend into the middle of the map for most who didn't actually live there—not to mention Columbus's college football. I enjoyed cheering on the Buckeyes; I had watched my first game with Todd and another good friend, Larry. There was an almost immediate familial relationship between the three of us. When we're all together, we might seem like a silly knock-off of the three stooges. And they helped me connect to the city like it was my second home.

Todd is a native Ohioan, originally from Cleveland, and Larry is an ex-Long Islander who may have left New York as a teenager, but New York never left him. Both these men love Israel and are active in Jewish causes throughout Ohio and the United States. I could go on, but it may begin to seem like I am procrastinating—so I'll get to it! I really screwed up, particularly with Todd, who was diligently running the North American ILI. I think it was because I knew how he would take the news.

Todd, a man who wears his heart on his sleeve and his mind on his mouth, would have been on the next plane to Sderot. I couldn't bring myself to imagine what it would be like to lose him, or for him to lose me. He and I weren't just dreamers but leaders who shared a vision of a better world. What would it mean to tell him he might be alone with that vision in just six months' time?

I had no more excuses. I made the call I had been dreading. The phone rang several times until he finally answered.

"Todd, where are you right now?"

"In a meeting, can I call you in an hour?"

"Of course, talk soon."

It was an hour of agony. 15 extra minutes elapsed, and I almost hoped he wouldn't call back at all. Then, of course, my ringer went off.

I told him.

"What?!" His words blasted out of the phone like he was right next door, not over 6,000 miles away. He has always been a doer, so after expressing his rage at the universe for the unfairness of it all, nearly breaking my phone speaker (not to mention my eardrums!) in the process, he quieted down and fell into problem-solving mode.

"I know I am far away, but tell me, what can I do? Do you need me to come over?"

I knew that would be his first thought, and it comforted me even though I knew it was impractical. Todd would want to help me—to help save my life—but I didn't want to steal his time, though of course I also didn't want to take his offer for granted. It was part of the reason I hadn't called—the same conundrum. Exposing myself to others was an uncomfortable burden to impose. The more support I had, the more needy I felt, and I wondered if I would ever be able to repay people for their kindness. What if it was all for naught and I still expediently perished? What would that mean to them?

I realized I couldn't be responsible for how someone else responded. I needed to be responsible for *my own* response, and I *did* need support. There was a way to handle this.

And I found it, like many other personal truths, in the quiet moments in between everyday activities, those brief times of introspection. To resolve this dilemma, I decided the best approach was accepting these gifts and blessings, and to return their investment in full, a sort of duty-bound gratitude. While I had a new appreciation for time, I also had this growing sense of gratitude for other things. This was a *huge* change for me. I needed help and I had to allow other people to do their good deeds and express their love for me. Despite my sense of discomfort and desire not to be beholden to others, God had other plans and I needed to listen to His lessons.

I was learning a key facet to personal leadership—a codified perspective for modeling what was overly protected in my mental fortress. Now I would soon be able to learn the next tool of accepting a rope as a lifeline rather than a prop for a mental tug of war. As with all the tools, there is an interconnectedness, and I found an especially unique relationship between the Fortress and the Rope that you will soon learn about.

Even with what progress I made on this journey, I needed to stay grounded, but it felt like one foot was on concrete while the other was in the muck. It didn't matter how many victories I achieved, this fight with cancer was being waged in the withering fields of my body. I saw it clearly as a tension between light and darkness—hope and determination versus doubt and despair. Doubt and despair are formidable enemies and I felt they were flanking me on both sides. Each day I would experience a terrible rise and fall pattern of determination and devastation like I was on a treadmill to nowhere. If I held onto hope for too long without wielded purpose—my hands would become charred, and the doubt for any meaningful survival would be a wildfire turning my mentality to ash.

But despair? That would be more like a lightning bolt strike setting my world aflame. Despair is an explosion like those I had seen on the battlefield with my own eyes at the First Lebanon War in 1982—I remember the bombshells exploding all around us. There was no warning before it blasted the ground nearby. So, you could potentially put out a wildfire, but an explosion would consume you too quickly for any escape.

Through dubious odds, I tried to consistently convince myself to uplift and affix my weary eyes to that vast golden-blue sky of potential. That was my daily visualization. I would see myself trip, stumble, fall, then rise, stabilize, and stride ahead. It didn't matter how much reassurance and evidence I had from the positive twists and turns life threw at me, or the choices and pathways I decisively walked; the doubt of self and success and the despair of decline and failure—these were the thoughts creeping into my meditations and any positive effort to reframe my outcome.

Uplifting my mental state was a constant climb because I felt desperate. The vision I had of myself was of someone hanging onto a rope for dear life, my metaphorical hands burning from the friction as I pulled myself up, using whatever strength and willpower I had within me, only to slip down on my ass again. It can feel like your mind mutinies against you, kicking you off the castle walls of your fortress—but with the growing sense of the next tool, the rope—I realized there was a critical link to the fortress—I had a grappling hook. I would envision a sense of triumph overcoming the threat of defeat and see myself as a well-decorated veteran of this thing we all call life. I would climb back on the ramparts and take back my keep.

All the while I was fighting negative thoughts, I wondered if I was crazy, and what remained in my cranium was just overcooked scrambled eggs. But then, I would have moments of inspiration. I wanted to live. I wondered what inside me was pushing me to transcend the challenge of such a horrible fate. I could have given in like the first four doctors had recommended. Their idea that I should get my affairs in order and live my life waiting for death made me angry. How small-minded was this? Maybe that was my soul reacting to the ultimate challenge. We all have a soul and what I like to call a "higher self," that knows our direction of destiny toward the mission on Earth and our potential. Mine wasn't ready to give up yet. I was happy I had gotten over myself long enough to call Todd and to reach out to those friends who I knew had inner strength to spare.

I never wanted to feel entitled to the help my friends were offering me. Entitlement is an expectation, and this can be dangerous when your circumstances necessitate flexibility and *letting go*. But now, I felt like I had so little left. I was shrinking next to the seemingly insurmountable odds and obstacles, and needed to adjust my perspective to see how blessed I was. I thought about entitlement differently. Maybe people are entitled to certain things. Or maybe you are entitled to nothing, including your dignity, so anything we do receive is appreciated as a gift. That was how I was going to shift my thinking. My fortress would not wall out help, and a rope would no longer be a means for conflict, it would be a tool for allowing others to pull me up and to help me climb.

Still, Todd's emotional response unnerved me. With all my lofty thoughts about allowing people to help, I still felt humbled when people showed me how much they cared. I never questioned giving to people, but this was a true revelation of what my reluctance was underneath to tell people about my struggle.

I reassured Todd right away that I was going to beat this. I felt like I was feigning confidence, but it even subtly convinced the cynic within me.

I got lost in thought for a moment as Todd tried to cheer me up with stories of our good times together.

How could I use these new insights as part of leadership training? Perhaps I would teach people how important it was and how much courage it took to model personal leadership for others, but in the same way you must model it as much for yourself. You need to be your own leadership guide and constantly reinforce your attitudes and behaviors like the solid walls of a stronghold. You teach what you need to learn, and you can't hold yourself exempt as you look at others and what they need to be good leaders.

Here's a way to illustrate this. As you are behind your fortress, you rally on its ramparts and hold steady in the face of whatever besieges you. You have rebuilt walls that support you but don't hold you away from those who are your allies. Now, you shout a battle cry from inside these newly supported walls holding your shield steady standing in integrity.

And for when doubt and despair appeared to be claiming my mind's keep for their own, I pictured another tactic for when you feel outside of your protective fortress without a way to get in. I saw people like Todd and my other friends throwing me a strong rope and pulling me up the turret to the top and embracing me with a warm welcome of friendship and support. This was a stalwart defense against defeat. I could see how the tools worked together to build leadership both for others and for me personally.

I returned to the conversation to hear Todd laugh after a particularly funny memory and some jokes we all had told around the dinner table. I happen to be a good cook, so we'd have many nights of good food, drinks, and political conversations at Todd's house to solve the world's problems.

If only everyone would listen to us, the future would be changed, and the world would see our brilliance. Well, maybe before we had the drinks.

I could hear that we were both feeling reassured. Our voices were not so pinched, and we were soon laughing together again. That was the Todd that helped me feel at home and happy.

"I'll probably become a little withered from a loss of appetite and the nausea—and before you say it—yes, Todd, I could lose some weight. The fatigue is already settling in a bit—it'll get worse. Oh, and I'm bald now."

He nearly choked with laughter. "Oh good, now people can really see how ugly you are!"

I immediately snapped back, "Todd, remember, between us as family, you're the short brother and I am the handsome one." We both laughed; I fought back tears at the closeness I felt.

On a more serious note, Todd, instrumental in the North American side of the ILI, assured me he'd handle operations in the states while I went through rounds of chemo, and he volunteered to postpone some of the fundraising events we had planned in the USA, a kind of unnecessary stress I wouldn't have to deal with, but it still stung like a hornet to table them. These events were like my identity. Postponing them made everything too real.

It wasn't long until Wilma, the operations director for the ILI North America working with Todd, called. Todd must've texted her right away because she rang soon after we hung up. Todd had beaten me to it. I couldn't put off telling Wilma either.

Wilma's voice was full of vigor and empathy. She was a devout Christian who gets along with anyone, and she sure loved Israel. She was the kind of person who was always thinking of the greater good, nearly forgetting about herself at times.

"I'm sorry it took so long—" I was about to apologize for my purposeful avoidance.

"Don't even say it," she interrupted. "Look, I got something to share with you. There's this macrobiotic clinic in Cleveland that we should have you visit, and I'm going to look for more ways to help. You really ought to attack this from all directions, like a whole health approach, Eeki."

"I like the sound of that."

"Knew you would. We're going to fly you in soon, okay? Todd said, let's have the serious part of the trip, then there's the fun part."

"What's the fun part?"

"You'll see when you get here."

"Don't let Todd get us into anything crazy."

"Can't promise that, but don't worry."

"I'm not!"

I was happy to have something to look forward to. I prayed I would feel up to making the trip as there were three chemo and (possible) biological medicine treatments that would be happening before I could prepare to fly from Israel to Columbus.

At the moment, I was worried I wouldn't make it. My body felt like it was starting to decay. Gravity felt twice as strong, and the fatigue was like a heavy blanket you couldn't shake off on a groggy morning. I had never felt this weak. It was eerie. I still felt like me, though keeping my mood above water was like pulling up my own iron anchor from the bottom of the ocean by hand. And I remember thinking how it was becoming harder to feel happy. This trip, if I could make it, would come at the perfect time.

I put my mind to work and would think daily about how my body would endure. I concentrated on this seed of thought and watered and guarded it until the trip dates were nearly here. And believe it is why I felt strong enough to travel.

There was something extra special about seeing Todd and Wilma in person after such a long absence. As childish as Todd and I could be at times, Wilma could be too. It felt like being reunited with childhood friends after so many years being an adult. The macrobiotic clinic proved to be helpful, treating my body from this angle too—any boost to my health would benefit my fight. The whole health approach, as Wilma called it, made sense. Or as my mom used to say, "It couldn't hurt."

It didn't take long to get to the fun part of the trip. This would be as important as anything else. On our way to Hocking Hills, a hilly region just beyond where the ice age glacier had flattened much of Ohio, we made a pit stop at a funky thrift store. We found little trinkets and a few interesting pieces. While trying to convince Todd to not buy anything, he snapped a selfie of us that I still look at every now and then. It is disarming to see but I keep it to remind myself how sick I truly was. I looked like I was on a fast track to heaven. But I held the expression that internally, I was warring against a fake fate.

We were winding up and down and around steep hills—Todd still hadn't told me what we were up to, and Wilma wouldn't budge either. They were ganging up on me.

"Todd, will you slow down? I can't tell if I am going to puke from chemo or motion sickness!"

We were laughing the rest of the way to a large cabin where they were renting canoes and kayaks. Stepping out of the car, I felt my head swishing like a whirlpool. I was going to put my head between my legs but then it went away. It was a firm reminder that I was still sick despite the fun I was having. All the joking around during the drive made me feel almost normal but my body made sure I wouldn't forget.

I could see their concerned looks in my peripheral as we walked in—their eyes sweeping over me to make sure I was doing okay. As I returned from the bathroom, Todd was deliberating over which boats to get. A big one for the three of us? It was plain as day how much effort Todd and Wilma were putting in this trip to help me feel better. I needed to show them I was okay even if I was not. This wasn't to deny my pain and struggle, it was to wrestle with it, to fight back. While my body was weary, my mind saw clearly. I knew what I wanted. "Why don't you two get the canoe. I'm taking *that*."

"The kayak?

A fierce looking colorful boat was leaning against the wall. A kayak is typically meant for only one person if it is true to form. It was the right kind of symbolism for the mood I was in. I felt sluggish and at first thought better of it. Was I being silly to try the kayak with its double paddle? Maybe I was being ridiculous, but it was not more ridiculous than the situation I was in. It was some crazy idea to fight back—to show them and myself that I have some life in my blood, not just cancer.

Downstream, we were parallel to each other. Todd, Wilma, and I had finally figured out our paddling rhythm. By this point, there wasn't much use turning back even if I wanted to, but for a few moments I really did. We'd have to get around the whole circuit to where we started. We rowed apace, but it felt like there were three people sitting on both ends of my little kayak as dead weight. I won't pretend there was much whitewater, but it sure felt like it.

There's something about surrounding yourself in nature and returning to the natural world beyond so much of it that has been tamed and domesticated. Like many things, the artificial world brings its conveniences, but we lose something at the same time. Nature always reminds us of the circles of life in a most basic and encouraging way, which especially inspires hope for those who struggle to stay alive. Here on the river, surrounded by tall trees that towered high above me, I found some primal semblance of the old, 'man versus nature' battle. Perhaps it was a kind of simulation. If only I could somehow make this into one of the ILI's workshops!

My shoulders burned and sweat beaded on my head. Red spots dotted my arms, probably a side effect of the chemo or poison ivy. If I had hair, it would have been soaked. But the real challenge was inside my head. Every few moments I wanted to quit and throw my paddle in the water. Todd kept humoring me along the way, which was less of a distraction and more cheering me on. Wilma was calling for Todd to stop randomly switching sides of the boat to paddle. The final stretch came into view, and I was suddenly struck by joyful tears welling up in my eyes, but I laughed them off. Strangely, I felt more energized than I had the whole trip. "Quit messing around guys! There's the finish line! You are all buying me dinner if I win!"

I was out of breath, yet my lungs felt so good. I won. Well, it was a close tie, but I won the battle. As we drew near the shore, I considered how the fortress tool is something we bring wherever we go. It is a defense against the crushing forces and infiltrating influences that may tear us down from the inside out. It is a shield we use on the offensive, emblazoned with our empowered self-image, intimidating and pushing back against the pressures against us. We become the commanders and guardians of our own domain, and we must reign over it with cunning and courage. Personal leadership involves sword and shield, offense and defense against our challenges and in the pursuit of conquering our futures. I imagined myself like an armored knight riding out beyond the drawbridge to meet my enemies on the field. Whatever way we try to personalize this tool, it must serve to ground ourselves in our struggle to win. There are many features to a fortress, and as we build our own, we come to find a greater confidence in our abilities. A greater *strength*.

That night at Todd's, we stuffed ourselves with a worthy feast. It was only until the next day that I realized I hadn't felt sick while eating. My body was following my lead.

A day before I went home to Israel, I was left to my own devices at Todd's house while dog-sitting. I had a few people come to visit me, but soon it was just me and the pup. While watching the television, I kept flipping channels, a few dramas with too many commercials. I needed something light. I found a comedy, but just as I was getting into it, it ended with more ads. Strangely, it was for the biological medicine commercial. My face grew blank. In Israel, it is forbidden to publish life-supporting medications in commercials on TV, like oncological medications. At the end of it, they listed a slew of side effects like an auctioneer, as if people could just place their bid on which one they'll get. Time slowed as I heard, "itching on your limbs which is preceded by non-itching rashes… pain and discomfort in the joints—"

"Wait, wait, what did they say?"

The dogs' ears perked up.

I lifted my shirt and my eyes darted to the spots on his limbs, but there was none on my stomach. I felt like I was becoming a hypochondriac. I wasn't sure if my joint pain was due to the kayak trip, age, or—

"YES!!! Yes! I got the rash! Yes!"

The dog jumped, barking at me.

I knew it. I knew all along, but now I could say for sure.

It was the middle of the night in Israel, on the other side of the globe, but I immediately sent an email to Dr. Onn, that simply read: *You don't have to worry, I got the medicine!*

It wasn't the placebo drug.

When Todd got home, we called Wilma over for a celebration. They had no idea what for, but they were ready to party anyway. That night, we had a toast. *To life!*

That night they looked at me differently. While we were saying goodbye, we were renewing our future with hope and courageous joy.

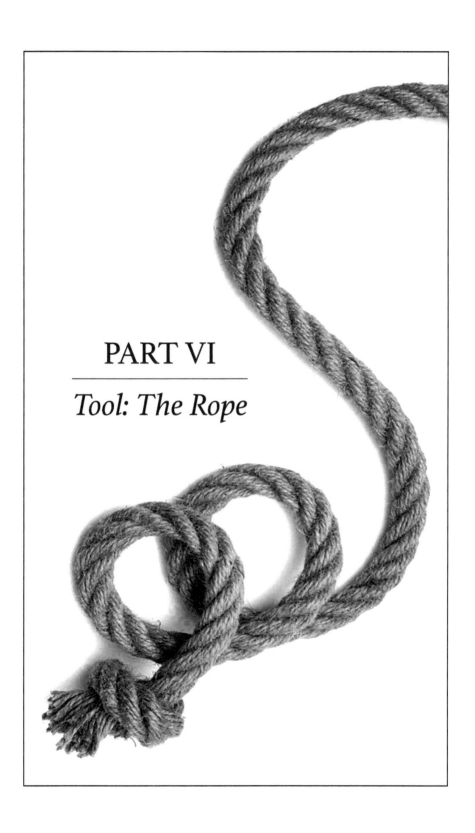

PART VI

Tool: The Rope

THE CLIMB

When you contemplate the tools in personal leadership, you view the mind and heart as separate: *The mind is the rider, and the heart is the horse*—two forces that stand against doubt and despair. But I believe there's a third entity; the soul in each of us, which is a unique essence at your core, no matter what source you believe it is from. From my soul, I would derive strength from an infinite energy to reach my goals, but it required it to be channeled through this rowdy partnership between my head and chest.

This was now my answer and anchor as I experienced this when under the greatest pressure. Before cancer, I could think of the idea of the soul and apply it to others. But until I felt as if my mind was falling and my heart couldn't take another step, I did not perceive that I could go beyond my limitations. Something inside of me drove me beyond my ever-expanding inner universe in unimaginable ways.

I wondered if this was a cosmic secret only discovered when pushed to the brink. Or maybe, had I applied the tools of personal leadership to myself during less challenging times, I might not have had such a deep soul-searching struggle. I had to plunge into the deepest end of myself.

I perceived the mind and heart as naturally limiting, bound to physicality, perception, predictabilities, and patterns. But because God gave me this challenge, or what you may believe bestows such things, I saw that the soul transcends these human limitations as an innate, boundless force that is often dormant and disconnected in many of us. For far too long, this included me. I make no secret of this; my journey showed me that unleashing the soul's inner power is a painful and arduous voyage with the forces of nature to contend with. And this journey never ends. Perhaps it is the reason we are here on this planet and why I was given a reason and a path so I could stay.

As the first couple of treatments were coursing through my veins, ILI courses came to a close. Matan and his friends, my students, were graduating at the peak of summer. So many things in life come in cycles, as it was with the annual end and beginning of the leadership programs. This end was their new beginning, and I considered again how my own life's renewal was because of my nearing demise.

My sister Bracha had been coming to my treatments despite the long schlep to get there. She was so pained to see me go through them, it was apparent that maybe they were too clinical for her, and too real. That "fake it until you make it" expression is thrown around a lot, and I found myself thinking of it then. It didn't seem right to me to artificially act a certain way to make us both feel better. Instead, I would create the experience I wanted without the artificial. I looked at it as both an art and science. In theory, the characteristics I wished to have for myself, and others could only be earned through action. For example, why is someone considered strong? Kind? Confident? Empathetic? Rude? Funny? Etcetera? There is some behavior, some action that one can point to, that defines that characteristic. The art is in the creative and clever ways we find this evidence for ourselves. We can change our character traits by reframing how we look at ourselves and the image we put into the world. If I wanted to be strong and confident and beat cancer, I needed to do things that showed this. In this case, to do was to become.

I would dare myself again and again to *do* what I needed to *be*. Living life was a process of becoming. With the help of my brilliant ILI team, there was a tidal wave of applicants to review and interview. No one would even blink if I stepped away for my treatments, but *my* treatment of challenges demanded I keep the train moving. This wasn't my stop.

The next crop of applicants needed to be planted before October's harvest of students, certainly a quick turnaround—that'd keep me busy. It would be some of the action I needed to build more momentum. Otherwise, it would be too easy to slip into malaise and hopelessness. That was not for me.

I reminded myself of what is at the core of the ILI training program. It was designed based on two foundational principles: leadership is a choice to make in life, and everyone can make the choice to become a leader—and once this choice is made, the expression of leadership is achieved through one's behavior, requiring the development of an array of special behaviors and tools. These make for a successful leader.

I considered how the tools I was developing during my fight with cancer were inspired and adapted by what already had years of shining success with students of the program. I realized I was not reinventing the wheel with my pursuit of *Personal Leadership*. And so, as I prepared for the initial interviews for candidates, I reflected on what criteria we used for the selection process. For students wishing to join the program, the team would first assess the level of commitment to become a leader, and second, the motivation to invest in learning and acquiring the tools and behaviors needed to be one.

The ILI has an interview tool developed by one of our longstanding team members, Ofra, who was a top ranked, military colonel of the human behavioral department of the Israeli Military HQ. This fifteen-page notebook would be used by about all 25 of us to guide and survive the days ahead. I kept thinking, *God bless you, Ofra*. We sure needed it, but with my body so worn down, I especially did to keep me on the rails.

After several interviews with many wonderful candidates, I sat down with one whose family immigrated to Israel from Ethiopia, Esther, whose story inspired me. I felt fatigued beyond reason, but I still needed to keep my composure. With a determined gaze not hardened by hardship, she described her family coming over to Israel by foot, and the challenges of culturally assimilating with her parents and siblings. This woman spoke the language of leadership; she had involved herself in a self-created social program prepping boys and girls for military service. At this point, I already knew she was going to be admitted.

Then in an offbeat moment—she told me her mother had died recently.

"Oh, she must've been young… what happened?"

"It was cancer."

I tried to hide my expression as a lump formed in my throat.

She must've shared a few more stories with me before I realized I was staring past her, casting my thoughts into a void. *Will I be there when she graduates?* The question echoed in a hollow space inside me.

We said our goodbyes, and I told her we'd be getting in touch again soon. I must've sat there for a good 15 minutes afterward, shuffling through my notes, eyes perusing over much of her life story. The funny thought of filling out my own form occurred to me. Or maybe I would interview *Sunshine. Where are you from?*

Before I began the chemo and the biological medicine treatments, I was already at the end of my rope. After all the interviews, I felt my grip slipping. I felt as if I barely pulled myself over the ledge to the first CT scan.

There was more reason to doubt. Dr. Onn was concerned the strict scan protocol of every two months would be too much for my body as the radiation would be exacerbating my cancer, and with an already weakened immune system by its nature, the chemo wasn't helping this either. The pharmaceutical company's study required this schedule of its research participants. The statistics were already bleak for stage-four participants. So, the company would get as much data as they could before many dropped dead. But Dr. Onn believed I'd die from the treatment's radiation if I lived through the cancer. Well, I'd be damned either way.

We already knew there was a positive trend before the chemo and the biological medicine treatments, but the excitement was short lived as I would fall into a fit and pit of doubt and despair until the next, reassuring milestone.

Cancer had been all over my body. Tumors thriving as I was barely surviving. I kept wondering if all progress would rebound and cancer would sink its last shot with the most defeating buzzer beater of my life. What an upset.

The CT scans felt like waiting for winning lottery numbers, so my childhood friend, Amnon, was my lucky charm for going to them. Amnon was the only friend who knew me for decades—sometimes it seemed like we had known each other since birth. There was a voice in me that suggested having him at the scans as another reassurance that I'd survive because he was always there for me and would not let me depart from this life.

I always believed he had good karma, and he made me feel like I did too because of our friendship. He was the kind of person you'd immediately feel comfortable sharing your troubles with, though he often was aware of them before you would get the chance to speak up. He would accompany me to all my scans like we were going to some casino to strike it rich. All bets were on the table. I'd beat this, but that greedy gremlin in my head would whisper doubts as if he was trying to psych me out and make me fold.

He was walking beside me toward the hospital. "Quit your worrying, Eeki."

I looked to our right for oncoming traffic as we crossed the street. The blazing sun chased shadows from every little crevice and angle of the building complex. "Not worried, just trying to make sure we don't get run over."

"I know you. When you stop talking, you start thinking. Lord knows I can barely hear my own thoughts when we're together."

My grumpy face melted, surely not from the heat.

Amnon took a seat in the lobby after I introduced him to Dr. Onn. A foreboding tension came from his office before I even entered the room. The feeling caused me to imagine a vacuum hose drawing me into a body bag. The doctor appeared more reticent than usual, reserved within his inner landscape.

We sat down. Like the last visit, I wondered if it would in fact be the last.

"I've waited to review the results of the scan. I thought we should do this together."

Ah, maybe Dr. Onn had his doubts too? "The suspense is killing me."

He managed to restrain his grin, but his eyes couldn't hide his amusement. He scanned the report. "The CT shows a little less than a *50 percent reduction*. Eeki!" His chair skidded back as if screeching with excitement, and the whole room seemed to stir. He rushed over and nearly choked me with a bearhug. He smacked me with a kiss on the cheek. "You see?!"

"We're halfway." My voice was a little crisp. All the shouting thoughts on the drive over must've winded me. They were now hushed.

"Eeki, the signs are there! You're going to get over this! Keep on climbing, keep the course."

A victory tune slowly entered my consciousness like a steady turn of the volume dial. "It's all thanks to you, really. I wouldn't have made it this far otherwise."

"On the contrary, this is you, and I knew it the day you first walked through my door, but I'm by your side all the way." He paused and gave me an up-and-down glance. "Now Eeki, when I told you to fuel your fight by eating well despite the chemo's effects, it wasn't to become a pig... I joke. This is a sign of health." I guess he noticed my developing pot belly. How could I avoid all the sympathy food that my well-intentioned friends kept bringing me?

Amnon was already smiling when I saw him, expecting success. *Jackpot.* My hug nearly strangled him. "My lucky charm, Amnon!"

This meeting was a boon to my mood and sense of mission. For me, a part of making milestones is recognizing and rewarding achievement. Even more, is to share this success with others. It was an opportunity to show my parents how strong and confident I was, but I had deliberately not yet told them of my cancer. It was a delicate situation...

◆ ◆ ◆

My parents were strong, resilient, and of my greatest source of reverence next to God. I had been praying in search of when to tell them. It seemed my prayers had been answered when I walked out of Dr. Onn's office, but it was much more bitter than sweet.

By this time, my mother had been diagnosed with Alzheimer's for about five years. She would forget your name the moment you left the room, but she'd still remember what was said. Her mind was like a titanium trap, and she held on for quite some time until its jaws slowly released. She could only get around in a wheelchair while my father walked with a cane—my father, a man who shouldered his family's burdens despite this. The truth was, I feared more than anything that the news of my possible death would spell their own demise. That my mother's last memory would become her most devastating loss, and that my father's heart would burn to ash.

Survivors. Would I live to show them I was one too?

I couldn't rely only on hope. Personal leadership is not solely driven by it. There is a medley of *middot,* Hebrew for character attributes, that are refined by your choices and actions. They are to each person's soul as a raw diamond—as you face the friction of challenges and pressures in life, you carve and refine yourself until you shine as you should, in your most pristine form. And not one diamond is the same.

Life is often described as a journey—surely, I have said as much—but it is also a climb, especially when you think about where your potential is to be found. There are many ropes hanging from the heavens to pull yourself beyond what you believe are your capabilities. There is consistent evidence in the world of sports that athletes are breaking previously unbeatable records all the time. Focused athletes strive to go beyond the expected limits, and they achieve new goals. So, when I say the soul has ambition, it is this inner spark of unrealized potential that drives you to seek growth, and its greatness is yours to obtain. But where does this ambition hide for most people? One can admire athletes' ambition but believe they are somehow beyond average human beings as if their souls possess some secret ingredient others don't have. This is not so. While you may not be meant for major league sports, there *is* something you are uniquely made for and can make yourself to be.

All the tools of leadership have led to this very question. Where is this untapped potential stored inside you? The question is what I can provide you with, but the answer is your cosmic secret to discover because it is only yours to share. But perhaps I can also show you how and even dare you to find it.

As my parents were aging past their 80s, I made it my commitment to take them on vacation at least once a year. They just loved it! And so, even with my mother in decline as well as my treatments, I offered them a vacation in September to the nearby island of Cyprus.

Cyprus is one of the most common vacation spots for Israelis. It is its own island country with beautiful beaches and everything one would want from a getaway. But for me this trip would serve many purposes, not least of which was to provide evidence of my vigor to my parents when I told them the news and to myself that I was really improving my health.

One of the ways I chose to handle my body's decline while everything, even my mind, felt like it was walking through a murky swamp, was to remember what I was doing before the *problem* surfaced. Except this time, it wasn't to correct or learn about past choices—it was to return a sense of normalcy. There were routines and responsibilities that built structure. I still dragged myself to the gym and kept up with the ILI's impending round of workshops that Rumi and my team were preparing for. It wouldn't be long before the current cohorts graduated, and I would be interviewing the next crop of students. Time moved forward, and no matter how much I would have liked to, I could not hold it still.

I sensed that I needed to maintain a certain baseline of living as I rebuilt my life anew—my growing fortress now was built on a more stable foundation, but I also needed to keep up production and momentum. Just as it was on the river in a kayak with my friends—when I was arguably at my worst on chemo—proving to myself that I was competent and capable was key. It was time to challenge myself again. The next rope was in my hands. *Time to climb.*

I knew the trip to Cyprus would be difficult, but I was determined. We all met at my sister's home for dinner one evening. My parents and I sat around the table as Bracha placed the dishes in its center.

"I have some important news to share." I said, grabbing everyone's attention. Bracha had impressed me with her ability to not drop the bombshell news on our parents, but she nearly dropped a bowl of hummus all over the table—she looked like she was holding her breath as if I was about to tell them what was in my lungs. My mom smiled while my father patiently waited, calmly curious.

"We're going to Cyprus to celebrate Mom's birthday in September! Clear the cobwebs off your suitcases!"

Bracha stood behind the counter, and I half expected her to duck as if taking cover from a grenade. She breathed a sigh of relief and gave me a raised eyebrow. Her expression read, *What the hell do you think you are doing?*

My parents beamed, but I could feel an air of concern as it swept over the table. We had begun to dish out food for each other. My father took a pita after everyone else had their share. "It's hard for us to get around these days if you haven't noticed, but it would be really nice."

My eyes bounced between my parents. "It's a short flight; we'll be alright. Bracha and I will take care of you—Mom, do you want to go to Cyprus for your birthday?"

"Yes!" She said it so loudly you'd have thought the whole neighborhood heard.

Dad was cornered and he knew it. He breathed one of those self-contained sighs, knowing it was futile to refuse now, though he'd quickly warmed up to the idea.

Bracha smiled. "I can't go, Eeki, but this'll be lovely for them. Can you really handle this yourself though?" The weight of that question was lost on my parents.

"We'll bring Mom's caretaker. All resolved."

There was too much talking and the need for more eating. I silently beckoned to my sister. She caught the hint and brought some dessert. It was already decided. I would book the tickets that night. I wanted a good experience for all of us, even if it would be the start of a Jewish goodbye. At any gathering, we need to start bidding proper farewells to everyone at least a half-hour before anyone intends to leave, which inevitably leads to long bouts of kibitzing, those little wisecracks and teasing about what we're doing with our lives and how we're doing it. Of course, there are also the heartfelt expressions of, "Let's keep in touch," and small conversations that carry on as we draw near the door. Finally, we feel fulfilled in our parting of ways and are permitted to leave—that is what this Cyprus trip would be. I wasn't ready to say goodbye, but I knew I needed this because of those "what ifs" that drift ahead of you, projecting into the future. At least, the trip might be the beginning of our goodbye with the hope that it would take a long time before any of us exited to our next stage of existence.

This trip was also an important way to ignite my ambition, a powerful force for growth, and I needed to express it. It wasn't just about telling them about the *big news* in a comfortable space, it was about creating joy when despair was smoking up the place. It was about spending precious time with family on Mom's birthday, a treat for them and a proving ground for my strength and courage.

I booked a tourist villa. You might think parents or friends would be the ones to spoil the person fighting cancer, but my motive was to spoil them. It may seem a bit backwards, but for me, it was the way forward. It was an action I could take, and it felt good.

I'd have to push Mom around in a wheelchair while my father kept pace on a cane. It would be a lot of work while my body was at its weakest, like my experience on the river in the Hocking Hills, but this made it even more compelling for me. When I dared to break boundaries, it felt like I could withstand a hurricane.

I loved seeing my parents happy and even adored their little squabbles, which never really seemed like real fights, moreso a way to impart how well they knew each other, how close together they'd grown. This was evident during our travel and as we finally settled into our rooms while my mom waited for my father in the bathroom to get ready for the pool.

"Yes, for the last time, I'm coming out!"

"You said that the last time and you're still in there!" Mom said. Her caretaker was as amused as I was.

As the sky dimmed into nightfall, I watched them floating in the pool outside our Mediterranean villa. The change in lighting along with the colors was breathtaking. I didn't mind losing my breath to beauty. At least that served a purpose.

We were having a little barbecue with a neighboring family also on vacation. I grabbed a bottle of wine and led my father to join me on our own. I opened the cork, poured the wine and gave him a glass. Then we quietly reminisced. My father liked to joke and tell stories to keep things lighter and more on the surface. His emotions were typically well-hidden, and he was a master of deflection if our conversations moved into territory he found uncomfortable.

As we sat in silence for a while, the large waxing moon cast its reflection over a long swath of the sea like a runway. It brought me back to childhood as I tried to find a flat stone that would skip at least two or three times before diving in the water. Dad looked a little tipsy leaning on his cane even while sitting, but he seemed wonderfully relaxed. Now I had no excuses. I had to tell him the truth.

"You've always been such a good kid," he said, waxing nostalgic.

I loved that he could still see that young person in me. Having never had children of my own I could only imagine how images of your child's life would be embedded in your memories as touchstones of a life together.

"Sure, you had your moments," he said with a laugh. "But I have always been proud of you and your work. And, I'm not just saying this as your father." He had told me this two times already since we opened the bottle, but it wasn't the wine talking. It was eerie, as if he anticipated something that I needed to say and to hear.

"Dad, a few months ago they found some tumors in my body," I said matter-of-factly before I could change my mind. Then I sat back and finished the rest of my glass. There it was, out in the open.

His eyes widened. "When did you get the news?" he asked.

"I have known for about four months now." Before he could object, I threw in, "I've been battling cancer and winning. I needed some time to understand what I was up against—"

"What, cancer? Four whole months you say?" He sobered up and I could see tears in his eyes. His expression was crushing me, but I held it together. I watched as he seemed to mouth something to the heavens. I could practically see his blood pressure rising. "Just like Moshe. Not again… It's a family curse, isn't it?" Although I felt a bit ashamed, I had almost forgotten about my cousin Moshe. It had only been a year since his death to cancer, and the family was still mourning. I realized I needed to reassure my father right away. Otherwise, he would sink into thinking of the worst possible scenarios, and I could easily find myself buying into them. I was only ever a thought away from doubt and despair, which always threatened to disrupt my focus on living.

"Dad, it's not going to be like Moshe! I just had a scan that showed the cancer has halved in my body. That means that one half of the cancer has been destroyed by me. The treatments are helping! I am winning the fight and we are here to celebrate." Maybe Moshe's losing battle and the pain that people felt in the aftermath could be turned into a greater reason for me to use everything in my power and toolbox to fight. I would also do it for him. My beloved cousin Moshe, named after *the* Moses, who had rescued and led the Israelites to the promised land only to be forbidden to enter it with them before his death, and didn't have the time to fulfill all his dreams. I imagined myself as Joshua, his disciple, who carried the torch beyond to finish what Moses could not. I would honor him and my parents.

"Why didn't you tell me sooner?" my father demanded. Now his sadness turned to hurt and anger.

"Why would I tell you if I didn't know how to handle it? I have help and everything I need, thank God. I just wanted you to be aware of it, and I believed now was a good time."

My father wasn't the best communicator, but maybe I wasn't either. He often seemed too cool and calm, like a mirror reflection of my own demeanor. I was glad he was showing real emotion, an appropriate reaction. Sadness, hurt, anger were all the right feelings at the right time, and they helped me cope. I felt like a boulder was lifted from my shoulders. Not only did I no longer need to worry about sharing the news, but I also felt connected to my father in a way I hadn't in the past. Even though I am fully grown I might well have been twenty again, just starting out. Only now did I feel my father with me as support. I felt less alone, and I slept better that night than I had since my diagnosis.

We were nearing the end of our trip, but there was one last excursion Mom insisted upon. When she got an idea in her head, she fiercely advocated for it. She and I were like one soul split into two bodies. It broke my heart that her mind was fighting to hold on because I remembered who she used to be. But despite her condition, her heart remembered everything. Bracha had a similar bond, but to our father. Dad and my dear sister were much more reserved while we were quite loquacious and temperamental; perhaps we didn't leave much room for them to speak.

"Eeki, I want to see the cherries," Mom insisted. "You told me about them before we left, and we won't leave until I get to taste them." Her remembering the cherries didn't surprise me. I knew this trip would be stimulating for her mind. It made me so happy to hear this, but it was bittersweet—the cherries were out of season.

"Yes, Mama," I added gently. "But I told you they grow in July and are gone by August."

"I'm sure there are some left," she insisted. "Get your father and I'll have my caretaker get me ready."

It was a decent climb up the hill for a good purpose: to make Mom happy. Lo and behold, there were no cherries, but it was a lovely spot on the small mountainside, with a quaint coffee shop that had a beautiful view of the sea. We had stopped by for a break. Dad and I were leaving the restroom, but before we returned to Mom with her caretaker at the table, he pulled me aside.

"You know Eeki, if I have to say Mourner's Kaddish over my son's grave, I think I would dig my own." His words gave me a heart palpitation. After an intense conversation, Dad would often reflect and come back later with a few choice words like a long-lost boomerang.

"It is easier to bless God's name when you are alive, so I plan to stick around for a while if you can continue to put up with me," I replied. What else could I say? I made a promise to my dad that I would keep. I would use everything in my power so my father wouldn't know the pain of losing a son. I noticed lately my prayers to God were more often thanks, as I knew I had tools within me to lead my life even though my set was not yet complete. There was still much more to discover and learn. And for this, I thanked God as well.

DARE YOURSELF

Amnon was ready to go gambling with me again when my next CT scan appointment came around, and Dr. Onn was waiting for us at the hospital's roulette table. I thought about how I'd rather be in a casino than the hospital yet again, and I nervously patted the steering wheel as we stopped at a red light, nearing the turnoff. "Alright, my lucky charm," I said, referring to Amnon, "what percent do you think it'll be this time?"

"You know this isn't a game of chance, Eeki. You told me yourself, when you weren't joking around that is."

"Ah, lighten up brother," I said. But I was the one who needed to relax.

"I bet you *think* you're funny, I'll put money on that." he said, making an effort at humor. I know he could sense my anxiety. It was dripping from me and would have been obvious even to someone not as observant and intuitive as Amnon.

"Folding on that one." I gave him a thoughtful glance. "You know, I believe everything is meant to be, as I have said before. None of this just *happened* by chance. But I'll tell you what, there's no counting cards when God's the dealer, so I can't game the system." Then I paused to think. "But I have been given all I need. This game is far from over." I was being sincere. I knew I couldn't cut corners, but it had much more to do with my personal leadership than with the medical protocols. They were working as they should. But I would not be able to game the system without a sincere belief that there was meaning to all of this. I had faith God had offered me an opportunity. I couldn't fake that.

Around a week later, I met with Dr. Onn to review the results. The percentage kept climbing. There was a 75% reduction in my tumors. The report's table graph showed the disease had all started in my left lung, but by this time had decreased by 50%. Where cancer first starts it is apparently the most stubborn, much like me. "Remember how I called it *Sunshine*?"

His eyebrows raised. "How could I not? It was my first time hearing such a thing, but I loved it. Make light of what seems like a dark thing, right?"

"Always, but we have a complicated relationship. I'm burning these tumors away, but *Sunshine* is more stubborn than belly fat."

Dr. Onn shook his head with a grin. "You're winning because you're focusing on healing yourself, despite what the medications are doing. Your mentality, your fighting spirit, is beating this. The fire comes from within *you*. The medications work *with* you and do not kill the cancer itself. You do."

I carried his words with me all the way home. It was as if the skies parted, and the next horizon was before my eyes like a sunny daydream. Amnon looked at me like I was crazy. Perhaps I was. *It was time.*

I had a wish-filled wildcard that would have all those pessimistic oncologists leaving the blackjack table, especially the one who had suggested putting my childhood dream into play before I lost everything. *I would climb a mountain in Iceland.* A sky-bound rope dangling from the heavens. That would be the ultimate test and metaphor for my battle with cancer. But I never saw it as a last hoorah while waiting for death. It would be a triumphant climb for not having given up and given in. I was reclaiming my life as God wanted it for me.

Before I let Amnon out of the car, I sprung it on him. "I'd like you to come with me to Iceland."

"What?"

"All expenses on me, lucky charm. You know I've always wanted to do this."

"Yes, I sort of remember, but Eeki, are you sure about this? You must be kidding."

"I am always serious. Come with me. It won't be until next year—there'll be plenty of time to get ready. We're going to climb a glacier!"

"I don't have a choice, do I?" He scrubbed the back of his head. "Someone needs to look after you. I'll take the job, but I'll pay for myself."

"No, you won't."

He shook his head with a smile. It would be a lot of work thwarting his efforts to cover his expenses. This was a gift I wanted to share with him.

I purchased tickets for July 4, 2017, exactly a year since the beginning of my treatments. I didn't dare set myself on cruise control; there was much work to do. I had reached one plateau and would need to continue climbing if I didn't want to fall. I dared myself to climb despite all the excuses and through all the resistance. I wasn't chicken, but if I backed out, my life might as well be a rotisserie spinning me around until I crisped into dead meat.

The ILI was in full swing and carried into that summer, another cycle reaching its end. After what felt like a short winter (not just due to Israel's climate), the spring months promised renewal, and I seemed to keep ahead of my worries, though I occasionally wondered if I'd be able to use my ticket when July came around.

I would challenge these doubts by visualizing my goals as checkpoints. There was always a milestone ahead of me, predetermined and actively pursued. This is a critical part of the rope tool. Negative thoughts were the gravity keeping me from climbing higher. Through the struggle I grew stronger. There was always a clear, achievable end and—like the cycles of ILI's workshops—another challenge was prepared when the other was achieved. And if we are to fall, the next ascent will feel even more redeeming.

When we left for Iceland, July 4 was a time of fireworks in my heart. Our first flight went to Vienna, Austria, where we had a little time to fill, not to mention shot glasses. We bought about five bottles of liquor at the airport because we heard it was more expensive in Iceland, and so we found ourselves sampling some of each like a couple of buffoons.

"*L'chaim!*" I downed a shot of Jack Daniels with Amnon, as we began to reminisce in a little corner of a bar in the terminal. He started getting sentimental, the lightweight.

"Eeki, I've come to realize how special this trip is to me." His face turned gravely serious. "Your battle… I'm with you, and whatever happens—"

"*Shush!* We're going to Iceland!" It must've sounded like a Viking battle cry as I filled us another round of shots.

He tried again. "Eeki, I mean it, this is a special trip that I want—"

"Iceland, Amnon! Can you believe it?! *L'chaim!*"

Another round.

"Eeki, listen to me, I'm getting worked up, you know? We'll take a lot of pictures—"

"*Skal!*" Another.

He shook his head with a crooked grin. I knew what he was thinking, the sap. These pictures and videos might be the reruns of our last adventure. I would do everything I could to make the most of my remaining time, with the hope that God would greenlight many more seasons of my life. *This will not be my swan song.*

Soon, we were hundreds of miles high as I wrapped a pillow around my neck. As I tried to nap, I could see Amnon in the window seat next to me, wistfully gazing out the window. His eyes seemed to behold some kind of sadness found within the clouds. I nodded off wondering if it was some prophetic vision he was having.

My journey through the trials of cancer began in one desert and seemed to land in another. Iceland was otherworldly. From the plane, it still felt like what you'd see on television or in pictures, removed from reality. As we left the terminal, cool and crisp air filled my lungs. The scent of certainty must've tickled *Sunshine's* nose. He became a kind of ghostly passenger, scribing my chronicles. I would carry him on my glacier hike and mountain climb to witness where this odyssey would take me.

The ride to our first destination was scenic beyond my imagination. I had often dreamed about coming here, but seeing Iceland for the very first time was something I will never forget. We stopped several times along the way to witness this majestic land. The bald mountains, lush landscapes, and countless waterfalls were blanketed in low-hanging skies of gray, strangely unfamiliar as if it followed laws not of this earth. I wondered what hid in the smoky peaks of these mountains. Snow splashed down their sides, some sprinkled with green, and the black sandy beaches seemed to show a world turned upside-down, a world of contrasts, raw earth with cities caught between the might of its landscapes.

The view was made of visual delicacies, and I would have been content to sightsee. But that was not why I had come. There was a volcanic mountain to climb, but first I would need to warm-up with a glacier hike on Sólheimajökull. I had planned for this hike to serve as an appetizer to what would be the fulfillment of a life-long dream.

Before this, we enjoyed a couple of days of easy-going adventures, but on the third day we met our guide, George, who rode with us to the glacier. He would accompany us on the hike. Of Scottish descent, he still looked like a Viking—he was a man of adventure and sincerity, passionately introducing us into Icelandic culture. He made us feel like we belonged.

This was the perfect place to challenge my reality. Of all the places I could have chosen, the unique Icelandic landscape made an immediate impact on my consciousness. My intuition had been right. Sometimes dreams are really signs guiding us where we need to go in order to grow.

I found myself daydreaming how to rebuild my life—inspiration was all around me, so many contrasts and wonders to expand my vision. I was able to step back and consider what the Eeki in Israel was doing and feeling. Before the diagnosis, I had been missing out on so many spiritual opportunities to become more than who I was. It was a good life with a decent pursuit of purpose, but now I could never go back to that without wanting much more. No matter the outcome of this trip, I would return home to make my life anew. I had to use what I knew and stand as an example for others. I had to show them through my personal struggle and triumph. I *would* succeed. I had to.

Amnon and I followed him out of the car and took a short journey to the foot of the magnificent glacier. It was like stepping out of the world I knew into a completely new experience. As we approached the ice, I was startled by the cold that crept into my skin through thick layers of clothing, but it was nothing compared to the icepick chill that struck my soul. I was far out of my element—not just because I was a sun-spoiled Israeli. This was a waking dreamscape where I knew instinctively that all my hopes and hurts would bear fruit. I would need to grow toward the sun, the light of my future, transcending all doubts. But it wasn't going to be easy. I had many built-up years of stubborn resistance. I was staring at the ominous Icelandic clouds when it occurred to me that they were just like my thoughts shrouding my optimism with cold uncertainty. That is why I needed this warmup. Heat rises, and I would need to ignite my insides with a sense of confidence and leadership so I could climb beyond my fear and despair. If I were to survive, I needed to walk beyond negativity. But of course, surviving wasn't enough.

I was going to renew my life path, and the perfect proving ground was beneath my feet.

The black, rocky terrain had ridges and ripples of earth in all directions—bluish-white ice, clear and crystalline and flowing at a pace unperceived by the eye. I wondered how this hike would compare to the climb of Snæfellsjökull, a volcanic mountain that had long pervaded my dreams. I trudged along in heavy boots, each step like stepping in molasses. I let my mind wander and my imagination flow freely. I envisioned my body slowing, melting with the gleaming, icy ground below me, and vanishing all together. I felt so small and insignificant, yet remarkably powerful.

Amnon's expression was the same as it had been on the plane. He was worried about me, and I couldn't really blame him. He saw through me. When our eyes met, I quickly turned away.

Although I was excited about the challenges ahead of me, I knew some of it was false bravado. I knew this hike might be but a stroll for some—but for me, it was a fight against my mind and bodily limitations. It wasn't just chemical weariness—it was as much the internal struggle of past and future me. This was the real tug-of-war. I was stubborn and wouldn't let go, even though the rope, this challenge, burned my hands like gripping fire. I saw what I could become but only if I obliterated my old way of thinking. This was not about survival; this was about achievement. I focused on what was at stake. I spurred my heart from a trot to full gallop. *You need to do this. Go. Pull yourself forward.*

I was using my mind as a muscle. The physical and mental pain increased as we marched farther on the glacier. My thoughtful old friends, doubt and despair, came to join us. These thoughts, I would push away. Doubt. *Push.* Despair. *Push.* I was willing away these enemy forces—the pains of growth—with each mindful thrust, like a hand knocking away distractions, while the other pulled me up this flaming, ethereal rope to a higher me. I soon realized I was being carried by nothing but mental fortitude. It made me laugh to think maybe I had some kind of mutated, psychic muscle in my head. No matter. I had to pull myself forward while pushing away anything that didn't fit for my personal leadership. I would use the same mentality required by that one final rep with a barbell—pushing beyond what you think you can do. In my workshops, I inspired other people to do it. I would have to do it myself. I was not planning on giving up, in fact, it was a conscious effort to focus on my goal of finishing this hike, especially if I ever hoped to climb the mountain on this trip. I outmaneuvered my pain as much as possible.

"Eeki, are you doing alright?" Amnon called back to me.

"Yes! Will you quit slowing us down? George charges by the hour!" I knew this was a fib, but I didn't want Amnon's realistic concern to break my effort at mind over matter. My little joke bought me some time before my dear friend would ask again. I persevered for another couple of hours on the hike. The body is amazing when in sync with the mind. I was totally exhausted but hit what I can only describe as a fourth wind. My engine was running hot, and I worried I'd gas out before the end and possibly need to be rescued. That would have been a terrible joke on me, very humiliating.

I was peeved when Amnon would slow down whenever he thought I was slipping behind, but this frustration was directed at myself. So, I kept pushing ahead, imagining magic hands dragging me forward by the collar with my dangling feet scraping the ice.

So many questions swirled through my mind. They felt like pesky buzzards waiting for flesh. I had no idea what would be waiting upon my return to Israel. New life? At least a little more of it? What could I bring from Iceland? A part of daring myself to do this challenge was to understand the threads of meaning that my hands gripped onto, an emulation of my war against cancer. This is a critical element to the rope tool. When there is no meaning in your struggles, you stunt your growth. And this meaning is for you to co-create with whatever force you believe guides the universe.

"This is the last stretch of the journey, my friends. How're your legs?" George visually assessed us. I felt like puffing out my chest, but *Sunshine* and I were both short on breath.

"Full steam ahead! Amnon, you better keep up."

He grinned but also saw through my struggle. I pushed forward.

Will I make it to the end? And back again?

I was in awe of the nature of change. The frozen waters and medley of stones I walked upon reflected to me a sense of grounding. I remembered my recent kayaking trip with Todd and Wilma—what would they think of me now? What was a rush then was a terrible slog now. This time there were no waters to carry me—I couldn't just flow with the river. Instead, my *moving fortress,* the fifth tool, was like steel spikes stabilizing me with each step. I knew I had to hold strong and protect my sense of purpose from any doubts.

I looked to the foreboding clouds and wondered if God was watching me through them, cheering me on. I wanted God to know how hard I was trying. That is how I felt as a child when I looked to see if my parents were watching me play an important game, only this was the championship.

The smog of negativity began to fill my head. There are many references to overcoming "enemies" or opposition in psalms and sacred texts—I began to think of my negative thoughts as enemies. My thoughts, my inner enemies, were hurling disdain and false claims.

You think this experiment of yours will make a difference? What's going to be different when you get home? Maybe this little vacation of yours is a warmup for the "big one."

I wasn't going to let them bury me. It seemed the more I fought, the bolder my enemies became, but perhaps they were only desperate. The old me was questioning my integrity and capability in ways I never had before. I was hiking a glacier, something I had hoped would show my personal leadership in action, and that I was ready for the mountain climb, yet I felt like an imposter. I had to fight back against myself, so I began to hurl questions at my thoughts to see where they came from. Maybe some part of me was planning to die, expecting my demise, while my more conscious mind had been trying to deny the possibility by filling my time with goals and achievements. I realized that fear was at my core. There is an innocence to this fear, and it wasn't my enemy. If I accepted that I was afraid of dying, I could reach out from the deepest part of my soul with strength and bravery to protect this part of me—as a leader would—and the only way to do this was to live my life to the fullest. Personal leadership must acknowledge fear and work with it, not against it.

I had to look at why I wanted to come here to Iceland in the first place.

What did you expect to find here? More time? What a joke! You're killing me.

What a punchline to my gut. Yet I countered with a new consideration: *You're just being impatient. It is not how much I have, but how I spend it.* This adventure was an investment in the new Eeki who would return to Israel. You see, the rope, our sixth tool, puts you on the offensive after your mental fortifications have been improved. I kept my calloused hands on this rope of challenge—this ambitious dare to demonstrate my tenacity and capacity to live. God wanted me to hold up my end of the rope. I didn't dare try to pull it away from Him. I showed that I could take the lead refining my soul with what time I had left.

The glacier trail's end would be a new beginning. My legs ached and burned. Everything did. It had been at least four hours, but it felt as long as the three days we had been in Iceland. Was I short of breath from exhilaration or *Sunshine's* suffocation? George pointed ahead at the finish line. The next moments felt as if I had taken painkillers—a jolt of adrenaline flickered throughout my body like static. Momentum picked up, and soon, Amnon and I were marching across the finish line. Our surroundings were majestic. It was an oceanside kingdom of clouds, heavenlike. I felt light as a nimbus. I may as well have had wings sprouting from my back.

The sun was concealed in clouds, though its light still generously poured through. George turned around and welcomed us over to a better vantage point. "We made it. Bravo, my friends!"

We had arrived. I smiled. It would have to do, George.

I began to pray, closing my eyes, feeling hot tears rolling down my cheeks. I looked all around me, trying to absorb my surroundings so I would never forget them. This view was like an island in heaven and would forever become a place I pictured to uplift myself at my lowest points.

I closed my eyes and held my hands up beckoning God to accept me. "God, here I am standing here. Did I prove to you that I can handle this? I am willing to struggle for this, and I am grateful for these trials you've set before me." I took a breath and looked at the horizon. "And I promise, God, I will always stand for others in this situation. I will always help others in this struggle."

Amnon was there next to me. We embraced. I gripped his shoulder and looked into his eyes. "Amnon, I was worried about you."

He coughed a laugh. "Shut up." We hugged again. "Worried about me like everyone else is for you, huh?"

"Always. Hang on, I need to say something." I pulled out my phone. There were many friends at home I wanted to spill my heart out to—I began a Facebook livestream introducing George and thanking him for getting us through the hike.

Then, my heart poured from its spigot: "If you are with me now and watching this, please take this video and share it with anyone that you care for that found themselves struggling with troubles that look like there's no way out. Show them so that they'll know we can always fight and overcome them. That we can always lead ourselves into a better future. You see, there's one thing that I made clear since the day I was diagnosed: I don't have cancer. My body does—and I control it! My mind controls my body, and so does yours. Take the steps you need to grow your personal leadership and stand against the threats to your life. Lead yourself and you'll prevail."

I was shocked. 15,000 people ended up watching it. It was such a blessing that I could share this experience and its message with them.

The next day we celebrated with an outing into the town. The cold streets were warm with life. I felt invigorated for the ultimate challenge of climbing an Icelandic Volcano. We had stopped at a tour service seeking to set up the grand finale of our trip, the stratovolcano on the other side of the country, Snæfellsjökull, known locally as the "king of mountains."

One of the reps took a good look at me and asked us what we had done so far on our trip. George was there too. Both beamed a smile seeing how excited we were, but the other rep must've heard from George about my war with cancer—he asked about how I was doing, and I tried to downplay the significance of it. I pressed him to sign us up for the climb.

The gentleman was to the point. "Not in your condition. It's too dangerous. Would you want to be airlifted from the mountain and ruin what has been such a lovely trip? Frankly, it wouldn't be a good look for anyone. I know this sounds harsh but come back when you've recovered. It's a policy I must follow. We will be waiting for you."

There was no refuting his position. What could I say? He was right. It took a few moments to orient myself with how I felt. It seemed like I was about to plunge into a freefall of disappointment, but it surprisingly turned into a bold sense of determination.

We made it a point to venture close enough to the mountain. It was on the other side of the country, but I needed to see it.

Amnon watched me gazing at Snæfellsjökull. I could see that sad, worried look on his face had completely transformed. As the mountain filled my vision, I knew this was no longer a dream. I knew I had found exactly what I had been searching for in this majestic land—the treasure I would take home to Israel: a vow to return and surmount the King of The Mountains. *See you next year.*

PART VII

Tool: The Parachute

THE FALL

I was still on cloud nine as the plane descended onto the tarmac of Tel Aviv airport. High strung as I typically was, I now felt like I could see the finer fibers of life; Amnon must've noticed something had changed in me atop the glacier. Even I could tell it felt like I was on something—and it sure was the good stuff. As I entered my old life feeling like a new me, it was as if a victory anthem welcomed my heart to dance.

Joy comes in many forms, a spectrum of colors that vivify life in the most beautiful ways. Euphoric as it was, I eventually realized I had learned nothing from the emotion. On that glacier in Iceland, I had reached the crest of cancer's crater mouth that had threatened to swallow me. I felt *Sunshine* there with me, so bright and yet waning—wait, waning? The skies around me darkened. Finally, I woke up.

Where did things go wrong?

My next round of treatments began a week upon my return to Israel. The nurse was about to plug the I.V. in my vein, but I wanted to do it myself. There was a symbolism to it that meant something to me. I wanted to aid my body in this fight, consciously rallying to our shared cause.

This positive outlook on my mind's influence over my health was now protected by the memory of my Icelandic adventure and the vow I had made to return for the ultimate climb with God by my side. I knew the research supported the benefit of positive thinking while fighting cancer and I was aware of the ripple effect of what each positive thought and action would beget. Maybe one extra step, one extra effort, an opportunity not overlooked—each addition cascading and pouring into the next. And when all else failed, having grace for when I felt frail would help me rise again. But the challenge of treating cancer didn't stop with my improved attitude.

Bracha spent the night helping me as the chemo weighed me down. Rumi's army of saints would come to help in shifts, typically eight hours, until I could convince them to go back to their own lives! The fifth CT scan was another two weeks after the treatments. At the hospital, I was drinking glucose for the scan while sharing my newfound sense of success with my lucky charm, Amnon—not quite as good as the Jack Daniels in the airport terminal, but it'd do.

"I nearly fulfilled my dream," I told him, "And I feel like I'm losing sleep from thinking of Snæfellsjökull."

"You'll go." Amnon smiled. "Hey, remember the doctor who told you to do so in the first place? He was one of the doctors who said you only had six months to live."

"I do have him to thank for that suggestion. Who knows, maybe he is one of the reasons that a year later, I am still here." I considered how much I wanted to prove wrong all those doctors before meeting Dr. Onn.

"You should tell him you're still around," Amnon said.

"Give me a second here." I grabbed my phone and drafted an email addressed to the doctor: *This is Eeki Elner, I don't expect you to remember me from our appointment a year ago, but I just wanted to tell you this email isn't from heaven. Your recommendation to fulfill my childhood dream was a good one, doctor.*

He would reply later that week—he *did* remember me, and I could almost hear the relief in his writing. I realized it must not have been easy for him to tell someone they had no hope of survival. At that moment, I let go of any residual resentment toward the doctors who told me what they thought was the truth.

After the scan, Amnon met me outside. "So, you're coming with me to Iceland next year? Things don't go as well without you around, you know." I appreciated his encouragement.

"I know."

I stared at him, eyes narrowing with a grin. "Well don't let me pump too much hot air into that head of yours.

"Better than the freezing cold on that glacier."

I shook my head.

I became accustomed to showing up to Dr. Onn's office with a smile on my face; *Sunshine* seemed to become shier and shier with each appointment.

I sat across from him as he began to pull up the results on his computer. The aging machine seemed to grumble from the effort. Dr. Onn's eyes darted around the screen as his brow scrunched. As far as I knew, he didn't need glasses. "Eeki, you've had remarkable success," he scooted away from the computer and squared up with me. "Sometimes we may plateau, but this is no reason to worry."

"What does it say?"

"The cancer is being stubborn. It seems it has hung on for dear life after you've really beaten it down. You've shown rapid and increasing progress on all four scans, a whole year of treatments and the tumors kept shrinking, but this scan says it's come back with a counterpunch. It has shown signs of growth."

I tried to swallow what I was hearing. It went down as a hard lump.

This wasn't something I could fix quickly. The fight was still on.

"What changed?"

"This happens. Hit the brakes on what is going on inside your head right now. There is still a lot we can do—and we will do."

It felt like I was being arrested for feeling happy and free. The King of the Mountains was a world away wondering if I'd ever return. Had I left the ramparts of my fortress unattended? The war was not over. Only until my death would it be done. I knew joy would come only as a result of living a meaningful life—not from chasing happiness. As long as cancer, my *Sunshine*, held me back, I could not stop fighting.

My thoughts were not like previous spirals, which saw me descend without wind resistance. I felt determined—and a sense of control. Still, I braced for a crash landing. Dr. Onn encouraged me to keep my eyes on the road ahead—if this meant the biological medicine had failed, we'd find something else to aid my fight. My battle plan allowed for setbacks. I wasn't getting diagnosed again; this was not my first hurt. I was not in trouble like a regular Eeki—this new version of myself was a war-torn veteran, proud and tempered, admittedly terribly impatient at times, and I was still bad at—*no! Let's stick with positive thinking!*

There was so much good around me, *and within*. When your heart sinks, your mind falls flat in the mud, your spirit is crushed, and the pieces are scattered in every direction, but you ought to remember your victories, your loves, your dreams, and feelings of hope.

There was no rope to save me now, at least at this moment, yet all I had built would brace my fall. My mind, body, and spirit were protected by my fortress; I had support from friends like Matan, Amnon, Todd, Wilma, my sister, and so many more who helped me aspire higher; and yet with what security all of this afforded, I needed to develop an immune system. Doubt is like a virus, and when life injures you, your own mentality can destroy you. It produces anxiety, depression, and much else, precipitating self-defeat. Is there no cure?

Your body must create its own.

When I don't push myself to be confident—this psychic-like propulsion coming from my mind's eye—I crumble. It is like conjuring a mental image of myself, seeing myself as a leader. I am my own avatar. I am controlling it, giving it the directions it needs. I am the puppeteer of my own body, pulling my shoulders up to stand straight and march rather than drag my feet. *How we see ourselves is how we see our outcomes.*

As part of this process, within my personal fortress was a mental trophy room—trophies lined the walls of all that made me feel accomplished and whole. These trophies were my achievements, the merits of overcoming pain and challenges. There was personal meaning in all of them; they showed me that I lead my life—my life doesn't lead me. I would not count myself out.

Sunshine didn't like the new me. I envisioned my cancer as one who watches a childhood friend change and grow while remaining stuck in the past. Perhaps this was a toxic relationship. The old me loved my old ways. They were comforting and familiar. But now I needed to see myself as a new person, much more capable and healthier. *Sunshine* was terrified of this.

With this mental framework, my mind aided my body, but the ground was quickly zooming in. I needed to land on my feet, or I'd be crushed like a tin can. But how?

I called Bracha and asked her if I could visit.

"Sure, but what's wrong, Eeki? There's that thing in your voice again." As much as it annoyed me at times that she could detect what was wrong without me saying it, I still appreciated this silent communication between us. She knew my inner self without me having to reveal it to her.

"I'll tell you in person. It'll also be good to see Mom and Dad while I am there."

"Of course. Drive safely."

I tried to tame my road rage, but the rising irritability came from my aching knees. What had been an unconscious discomfort was now a front-and-center pain. I tried massaging them out, but there was no relief. *So much stress—now my legs are dragging me down too.*

It was August, almost one year after telling my father about my cancer. I had told him then because I felt strongly about my fight, but I was struggling with my optimism. It felt like I had forgotten this cancer was trying to kill me, but this thought turned into a sign. All that I had accomplished this far—it was my parachute. This wasn't a fall from grace, but a test to show how I've grown.

Bracha welcomed me inside her home. Without even touching, I felt the warm embrace of my family. We sat together at the table. Mom and Dad were upstairs.

"It's about the test, isn't it?" Bracha's voice was lowered as if saying it out loud would bring the dreaded *kein ayin hora*, or evil eye. We typically say, "Don't give yourself a *Kina Hora*," the words somewhat slurred together. It is usually said quickly, when you speak of something good, so as not to bring about envy, which might lead to the evil eye. But in this case, I realized Bracha already knew the news was not good. She likely lowered her voice so my parents wouldn't hear. We had both learned early on to protect our parents from any bad news. We had taken on responsibility for all their suffering, so we turned to each other for support when life was too much.

"Yes, the scan wasn't so great this time," I answered, still trying to sound hopeful. We could be honest with each other but always tried to downplay news that was too terrible to think about. It was a form of survival for siblings who could sometimes feel each other's pain.-

"The cancer is fighting back," I blurted out. "I'm worried we'll have to change the medications if we don't see it improve, but once I stop them, there's no going back. I'll be out of the research program."

Bracha reached for my hand, and I could see she was starting to cry. "So, what do you think you'll do?" She took a labored breath and my heart ached for her. I would have felt the same if our roles were switched. But I realized I had painted the wrong picture for her. I hadn't given up. As I lifted my chin, the light from the window shined down on me, forming a beautiful kaleidoscope. It reminded me that God was on my side, and I could not lose hope.

"Dr. Onn and I are going to push through this and hang onto the current plan. I want to do what I can before we make any big decisions." Bracha didn't look convinced, so I added "the treatments aren't the cure, they only aid my body in finding it."

This seemed to lighten her mood. "It's been quite a rollercoaster, Eeki. We've come this far though." I was relieved that she understood I would continue to fight, and this visit was not to say goodbye.

I heard steps on the stairs and knew my father would be worried. "Eeki, I didn't know you were already here," he said, embracing me. "Bracha told me there was a problem." I could already hear the worry wheels spinning in his head.

I shot a glance at her. "Just a possible detour. Come, join us." I helped him into his chair and set his cane against the table. Other than the cane, he still looked every bit the solid man I had always admired. "I told Bracha the test results showed the cancer was growing again, but this doesn't mean it will continue this way. If it continues, we'll seek another way to treat it. In the meantime, I need to keep myself healthy and help my body do its job."

Dad thoughtfully paused. "Are you going to tell me not to worry?"

"Would I ever be so bold?" That got him to smile, if only slightly. "I'll show you instead by staying healthy so you can see this is just a temporary issue."

I left my sister and father to talk and went upstairs to visit Mom. She was in bed with the television on and the window open. A light wind rippled the white curtains. I lowered the volume as she sat up on the edge of the bed. "Hi, Mama." I yearned for the strong connection I had always had with the mother I loved. She was always the most precious jewel of my life.

Thankfully, her eyes lit up when she saw me. "Eeki Shmeeki," she said playfully. She gestured for me to sit next to her and planted a kiss on my cheek. I put my arm around her shoulder and leaned close. I felt some part of me could at last rest. A curious look lifted her eyebrows like the wind had whistled a secret. "Where's your father? He told me he was going downstairs."

"Dad is just talking with Bracha, conspiring against us."

Mom seemed to miss the joke. "Oh, they're talking about your cancer?" I felt like all the air left the room. *How does she know... did Dad let it slip?* I couldn't speak for a moment. Since Mom was diagnosed with Alzheimer's—aunts, uncles, cousins—we all chose to keep bad things from her for fear of making her condition worse. A daily and nightly thought of mine was that I had to survive this, or she wouldn't. My mother was a holocaust survivor, but life still had more challenges for her—including raising me. It was only a couple of years ago that she broke her pelvic bone from a fall. She used a walker and a wheelchair on difficult days. She couldn't cook anymore, which frustrated her to no end. And more and more she relied on her caretaker to do basic physical tasks. She somehow knew about the cancer when all this time I thought she'd die the moment I told her.

"Yes, but it is all okay. Nothing's wrong. Everything is going well, Mama." It nearly killed me to conceal my troubles like I had so many years ago during my trauma, but I needed to be strong for her and handle this on my own if I were to survive. It was a different context, and I couldn't let the past distort the present, especially when the stakes were so high. So, I rationalized that it really was all okay, even though the scan results were real.

She looked me straight into the eyes with her signature look—she knew I wasn't telling the whole truth.

"So, everything is okay?" She waited for a different answer.

"Yes, of course. I'm in the final stretch. The worst is behind me."

We hugged, but she seemed to take longer letting go.

"Mama, remember the tree house I practically lived in after school?"

Her eyebrows raised.

"I was eight—all the kids were supposed to go home before sunset—my friends had left me asleep up there, remember? I woke up and it was dark, so I climbed down the tree like a monkey and ripped my shorts all the way to the waist."

She burst out laughing. "Yes, and you were covering your little *tuchus* to hide it from the neighbors as you snuck back home. You were so embarrassed that I couldn't even punish you for making me worry." Our laughter must've had Bracha and my father thinking we were scheming against *them!*

Laughing with my mother was something that relieved even my deepest fears. Mom was strong, and I knew I took after her. In her mind, more memories grew.

The turbulence continued in the following weeks, from the summer to the fall. I imagined some natural force wrestling against me—my only choice seemed to be to ride the waves without being swallowed by them. I was now consciously aware of the daily pain in my knees. Each day felt like someone was twisting a corkscrew another crank deeper.

I felt déjà vu as the final round of ILI selection interviews wrapped up before the upcoming school year—barely a month away. Garik had already been helping me with errands over the past year, but because of my knees he started coming over several days a week to aid me. Because I had undergone a full year of treatments, social security would pay for a caretaker. I knew Garik could use the work—as long as he didn't grow sick of me.

Every Descent is Meant for a Greater Ascent

The Jewish new year, Rosh Hashana, had arrived. The belief is that this auspicious day is when our lives—all that will be—are inscribed in the Book of Life, only to be sealed a week later, on the holiest day of the year, Yom Kippur. Many would wish each other a sweet new year: I knew the customary apples and honey would be waiting at my Bracha's house with my parents. To keep myself from being bitter, I'd take an extra helping of those apples.

My knees hadn't stopped bothering me—in fact, they only seemed to get worse. Garik pushed me to see the doctor, and I told him I'd go after the holiday. He wasn't happy about that. Just as I thought he was about to force me to go to the hospital, Bracha called and eased his concern. She'd take care of me; I heard her say. I'd stay with her over the weekend.

Bracha might've thought twice about delaying my hospital visit when she saw me. I relied heavily on painkillers and laid in bed icing my knees the night of the Rosh Hashana. They looked like red apples themselves. The pain came and went; each time I readied myself for a trip to the ER, the swelling seemed to settle down. The pleasant moments with Mom and Dad sustained me. I hid my pain from them.

Garik picked me up the next morning and I didn't bother telling him how bad my knee pain had been. I was sitting at my kitchen table rubbing my legs when he looked over at me as he put away groceries.

"Eeki, when are you going to go to the doctor?"

"I will see him in a week."

I struggled to stand, gripping the chair for leverage.

"You need a cane."

"A cane?! Are you serious? I'm too young for a cane."

His eyes flared with unusual anger. "Shut up. What does that have to do with being young?"

I sighed with frustration. "I don't know where to get one... oh well."

"Can you wait here for a while? I'll get it."

"Garik, it's okay. I don't want you driving all over the place trying to find one."

"I'll find one. It'll be good to have one around."

"Thank you." I struggled with the idea. Something so simple held a terrible symbolism to me. Garik was right. I needed to shut up and stand up for my health.

He was back in two hours with a cane. Before he could show me how to use it, I jokingly grabbed it out of his hand and tried it out. A pain shot through me, but not from my knees. It was a simple thought that had pierced me: I wondered what my father might think now that we both had one. I put the cane aside and pushed through the pain.

This downturn in my health seemed to have no end. What would become of me? Was my fate sealed? What choices did I have anymore?

The day of my appointment with Dr. Onn arrived at the end of October. He winced when I walked in with the cane, showing him my bulging knees. "Eeki, what happened?"

"Injured myself jumping for joy."

He looked at me with the same expression one gives to someone who made a bad pun. He examined my knees, but he seemed puzzled. "Eeki, I really have no idea what this is. There's a specialist I know—I am going to call him and get an appointment set up for you. Please go see him. Maybe it is related to the medicine, but maybe not."

I carried his confidence with me until the appointment with a Dr. Gidi, one of the top knee specialists in Israel. I was surprised by how quickly Dr. Onn had gotten me connected. Was he not sharing how serious this was with me?

Dr. Gidi welcomed me into his office. "It is nice to meet you, Eeki." His eyes darted to Garik, who had become my chaperone.

"It's nice to meet you too," I said. "This is my caretaker, Garik."

They shook hands. Garik strained a smile, seemingly uncomfortable in the room. "I'll come out to get you when we're done."

He closed the door behind him.

"So, you can obviously see these grapefruits growing out of my knees."

He didn't hide the curious reaction on his face. After an examination, Dr. Gidi tried explaining in more or less the same words as Dr. Onn: he didn't know what was causing it either. He ordered an MRI, and the results came back with nothing. No damage to the bones, joints—there was nothing to explain it. A question with no answer, but one my life may depend on.

"For now, I'll extract the fluid to reduce the swelling and we can continue to monitor it while I explore what the possible root cause is."

"How does that work?"

He retrieved a massive needle that reminded me of a fencing sword. I looked at the door and nearly cried out for Garik to rescue me, but a bolt of inspiration struck me.

"Are you okay? Don't worry, I will be putting an ointment to numb the pain."

I took a deep breath. "Don't put it on me. I can handle the pain. There's no good in fearing it."

"I admire this, but are you sure?"

"I insist. Just don't kill me, okay?"

"That's not part of my job, fortunately."

I laughed. When the procedure was over, I noticed my knees still ached but looked markedly better.

"We may need to keep doing this for a while. Let's plan for every two weeks, but call me, and I'll have you in the same week if you need to get the fluid removed before then, okay?"

What doesn't kill me can only make me stronger, I supposed.

My symptoms keep spiraling out of control and I feel paralyzed—what can I do? Is it pointless to struggle anymore? I needed to counter these negative thoughts. With ILI workshops just around the corner, I had to relocate my inner leader, stand back up and fight back against the laws of nature, gravity itself. *You'll manage this, I thought. I had to.*

I didn't take the cane to the first ILI workshop, but not out of pride or embarrassment. My pain had surprisingly reduced, though I wondered how long it would last. I noticed some of the new leadership students walking toward me in the hallway. We quickly exchanged smiles, but as soon as they left my line of sight, I winced. A surge of pain stabbed my knees, but I felt an emotional pang as well. How far I had fallen; I felt like the sky had been right there, so close I could almost feel the clouds on my fingertips. Now it was like I was watching myself plummet to the ground, the distance between myself and my aspirations growing wider and wider.

My mental tools had led me to this very day. They previously helped me trample my fears, and triumph through challenges. And they would do so again. This pain, both physical and emotional, could overcome my mind's will. I remembered the idea of myself as an avatar and began speaking to this image of self. I guided myself through the hurt, confusion, and darkness. I was a mentor, a guide, a trusted voice, and I called myself to action. *I am going to walk in there and show them what I will show myself.* Call it your inner monologue, dialogue, or simply the experience inside your head—I would use this to curb the catastrophizing, slow my descent, and parachute myself into a position to act. *Your job now is to teach these students. Aim your sights on what's right in front of you.*

Garik's voice barked in my head—*go get the cane!* Definitely not the persona I would have consciously chosen for my thoughts, but my mental Garik was right. Without my cane, the pain would hold me in a vice. I had a mission and would not tolerate distractions during this workshop—all four hours of it. I walked in with the cane and the leadership students' eyes instantly locked onto it. The concern that emanated from their collective gaze nearly pushed me back outside. I explained to the students with certainty that I was okay and left no room to refute this.

I saw Dr. Gidi each week as he and Dr. Onn contacted everyone they knew to find the problem with my knees. I had already experienced one side effect of the biological medicine—the rash—but not even one research study could explain my knees. Dr. Onn still pursued in answer despite not having any leads. All the while, I didn't know whether the cancer was persisting. Would it take me out while I was weakened?

The next CT scan was scheduled for late December. I had wanted to bring Amnon again, but there was a problem. Days prior, the pain unleashed its greatest fury. Garik had upgraded me to a walker, this time per my request. I could barely walk, and the cane only helped with short distances. Garik accompanied me this time. Would I be as lucky as during the first scans? I called Amnon just in case.

A sense of foreboding overwhelmed me as I entered Dr. Onn's office. The last scan had knocked me out of the sky. *Keep the course, I thought, this is no time to slow down. You'll crawl to the finish line if you must.*

Dr. Onn seemed just as eager to interpret the results.

I wondered if I had done enough to alter the course of my descent. I knew I was using all my tools, and by putting them to work for almost two years, they must have had *some* impact. It was never up to the treatments to save me. It had to be me.

"Eeki, the cancer is on the retreat again. A 50% reduction from the previous scan!"

I stood up from my chair to cheer and nearly fell over as my legs screamed. Some nasty words fell out of my mouth before I managed to smile again. "Didn't mean to worry you, doctor."

"It is not the cancer that worries me." His eyes fell to my knees. We summarized what we had ruled out so far, and he accounted for the conversations he had with Dr. Gidi. "We suspect it is a side effect of the medicine, maybe not the most surprising hypothesis, yet we both believe it may have something to do with your nerves. Your immune system has been boosted to fight the cancer, but it may have started to attack your nerves. We can't be sure until you get an EMG. It seems you may have gone to battle with a double-edged sword, but we will find a solution."

"We will. I'm not worried about this, but my hope is to endure this pain. Nothing touches it. I need to beat the cancer first."

"That brings me to another consideration. I am thinking we should go another few months on the treatments. It is working, Eeki. The tumors are shrinking, and we know your body can handle it, despite the difficulties. A few more months, and maybe the cancer will be eradicated."

"I knew this was a conversation we would have, and I had already come to this same conclusion. Let's finish them in April. An auspicious time, don't you think? It'll be my renewal."

"Eeki, you are already a greater man than the one who walked through that door over a year and a half ago. Your life changed the moment you chose to fight."

"It isn't meant to be one long war though, is it? We thrive despite the enemies and threats pitted against us. Maybe it's the Israeli in me."

"It is what you make it. You've shown me this." Dr. Onn stood and helped me to my feet, accompanying me to the waiting room. Garik's brow perked up, awaiting some sense of the results. It was a rare sight to see the man's nerves at work, though maybe mine were shot.

Garik drove us home, and we shared a drink, celebrating the successful scan. I had updated Rumi and the ILI, family and friends, all of whom were thrilled by the news. I began to feel an upward change in trajectory. I fell from what felt like heaven after my trip to Iceland, but now I arose. I had direction yet again—I found an artful balance between the good and bad. The secret is *everything is for the good.* Even the bad works in mysterious ways, like my *Sunshine.* I would strive to find this positive, latent potential in all things.

Time moved forward even as I struggled to do the same. It was nearly February, and the pain persisted. I was catching up on emails and would work for a few hours before Garik arrived to help me run errands. I pulled myself up on my walker and maneuvered to the bathroom for a shower. I tightened my chest for breath, bracing each step as if walking through lava. I noticed my head throbbing from the strain, trying to keep my attention from falling. In the bathroom, taking my clothes off felt like I was squeezing through a body-tight cavern, nearly suffocating from the effort.

As I turned the water on and transitioned to the shower chair, my knee gave out and I collapsed into the tub like a rag doll crumpling in on itself. Hot water blasted me as I howled in agony. My phone was in my pants pocket, resting on top of the toilet lid. I wouldn't be able to reach it without getting myself over the ledge. I hefted myself over, far enough to snag it with a finger and pull it back into the shower tub. The pants were soaking as I dialed Garik.

"Garik, please help! Can you get here now?"

"What happened? Eeki? Hello?"

"I can't stand!" I was speaking in Hebrew, which Garik still wasn't the most fluent in.

"I don't understand, Eeki, what is going on?" His tone sounded as if he thought I was prank calling him.

"I can't stand. I am not joking. Please come over."

It must've registered with him when my voice broke.

I was sobbing. It was at this moment I knew I wouldn't be able to walk once I was out of there. I sat myself back and let the water run over me, concentrating on the sensations rapidly rippling over my skin.

Garik arrived to pull me out without even shutting the water off. He helped cover me and I just breathed my way through those moments. He didn't speak of it once we were sitting in the kitchen. I was looking through my phone, my vision blurred, my brain not processing what was filtering through my retinas.

"Stay here, I'll fix you something to eat and come back with a wheelchair."

"I was just able to shower yesterday. I'm paralyzed, Garik."

"You don't need to shower. I'll help you take care of it."

My head hung as if I was a flimsy toy losing its stuffing. "Looks like we'll have to postpone our errands for later."

"Whatever you need, I'll bring it back. You need to get some rest."

"Would you help me to the bed?"

I lay down with the television on in the background, but it was interrupted by my thoughts. *Do not fear the pain.* I don't know why I thought this, but it reverberated throughout my body. The fear of pain inevitably becomes chains. This pain was physical, but if I feared the emotional turmoil, I would sink into despair like quicksand, struggling to climb out, when in fact, stillness and composure would see me through—I would walk again. There was a battle going on, and I would win the fight. I could not be overtaken by this. I resolved to do everything I could to keep up with my responsibilities, and lead myself to victory, whether I could use my own feet or not.

I called Dr. Onn and made a quick visit with him. He couldn't hide his astonishment. He called everyone he could. No one knew what it was or what to do. I would need to be patient. I considered how I had been *a patient* for such a long time. I needed to get back to the ILI workshop and show myself my other side.

The next day, Garik drove me to the ILI center for the workshop and helped me into the wheelchair. I rolled through the hall waiting for the first student to spot me. It was very difficult to sit with my knees bent and the pain flaring up, but I didn't want to stay home in bed all day. Either way I would be in agony, but this way I could do something worthwhile with it. It was an opportunity to show strength at a time of perceived weakness.

My students looked as if they laid eyes on a zombie—wheeling in, I met their eyes and watched them take the sight in. They saw me go from a cane to a walker, and now I couldn't stand on my own feet. They would see this as a bad omen, a terrible progression. I would show them differently.

Body language says a lot. And while my body appeared to be in bad shape—no, my weight was fine—I communicated confidence by believing in my strength. It requires mental buy-in. The cynical side of the mind will try and talk you out of it; you may feel you're being baited into a scam. But beyond the simple affirmation, *I am strong,* you must conjure a mental image that speaks your intended message. Through my physical presence, my feelings followed, rallying from my mind's battle cry.

I asked my students to join me on the floor, explaining it would be painful to remain in my wheelchair. We sat in a circle, and I stretched my legs out, and began the lecture before the simulation took off. All my focus was on experiencing the class with them, and not unintentionally making it about my pain. I did not fear the pain would ruin it, but I respected it was there, because fear would draw my focus to it, knocking me off balance, while if I somehow ignored it altogether, I would forget that a battle was at hand and perhaps let my guard down.

I felt redeemed from the shower incident. It was a humiliating experience, but Garik made no mention of it. I recalled how the battle plan tool was adaptable, the expectations could fluctuate with whatever the situation called for. I needed to accept where I was so I could set my sights on where I wanted to be. The fall became a process; its descent still led forward.

February arrived. There were only two more months of the treatments, and my next CT scan results were awaiting me in Dr. Onn's office. This was a critical moment. I had been fighting for almost two long years, far beyond when those other doctors predicted I would die. I had risen and fallen, and it was too soon to tell if I would stand again in both senses of the word.

Dr. Onn's eyes betrayed him when I rolled into his office. He made no mention of it. I think we both felt the time-churning rhythm of each moment before the results were revealed.

He opened the folder, and I witnessed one of the most beautiful smiles in my life. A breath of air released from him, but I still held mine.

"Eeki... you've won. The cancer is gone."

I sat there for a moment, looking into my soul. I'm sure to Dr. Onn it looked like I had just had a profound epiphany. My chest was a dam about to burst.

"Yes! Bless you, God! Bless you, thank you, thank you, thank you!" my shouts could have resuscitated someone like a defibrillator. Dr. Onn came over to me and gave me a hug, and we held a strong embrace like brothers at arms, finally facing victory.

There was a somber look that melded on his face as he withdrew.

"It is a marvel what you have achieved." He drew a breath. "But it came with a cost. Life will be very different without the ability to walk."

I loitered around the thought. He was right. I would need to adjust to this new reality. Would my vision adjust to see this new Eeki in a favorable light?

I couldn't sit down on the bench. This was only halftime. There would be no victory lap, and I needed to see this as the new threat it was. It was me versus fate. And while it may seem like a fight between David and Goliath— the underdog versus the big, bad wolf—fate has a weakness, and it is belief.

If I believed this was my lot in life, that this was my compensation for all my hard work—if I believed I didn't have a choice, and God wouldn't want me to make my own decisions as His child—then as fate would have it that way, *here I am*. But fate is no deity that I ever worshiped, and I believed I could find a way to improve my condition. It was a hard landing as my mental parachute kept me from catastrophe, but I would find a way to get back on my feet and lead myself again.

Bittersweet was the word. It was a bittersweet new year, but this tale in the Book of Life was not finished. I had long shared my journey on social media and found it gave others a means to access what I hoped would be a source of inspiration. Coinciding with conquering cancer, my ten-year commitment to live in Sderot was nearing its end—I had chosen to build the community around me through the efforts of the ILI, teaching personal leadership and crisis management. In every Israeli's heart is a combat readiness for whatever terrors seek to destroy our way of life. I was at war in my own life, and I had considered what times of peace may entail. It became clear that peace for me was giving a piece of myself to others.

The universe sent me an angel. Michal, a doctor and close friend in the US who I had known for almost 25 years, had seen one of my posts about my knee troubles. She called with what sounded too good to be true. She knew of a special treatment for treating damaged nerves provided by only two specialists in the world. One was in Italy. That sounded nice, but the other happened to be in my old stomping ground, Tel Aviv. The treatment utilized magnets in order to affect the nerves in such a way that could bring them back to function.

Dr. Karepov was originally from Ukraine. He mostly worked with vets from the Israeli Defense Force (IDF) who were wounded in war. The treatment was in fact developed in Ukraine, and apparently, he had obtained the reputation of making people walk again like a magician.

I made a quick call to Dr. Onn. He was still distraught over the situation. I could sense this mystery in my knees had troubled him. "Eeki, I don't know of any medical research to support these things. But I will support whatever you do."

This was all I could ask of him. I spent three more months wondering if I'd ever find a way to recover what I'd lost. I spent it nurturing a deep sense of gratitude for overcoming cancer. It was a new dawn, but *Sunshine* was now in my past and he got to see my descent into this chair—but he would never know what became of me. He was no more. I wondered if, in some way, he had given me some light, some truth, like the passing of a pen instead of a baton, for me to write the rest of my chronicle.

The biweekly treatments began in July 2018 and would continue until December—ten weeks total. It reminded me of where this journey began, my ten-day Passover stay at the hospital. It took ten plagues for Pharaoh to finally release the Israelites—leading to their liberation. But just like the ancient Israelites, once they were freed, they still had to break the slave mentality that plagued them. With God's help, I would use my personal leadership tools to similarly free myself from mental servitude. There were three tools left for me to implement, but I was still recovering from my fall.

When I arrived at my first appointment, I was directed to a magnetic bed. The bed's magnetic apparatus had two arcs that reached from one side to the other. Essentially, the magnet tension between the two arcs would "pull open" my knees that had become dormant and would not tell the muscles to contract.

The magician, Dr. Karepov, looked me straight in the eyes. "You'll be able to walk in seven to ten treatments."

I hefted a laugh. "You sound so sure. I like your spirit, but is it really that easy?"

"Perhaps if you believe it is."

"I do."

Garik rolled me in and would sit nearby watching the procedure. I lay down in the bed looking at the two half-circle rings, one over my chest and the other near my knees. I didn't feel much from the magnets, and I was disappointed that after nine treatments I was still paralyzed. During this time, I kept to my work at the ILI. Another cycle—graduation and a new crop planted. I still needed a wheelchair, and there were some days of agony. I had to get Rumi to help me find a replacement.

There is research to suggest chronic pain can create changes in your brain. Day in and day out, I kept to my tools, kept choosing to fight, wore my leadership, and accounted for the past experiences that had led to my present. I strategized and maintained my mental fortress to wage the long war, daring myself to believe in my capabilities. I could—no, I would—walk again. I might yet climb Snæfellsjökull.

After the tenth treatment, Dr. Karepov suddenly asked Garik to leave the room. I was upright on the bed and the doctor stood before me. "I want you to stand up."

I didn't feel any different, but I obliged.

I balanced myself on the edge of the bed, feeling I had peg legs. It wasn't so painful, but they felt weak.

He took three steps back. "Okay, walk to me," he casually directed.

"What? I can't do that."

"Don't be shy, Eeki. Walk to me."

I looked at the door. "Let's get Garik in here."

"You don't need him. Let's go."

"Garik!" I called out again as the doctor plainly looked at me. "Alright, take a step closer so you can catch me." He did, and I took a step. And another. I took one more, feeling like a waddling duck. He stepped back. "What are you doing? I am going to fall."

"Keep going."

I took another step and another hoping to grab onto him and shake the madness out of his head. Soon, I had taken ten full steps without the use of anything but my own two feet. "Oh, my God." It was all I could say. I walked back to bed and held on again. I couldn't believe what was happening. Garik came in and his eyes widened.

"Eeki, are you alright?"

"Yes, the doctor is just a quack like me. What kind of magic is this?"

He grunted a laugh. "No magic, and I'm not sure I can take that as a compliment."

I was able to walk over to him and strongly hug him.

Even though I had fallen far from what had felt like heaven, I was able to manage my mentality, not to let the pain change me, and slow my descent. Now I could move forward to my full potential. I could not spare any time for doubt; I trusted myself, using the memory of pain as a stark reminder that I was not where I should be. I needed to persist, resist complacency, stasis, and surrender.

It was only a few weeks into the next ILI course. I grabbed my cane and climbed out of the car. I walked into the classroom with bright eyes, witnessing what I felt was one of my greatest triumphs.

This was my great ascent. For every descent is meant for a greater one. I had used my fall as a backwind to soar into a new space, a higher height. There was a sweet truth that resonated with me at the turn of the new year: I would live with the readiness that at any point, rockets could descend upon me, but I would never surrender. I would seek to live peacefully despite the threats that sought to rob me of it. This was something to be ever grateful for.

PART VIII

Tool: The Compass

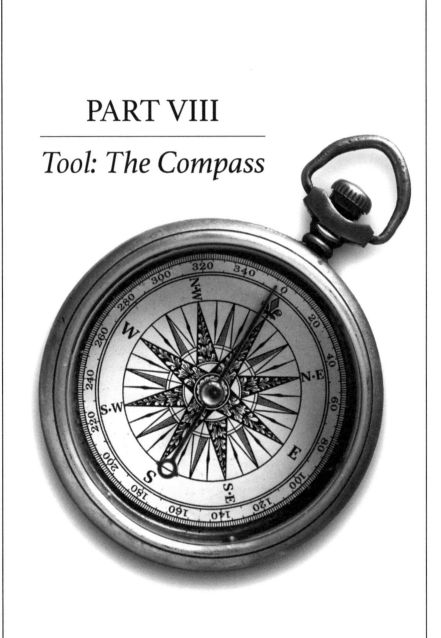

FROM A WHEELCHAIR
TO RUNNING A RACE

I was walking in the land of the living with a limp and an insatiable hunger for life. It made me laugh to think about what I must have looked like; I was the walking dead, but no zombie. Each time I won another battle against time, I left feeling bloodthirsty, but for more life, not death.

After living well beyond my deadline, a form of rebirth occurred. I felt a cosmic change in my being, like a solar nebula birthing a sun. This was a transformation of self, and I began to fully understand what Dr. Onn had meant when he said I needed to change my ways to survive the cancer. But I don't think he could have possibly known the extent I had undertaken to fulfill this quest. To survive, I needed to focus on fulfilling my life. But was this a case of taking the cart before the horse?

Despite how far I had come in the evolution of my personal leadership—of who I was—I still felt unbalanced in life. Something was missing. *Sunshine*, the little cancerous lump in my lung. Cancer was the challenging catalyst that grew a better me. Now that this war was over, I felt like a wounded veteran all over again.

My life's landscape felt like it had terraformed. I had evolved, but my sense of environment and circumstances did too. What was I fighting for now? I saw an interesting dichotomy between allowing life to lead me instead of leading it for myself. I needed to maintain and reinforce my progress so the cancer wouldn't return. Now that it was gone, what did God have in store for me?

I would never allow myself to go back to how I was before. I was awakened to a bigger destiny and saw the light, but my eyes felt like they were still straining from the glare. *What is ahead of me? Which direction do I go?*

Part of my leadership journey was realizing the answers were only to be found within. I had every reason to feel stronger and more confident now, but my old nature was to allow problems to become perils. With the survivalist mentality, I had to hold onto what I had, control the outcome as much as I could, but what about reclaiming what was lost? The limp in both of my legs was a difficult reality to accept.

Was this the reality I wanted? No, this weakness in my legs was not a fact I would let define my identity.

I had fallen deeper in love with myself and who I was becoming—an unexpected blessing from this arduous journey. Although not many people knew it, I had spent too much of my life seeing myself as a suffering survivor, clinging to what I could to ground myself while knowing there was a healthier way to live. I felt my traumatic childhood had branded me for life. In retrospect, I know the abuse I suffered wasn't my fault, yet it deeply affected how I saw myself. Through my battle with cancer, I had forged a different self-image. It was love at first sight with the new Eeki in the mirror, but I knew I needed to give gratitude to the old me, the Eeki who chose to better himself. And, had I not been given this challenge, I never would have known what it was like not only to love the person in the mirror, but to feel in love with the person I was growing into.

Still, my current reality depicted a weakened version of myself. I couldn't remain in this year-long period where I struggled to walk and physically function—I couldn't get stuck there—I wouldn't agree to it. I began to tinker with the various parts of my inner compass, and it occurred to me: there was no clear path ahead. Instead, I was facing a vast frontier with no clear destination in mind. The needle of my inner compass was spinning wildly, and I had no idea how to find the true north. *Where am I going?* The question baffled me. There were simply innumerable choices ahead of me, an infinite grassy plain, with each blade a possible decision.

I needed to ask myself what was next, but it wasn't a question of *where* I needed to go, nor was it a question of *when or how*. More useful was *who. Who am I?* I am a leader. With this in mind, I asked the most crucial question: *What is my true north?*

I needed to know because there was no pull of destiny anymore. I needed to push myself toward a new destination rather than slip back into survival or even contentment. The human body loves balance. It actively pursues homeostasis. But comfort causes the body to work against itself. If I hadn't changed myself through discomfort, I would not have learned anything and had nothing more to teach others. I was still physically weak, but I was not the same man. It was a blessing that the cancer was in retirement; hopefully, for good.

The first idea I came up with was my old plan to leave Sderot after 10 years to return to Tel Aviv. After a destiny-defining decade, it was time. My parents also weren't getting any younger. The cross-country trip to visit with them in Haifa had kept me away far more often than I would have liked. My inner compass literally pointed north. *Haifa, could be nice…*

This move meant it was time to say goodbye to some of the most important figures in my life: people who had marched into battle with me against my cancer from the day it was discovered to its last breath.

Garik, Judah, and my beloved friends from Sderot—I would miss them. I knew it would be hard to remain active parts of each other's lives once I moved. There needed to be a proper send-off.

I hosted a farewell party and invited everyone. 30 minutes before anyone would arrive, I tried to prepare myself not to cry. It was the last evening at my home in Sderot. I had become so accustomed to their regular presence in my life. I would need to do my best to keep up with them hereafter.

A knock came at the door. Of course, someone was early! Garik came in with armfuls of groceries. "Garik, what is all this? Everything is already prepared."

"It's okay. Don't worry about it." He haphazardly set down a few packs of dates and bottles of wine next to my neatly organized spread.

I left it as-is and smiled. I would sure miss his quirks. "Come here." I gave him a hug and thanked him. Judah and several others arrived shortly after. I was happy to see everyone making themselves at home, though it was bittersweet.

I tried not to tear up as I prepared drinks for a toast. I could hardly imagine my life without the people who were there for me when I was in greatest need. They were willing to do everything they could to support me because I allowed myself to break my old rules that walled others out. I invited them to stand by me, and they did so with haste.

I felt the warmth of a hand on my shoulder as I poured wine into glasses. I could tell immediately it was Garik. We used to joke about the temperature of his hands, as if they could smelt iron if he held it. I turned around, and before I could express how much I cherished his friendship and would miss him, he said, "Why are you using the glasses? Use the plastic ones."

I burst out in laughter, "One good thing about you, Garik, is that I don't have to worry that you'll ever change. You are still and will always be the older brother that tells me what's best for me."

Two hours later, as I walked everybody to the gate with well wishes and goodbyes, I noticed that Judah had stayed behind. Once everybody left, he came closer, looked deep into my eyes, and said, "Don't you ever take me back to that moment again where you and I found out you had cancer. You have gained new life, and now you need to set an example for all of us."

I wanted to say something smart, but I shut my mouth as I realized those life-altering moments that only he and I shared were eternally etched into my heart. It was with him that I started this journey and especially through him that I understood what people really see in me and are willing to do for me, that is, if I welcomed their love and generosity and offered my own.

The next morning, packed with my last belongings, I headed up to Haifa. On the drive I reflected about the past 10 years, feeling my inner compass begin to stir, and it was clear what it was pointing toward: precious time with my parents, but this was but a large piece to a greater whole. I smiled at the thought of seeing more of my mom and dad, but considered like-father-like-son, we both would have a cane. There was nothing inherently wrong with this, my body was still recovering, but it would remain stagnant if I didn't rise for another challenge. Suddenly, an idea jolted my heart and my mind.

After the brutal beating my body endured during and after the treatments, my body needed a new direction of its own. I needed to take charge and follow my compass away from what pained me. I needed to regain control over my body and the only pathway to recovery involved one thing: sports.

The cancer had ravaged my body to the point where it seemed a nearly impossible task. It would take time, and rehab, but if I fought, I would win.

By the end of my rehab, I wanted to join Cross Training. I knew there are some "crazy sides" to the Cross Training community, at least, according to some, but I also knew that it would push me out of my comfort zone, which, paradoxically, was becoming a comfort zone unto itself. Plus, I wanted to share my journey and achievements with a community.

My inner compass would help me map my goals and find the areas where I wished to grow. I was not naturally pulled toward these targets of mine; instead, I needed to push myself to pursue what gave purpose to this pain. This would be a new chapter in my life. It would mean not just "being into fitness" like I was during most of my life—I would need to recover first, and then find a new perspective I had never seen before.

My compass needle steadied. I had determined a direction in which to travel, but in the back of my mind there were doubts. *I just learned how to walk again. Why do this? Why not just take my time?* My heart bucked at these thoughts. It wanted to race toward what was envisioned. *What would it feel like to achieve this and rejoice!*

The partnership between my mind and my heart had become strained after so much strife. The heart needs guidance, and the mind can become blind to the passion necessary to pursue life. The compass was useful if they could not agree. I wanted to find a resolution before my road trip ended. Judah's face popped in my head, and in the most comical fashion, I imagined him with Garik's gruff voice. *The compass is the soul.*

This, this was the golden truth. The compass tool is an expression of the soul. The mind and the heart can fight over its direction, but it is not them that determines it. I could make a choice that superseded those in this conflict for the greater good. My soul said to my mind, you don't have to wait, though your judgment is sound. If you work with your heart, I will take you both there. The soul is the mediator and great equalizer; it is where your personal leadership resides. In unison, I reasoned this whole-hearted approach could not wait, and it was exactly what I needed next in my life.

With the magnetic treatments for my knees and learning to stand on my feet again behind me, the move to Haifa, closer to my parents, would be the perfect place to focus on my goal. I got my own place with a majestic view of the Mediterranean Sea. The sunsets were the perfect backdrop for deep reflection, and one evening, as I watched the sky change colors, I considered how I left Sderot feeling gratified with that part of my life concluded. The move to Haifa had opened my life's path, offering innumerable possibilities.

I brought up my plan to one day join Cross Training to my father.

"Sports?" he said incredulously. "You just got out of a wheelchair." When he said it, I realized how crazy it must have sounded. But to me, it was already a done deal.

While I enjoyed humoring my father, he noticed the serious look in my eyes. "It is the same as before, Dad. Surviving is not enough. This is the next step for me."

He didn't have to say a word. His mere presence was an affirmation. He gripped my shoulder and looked at me. "Show everyone what you can do. Just remember, you're not a little kid anymore. At least, your body isn't." It warmed me to hear the encouragement, albeit tempered with fatherly advice. Only in recent years had he come to accept how headstrong I was, but he couldn't help but show me his concern.

Mom understood very well what fighting cancer meant to me, despite her Alzheimer's. This was my rebirth. This was finding meaning in life after near death. I had always felt a spiritual link between us. I drew courage from her, and her admiration and adoration she gave during these difficult days was like rocket fuel. But I felt at times my efforts were more to uplift her spirits than my own. She was so down to earth compared to us all. She was so strong, and she didn't necessarily need to be uplifted. Unsurprisingly, she was elevating us all.

I was also gratified that throughout my journey, the fruits of my personal leadership challenges were ripe for others to pick. My story seemed to spark something in others, illuminating the dark crevasses where their own strength could be found. My journey with cancer and struggle just to get back to what had been my "normal" made me much more deeply empathize with others. When I saw other people encouraged by what I was doing I became incredibly curious about what it meant to them. As it became clearer, it fueled my efforts to carry out what I had set out to do. It was a reflection of their own potential. Something spoke to them saying, *there is more within you*. And my parents with their unconditional support were part of this desire to inspire. I felt so blessed. With all they had been through as survivors, they looked at me with love and dedication. They believed in me.

My compass gave me the direction. It was time to take the first step.

FORGE YOUR FUTURE

Only a few weeks after I began walking again, I called a graduate of mine from the ILI who had quickly become a brother to me as he began to hone his own personal leadership. Yiftach Abukrat was nearly half my age. During his leadership training with the ILI, he founded his own fitness studio that had been growing in success. He had received his proper credentials and was an effective personal trainer. His location wasn't the easiest place to establish a business, but he wanted to support his hometown by improving the health of the community. The business was thriving, which was a testament to his ingenuity, and I would have to say, his leadership training. He had kept up with me and my travails through cancer and recovering my ability to walk.

"Yiftach, are you busy?" He had answered the phone, but I could hear him rustling something in the background. "Yiftach, get off your *tuchus* and listen to me." He was more of a younger brother to me in the figurative sense; it was hard not to give him a hard time.

"Yes, Eeki, I'm here. What's happening?"

"Okay, I need you to sit back down and listen to me carefully."

"You just told me—"

"Listen, I want to rehab myself through sports. I want to be a strong athlete, and I need your help."

He was silent for a long moment; I felt like I could hear his heartbeat on the other end of the phone like a ticking pocket watch. I braced myself for some ribbing ridicule as I thought he might be thinking it was a joke.

"Shouldn't you ask your doctor first?" he asked with grave concern.

I paused. I was a little disappointed in his response. I had made my mind up to see myself differently and I wanted other people to do the same without hesitation. And before cancer, I always had a playful rivalry with Yiftach. In my mind, the leadership training never stopped between us—a sort of a friendly competition. I wanted him to see the curated qualities of the old Eeki before cancer but also the new person I was becoming.

I also understood where he was coming from. I had shared with everyone about my cancer and the pain I had in my knees and nerves. And my close friends had all had to have imagined I could have died. I had to accept that his concern was to be expected; it was coming from a good place. So, I explained how my mentality creates the reality I wish to see.

I wouldn't profess that *anything* is possible, but I would never say that anything is *impossible,* because as soon as I did, this reality would be created. It's not a physical condition but a mental one that makes decisions, and this is what would lead the way.

"I know you probably don't get where I'm coming from," I said. "Because you don't exactly understand what I've gone through over the past few years. I know you care very much and want to be cautious, but I want you to be my trainer. There is no one else. I need to rehabilitate myself."

"Eeki, I know very well what you have been through. And you know I believe that the mind can change the outcome. But—"

"Don't but, Yiftach. Don't *but* in the middle of the sentence. There's no discussion about it, and I *did* ask my oncologist about whether I can do sports. But first of all, it is my decision."

He was a busy man, and I understood he may not have time to conduct personal training with all his groups, but with the chance he might allocate special time for me—I made a hard ask. I only trusted him because we shared the same mentality, and this was an opportunity for us both.

"Of course, I will do it," he replied. "I won't go easy on you, brother." He laughed and told me he needed to finish his breakfast and that I better prepare for some hard work. It all felt right. This was the direction I was supposed to follow, and I knew it would change my life for the better.

We scheduled our first session in a couple of weeks. I knew this was going to be a long road, and likely painful. But this was where my compass pointed to, and I would lead the way.

It was a dreary rain-soaked day as the taxi bumbled along to the gym. I got out of the car with my cane, noticing a couple of sweat-soaked gym goers leaving. I decided not to use my cane as I walked through the doors, but then I saw there was a flight of steps.

I stared at them for a moment. *Are you delusional?* I began to ascend, trying to avoid using the railing like a childish challenge. My muscles were weak. I hadn't used them in months. It was going to be a long way up—both the climb to the gym on the second story and to my goals. *Can you actually do this?* Yes. In my new reality, the pain would not stop me from getting into better shape. It would be the fuel for change.

I walked in to see Yiftach talking with other trainees in the middle of their group session. He spotted me and smiled. "Eeki!" He approached and grabbed my hands. "Welcome to the first day of your new life."

We hugged. I was very proud. "Thank you."

"Wait here, I'll bring a few items for you to work with."

I looked at the other trainees, seeing how strong they were. *This is what I want to look like. I will not let the doubt crawl in my heart.* I was excited.

I guessed they were mostly in their early to mid-thirties. *Do you really understand what you are saying? Are you serious? Because if it is only words, then it's all nonsense.* The very first moment in my cancer journey was a choice. But action had burst forth like the Big Bang to set me in motion. Words must be given life.

I was determined. I held this compass in my heart, and knew I was moving in the right direction. Each effort was an exertion of mission-driven action. I commanded myself to be fully committed to this. If I took charge, I knew there would be only success.

He brought some cones and a PVC pipe.

"First, I want you to sit down on the floor. Then, stand using these motions."

"Really? Should I warm up crawling like a baby?"

He slapped me on the back with an annoying grin. "Let's go. There's lots to do!"

He attended to the other trainees while I sat down and stood up. Was this some kind of brotherly revenge? I fondly considered our sibling-like antics over the past couple of years. Was this an exercise in seeing which one of us would drive each other crazy first? I wasn't sure who would become Cain or

Abel—what had we done?

The warmup wasn't as easy as I had thought. I fell over and rolled on my back on the first few tries. I used the pipe he gave me to leverage myself up, then I got a couple of reps without it.

"What's next?"

"Some slow marching around the perimeter and then you're going to dash between these cones. See you here in a few laps."

After the first lap, I felt beads of sweat dotting my forehead. I swiped them away and kept marching, awkwardly stomping a few times. I was not one to get embarrassed, but I wavered between seeing this as a joke and something serious. The more solemnly I took it, the more frustrated I became until it cemented in my head. My body was relearning all it could be with awe. But it was because of my mind and its higher expectations. The limits of my mental universe were expanding beyond its limits—and I knew my body would follow.

The pain began to flare up. I jumped from side to side between the cones trying to touch my toes. I fell on the ground over and over again. Then, a new exercise: Yiftach had me stand in the middle of 12 cones in the form of a clock. Jumping to each hour and back to the middle. It felt like 12 hours of falling.

I kept picking myself back up. Did he know I would need to do this from the beginning? I performed some air squats, concentrating on the depth and muscles involved. There could be no distractions. I couldn't worry if I looked like a gym court jester. I pushed my body until the session was done, then crumpled on the bench, feeling the need for a beach towel to remove my sweat.

Yiftach seemed very pleased. "Take a day of rest, and I will see you here in two days." He gave me a slap on the back. "Go shower—you stink."

"I'll get you back for this." I still had enough strength to lift a toothy grin.

On the taxi drive home, I had the window rolled down for some fresh air and some perspective. This was how a new era began.

"Hello, hello, isn't this the address?" the taxi driver asked, breaking my daydream. I must have looked lost, or at least lost in thought, because he then asked, "Are you okay?"

"Oh, yes. Sorry." I wasn't sure how long I had been staring at my apartment building because in that moment I had lost concept of time. That had been happening to me fairly often. There was so much to consider, and I was in a constant conversation with myself, willing myself to hold fast to the vision of a healthy, fit self.

I got up and out of the car slowly, my body hurting. I used my cane for leverage. The driver kindly lingered as if anticipating I might fall. I imagined how I must have looked to him, and it upset me. It was only a few more steps toward the elevator and to the stairway. I lived on the fifteenth floor. *No, this must not go on, I must do it. Just one today.* As if mocking me, the stairs presented a challenge. I wanted to catch up with the other trainees even though there was no real comparison between us. As much as it hurt, I pushed myself to take one flight of stairs. A neighbor looked at me curiously and I decided one flight was enough for the day. I then entered the elevator to the fifteenth floor. But I wasn't about to give up. The stairs would become my challenge and I would master them.

This is what I must do.

Yiftach was 25 years younger than me, stronger, and healthier, but he was still sensible and understood my situation. Slowly but surely, he would build a beautiful program for me to rebuild my muscles. It took about five months of seeing him twice a week until I would be ready for the next leg of my fitness journey. Each time I got home I felt stronger and hurt less. I would add another floor to my ascent up the stairs every time. I was feeling good and more energized. It reminded me of my promise to return to the King of the Mountains like a mental training simulation.

But there are some things in life you can never be prepared for.

It was a Saturday morning in February, my family was having a Sabbath brunch. Bracha and her husband and our parents had just finished eating. I was cleaning the dishes when I saw my father grasp his stomach as he stood up from his chair. Mom was in the living room speaking with Bracha, unaware of what was happening. My father was wincing through the pain, an expression I had many times as I tried not to show my pain to others. I knew that look, the restrained expression, and the hope that no one would see—not just the discomfort, but also the weakness. I would never see my father as weak, but I understood why he was trying to be so strong.

I went to clear more of the table but gave a pat on my father's shoulders. "Join me in the kitchen for a moment?"

He looked at me as if I caught him doing something wrong. He knew I knew.

I glanced over him at Bracha and Mom, still together on the couch. As intuitive as my mother was, we all still did our best to keep her from worrying—anything that might affect her health. "I've seen you bothered by your stomach more than twice now. We should have you see a doctor."

"I know. Just wanted to spend a little time before I did. I'm sure you understand."

What truth spoken from his gut! I did understand, but I didn't want to. It brought me right back to the moment when I met the little lump in my lungs, *Sunshine*, nearly four years ago.

"Just a check-up. I'll get it scheduled, okay?" My dad didn't fight me on this but seemed to appreciate me being proactive. That is when I knew something was seriously wrong.

I told Bracha of my concerns, and she doubled down on them as expected, but she knew just as well to contain them in front of Mom. Even though Mom's awareness was spotty, she was right on the mark with emotions. She could sense trouble and would become worried. That would not be good for her. Better she be bathed in the warm waters of denial.

As expected, the doctors had him get a CT scan and MRI. Before long, my father and I were back in the office sitting side by side with a doctor examining the results behind a desk. I had become fluent in reading doctors' faces, especially in situations like this. The doctor didn't hide his expression well. He stalled for a while, but it was obvious he knew what was happening and it was not good news.

The doctor looked at us both, speaking as if to each of us.

"It is pancreatic cancer."

Dad was unfazed. He stood there digesting the news. He surely must have known just as I had before any doctor told me.

I wanted to slam my fists on the chair. He was 88. Of course, I knew the privilege this was. The Nazis didn't kill him, but now it seemed cancer would. He would fight it, and I would aid him. I suppose I saw myself as some sort of veteran being called from the reserves.

We would keep this secret from Mom.

***

The studio gym became a gladiatorial arena. I wanted to show my father the warrior I had become. He was there to witness me conquer cancer, walking now without a cane—but there were enemies trying to infiltrate the fortified walls of my mind. My training with Yiftach became a battle of the brain and body. There were challenges physically and mentally. My father was fighting for his life, but I knew it would help him to know not only that I was okay, but that I was thriving. With my father's diagnosis, I needed to keep my spirits high, and showing myself a sense of direction and control kept me in flight.

I credit Yiftach and his training for helping me learn to walk again. As April and the holiday of Passover rapidly approached, I realized it had been four years since this saga began. The early morning air felt fresh as I left the studio after a hard workout. It was another Saturday—what should've been a day of rest. Instead of the usual Sabbath family lunch at Bracha's that I'd grown quite accustomed to, I went home to rest my legs.

I woke up to several missed calls and a voice message from my sister.

"*Eeki, you better come over right away. Mom isn't feeling so well.*" I had been anticipating a dreaded call about my father's condition, but this was a surprise. I think I could only wrap my head around one of my parents being unwell at a time. Up until then, aside from the memory loss my mother seemed fine.

I immediately called Bracha. "What's wrong? Is she okay?"

"Just come over here right now," she said, sounding breathless. She hung up and I raced to my car.

I was speeding as fast as my thoughts, thanking God the traffic was light, though the fact it was Shabbat may have helped. I jogged up to the door and let myself in, there were two paramedics lying Mom down on the floor. I watched in horror. My father and sister were standing in the corner, crying like pale ghosts. Mom's caretaker was there too, tears streaming down her face. I rushed to her, knowing she might have the composure to tell me what was happening.

She spoke before I could ask. "We were sitting around the sofa, and then we just heard her give her last breath." Her eyes trailed back to my mother. "We immediately called the ambulance." It took me a few minutes to comprehend what was happening.

She underwent nearly ten minutes of CPR with a chest compression system. It seemed senseless and that my beloved mother had had enough.

My jaw tightened. "It's her time… What are you doing to her? She's ready to go." I looked upon her. "It's her time." I felt my face becoming clammy.

One of the paramedics looked up. "We have a heartbeat."

Mine nearly stopped. Mom was always a fighter, but I had already assumed she had passed.

A third paramedic arrived and brought in a stretcher. I helped them carry her to the ground floor where the ambulance was waiting, but halfway down the stairs, I could see she had stopped breathing again, her grip slipping from this world. "Stop! She isn't breathing!"

One of the paramedics quickly shifted directions. "We have to take her back up."

I shook my head. *What for?* A part of me insisted it was her time.

"Come, let go."

They began to perform CPR again as I shuddered, noticing Bracha trying to console my father. I looked around at the whole spectacle. "You're just breaking all her ribs! She's trying to let go."

Bracha shushed me. "Eeki! Don't talk like this. If you don't let them do this, Dad is going to faint."

"Why is he going to faint? Because he doesn't understand she is passing away? She's ready to depart. What is going to be left of her even if they get her heartbeat again?"

It was painful to see Mom like this. There was dignity I hoped to preserve and her will I wished to honor. We already knew this day was coming, but some things in life cannot be imagined, only experienced. I maintained my composure for her sake. I wouldn't lose my mind, not at a time like this.

Everyone was in shock, but in my heart, I knew what Mom wanted me to do. She wanted me to give her a kiss on her forehead and let her go. She would trust me to know what the right thing to do was at such a moment. But I couldn't make them stop because these were the orders the paramedics had to follow.

They finally brought her into the ambulance, and I followed behind them all the way to the hospital. Bracha and her husband had insisted they should stay behind Dad, considering his condition. Mom went straight into intensive care. An hour of anxious waiting in the lobby. The doctor came out and approached. "Are you her son?"

"Yes," I said bracing for the news.

"Look, I need you to give me permission or not for if her heart stops again, we won't resuscitate her. With her condition—"

"Doctor, not only do I give you permission, but I also forbid you. If it is time for her to go, she should go. She doesn't want to live life where she is incapable of doing anything."

The doctor looked at me and gave me a hug. "It is unbelievable." He took a breath. "I have great respect for you telling me this. In nearly all these situations, I never get an answer like this. There is really not much we can do—even if her heart recovers—the rest of her body is shutting down. However, this might sound… many make such decisions from the wrong place."

The last year of my mom's life wouldn't drain her of her dignity. She had fought all her life and had seen her fire carried on through her children. She saw me survive cancer and walk again. She saw me smile in the face of fate and outlast the darkness. She saw the dawn as her life came to dusk. A memory quickly flashed in my mind of her with both hands on my cheeks. *You are my son.* I remembered the look in her eyes as a reflection of souls.

The doctor turned around to face me as he returned to the intensive care unit. "Would you like to sit with her?"

"Of course."

Mom looked peaceful, as if watching a pleasant dream play on her eyelids. The doctor brought me a chair and I thanked him, then sat down and gently grabbed Mom's hand. I sat with her for four hours, telling her all the funny stories we had recounted hundreds and hundreds of times. I told her once again I could never repay her for all she gave to me—and I remembered how she once said in response to this, *but how can I repay God for what He gave to me?*

The doctor came in around midnight to have her brought up to another department and asked me if I wanted to go with them or go home. I knew she was about to arrive at her last stop before she left her life.

I stood beside her for a time after the doctor shook my hand and left us alone.

I stroked her hair. "Mom, if it is your will to depart, I understand. Then it is your time, but if you want to stay, I will be there for you and do everything to make you comfortable. But it is up to you. If you do depart, it will be with grace."

About eight minutes later, like the number of candles on a Hanukkah Menorah, she gave her last breath, and her flame went out. The room fell still and silent as if I was suddenly adrift in outer space. Did I stop breathing too?

I kissed her forehead. "I love you, Mom." I gazed upon her for a moment. My vision blurred. I don't remember when I ended up in my car. I hadn't turned it on. I reclined the seat and felt my soul shiver. A cold swept over me and I suddenly felt crushed like I was buried in an avalanche. The impact of reality was like an icy comet blasting a crater in my heart. My mind fissured and shook.

I made a call to Bracha, who was at home caring for Father. "Bracha..." There was a pause. And then we began to cry.

It was well past midnight. All I remember about the drive to Bracha's was the pain in my knuckles wrapped around the steering wheel. I would've liked to have said I woke up the next morning, but I didn't sleep at all. The next day, Bracha, Father, and I quietly sat together, gazing at all her pictures, sharing in the collective pain of loss, but trying to fill it with pleasant memories. Bracha seemed to absorbed father's pain while managing her own. I could see something was missing in him that morning—something inside him never saw itself through the night.

Since the moment Mom took her last breath, I still felt like I was floating farther and farther away from the earth. My navigation system felt shot, but as I perused old photos and shared many memories with my family and friends who came to see us, I found a particular picture of my mother that, to this day, I still keep in my wallet. I was in the upstairs bedroom, looking at where she had sat when we hugged after she acknowledged my cancer diagnosis. An angelic light turned on in my head.

I looked at the picture again. It stilled my heart. I had already learned how ephemeral life was when *Sunshine* had entered mine four years ago—he had lived for only so long too. There are over three billion bloody beats in an average lifespan. If you start counting, it may frighten you. I didn't know how many I had left, but with my mother's last breath, I knew there was only one heartbreak like this. It was the faint, last flicker of a candle blowing out. Every beat—every moment—has a purpose.

It was then I learned how nihilism is an arch-nemesis to personal leadership. How could anyone believe that life is meaningless? If her loss was meaningless, if all experience was a collection of coincidences—if my waged war was without purpose—then I would never have lived to see this day. And she would have died without her son.

I was knocked off course for a moment, dizzy from existential dread. But I recalibrated my trajectory and thrusted onward toward what felt like a new galaxy. *There is honor in this battle. Now, hers too.* It was hard to push through the pain that day and the next, and the next. My sense of the future was clouded, but I still had my compass. The fog of war is born from despair and doubt—not by similar emotions like anger, sadness, anxiety, that is, unless I let them rebel and turn against me. I needed to be a good leader, to control them. And to each of my emotions was a particular need, some more obvious than others: so still, I asked, *what was the reason for this pain?*

Loss. I could let my mother's passing vacuum up what was left of my life or respond and fill the gaping maw with a purpose. I would still grieve whether I wished to or not, but I believed Mom would yet see me live at my very best. This meant carrying the torch she had bestowed upon me.

Rebounding from Loss

M y determination only accelerated in the days to come. I met with Yiftach and requested to join the group training at the Cross Training "box." It was a bit of an aggressive wish, but I had become rather accustomed to circumnavigating the mental security checks that filtered what I was or was not able to do.

In this case, it was Yiftach who tried to flag me down. He scanned my body as if I was trying to get away with something. "I'm not sure you're ready yet, Eeki. They're training, but you're still rehabbing." Before I spoke, I could already read his expression knowing he already knew what I was about to say.

"Listen, Yiftach." As I spoke, he grinned slightly. "I'm serious."

Maybe he was right, but I had become much more in tune with my body after nearly losing it. And running from everything that seemed to seek to limit me. This was a calculated risk. I had to push myself.

"In this case, it is not about my body, it is my mind. And if my heart is also there, my body will follow. I know and feel I am ready if you'll have me."

He gave me a strong hug. In this moment, we saw the leader in each other. He knew what this meant to me, what I had just lost, and what I stood to gain. The next week, as a 58-year-old man in a wheelchair just seven months ago, I arrived at my first Cross Training session attended by a lively bunch of 30-something-year-old trainees. On the drive there, I had noticed my hands burning despite not gripping the steering wheel. I already had a suspicion of what it was.

I suspected my hands were suffering from the same damage as my knees. The training felt twice as hard as my private sessions, but there was a camaraderie that uplifted the spirit and seemed to lighten each lift and exercise. I struggled to keep up at times, my aching hands holding me back, and by the end, reminiscent of my first session with Yiftach, my body and ego were bruised.

As the earth was enveloped in fear by the Covid-19 outbreak, I was still in a battle with bodily affliction, but it was most of all a mental condition—I would continue to quarantine my negativity. My natural immunity had been developed by this point. My increased resiliency was only because I had been infected with doubt and despair, and I chose to fight it. My mental immune system was strong, and my sense of direction was clear.

Still, there was no telling at the time what would unfold during the pandemic. Everyone at the gym was concerned about the impending lockdowns; it seemed mostly everyone felt like life was shutting down. I had been able to attend a handful of four-times-a-week group sessions, quickly forming friendships over the course of the month until the gyms were ordered to close. Among the many hardships, I venture to say this sense of loss, the unprecedented disconnection from people and places of life, was the most collectively felt.

Having just overcome cancer, I wondered what such a respiratory virus could do to my weary lungs. There was too much history of victories now to be thwarted by fear. While the lockdowns were in full effect, I kept building upon a basic workout plan I put together so as not to lose my progress. The only thing worse than stasis is regression. Yiftach and my new clan of gym rats stayed in touch during the lockdown, but I could tell there was an incredible tectonic impact on their morale.

My neighborhood in Haifa was a lively, family-oriented area. A soccer stadium, a mall, and some major tech business centers crowded the coast of the Mediterranean, but now it was desolate and eerily quiet. What should have been a time of lively renewal, spring, never took off the ground. In Israel, the lockdowns would persist over the summer, but so would my training team.

Around May 2020, I sent a group message to everyone I knew at the Cross Training studio in my neighborhood asking if they'd like to join me for some social-distanced training outside the gym. Gatherings weren't allowed, but in this open space, we could work out independently. Everyone behaved as if they got the last tickets to the world championship game.

I shared my workout plan with everyone, but after a few sessions together I asked one of my closest friends, Emanuel, if he could plan the workouts since I was still fresh and not really knowledgeable in Cross Training. He flashed his signature, comforting smile. "Of course, Eeki, but it's not going to be easy for you since my ideas of exercises are a little more extreme than what you've learned so far…" My eyebrow curled as I looked him straight in the face with a grin. "Seriously Emanuel? You think I want you to do less than what we Soviets can handle?"

He laughed and gave me a squeeze on the shoulder. "The Soviets! We can make our own little clan!" It was the day the "Soviets" were born! It became the name of those whose parents came originally from the Soviet Union and were educated in the spirit of Soviet sports culture: the highest discipline ever. Work until you drop dead. So, a few devoted Cross fitters—Emanuel, Costa, and Max—became some of my closest friends.

We trained outside the whole summer because of the lockdowns. Covid was terrorizing the city, but as the virus affected every aspect of our lives, we fused together as a family.

It is true that through difficult times form the greatest bonds. If there was any tool that served my sense of leadership that summer, it was the compass. No matter how confusing our twisted times felt, there was some direction I could move. Life never was at a standstill despite how it felt.

Eventually the lockdowns lifted and so did all our ambitions. For me, it was time for another dare—another rope to climb. I rifled through several possibilities and realized I would also need my compass in order to follow through. Fall fell into winter, but I was getting back up, building strength and doing box jumps—which seemed a little quirky to me at first, simply jumping on and off a box repeatedly for exercise, but they proved to be quite a workout. Still, with the growing pain in my hands and residual in my knees, I had some resistance to face. Some days I wondered if I had become so accustomed to the pain or if it had actually lessened. Regardless, I was mentally and physically stronger. And at the same time, my father weakened. He was withering away in both body and mind.

The doctors had put him on chemo despite deeming the effort quite futile. He could barely keep a meal down. The loss of the love of his life left a gaping hole in his heart, and the cancer continued to spread. A growing dread amassed upon the raw wound my mother's death had caused. At times, it seemed the more I fought, the more I lost. This would cause me to doubt my reputable prowess—I had waged war and won, but it had left its mark on me. Maybe I'd lose my way; maybe *I* would be lost.

But the mental side to my compass would guide me to more positive thinking. My heart was magnetically drawn toward silver linings, ambitions, and meaningful decisions because I attuned myself to them. Think about the times we get an idea in our head: inspiration strikes, or there is a difficult decision to make. Your mind can often smack your heart silly, or subtly naysay until you say no.

The indecision created between your heart and mind distracts you from the real enemies. When they stop working together, you stop working and start to weaken. The cohesive bond that keeps them together—that keeps you rising toward your potential destiny—your personal leadership. The compass is not isolated or solely contained in either. Instead, it serves as its own uniting, guiding force, sourced in the very essence of who we are. *I am a leader.* And so are *you.*

And I felt as such because with all the tools leading to this one, I had drawn out my inner essence and renewed my sense of self despite the threats that sought to diminish it.

The compass is a tool buried deep in the sand. On your voyage to its discovery, the prior seven tools serve as a shovel to dig it out. When I beat cancer, I found it encrusted in dirt, so I polished it off and saw it was pointing to me not only rehabilitating myself, but also challenging my status quo: I wanted to compete in sports. I wanted to become and create while all too many things were crumbling and vanishing in life.

As Jews outside of Israel pray toward the east, toward Jerusalem, I found my "true east" was God's magnetic pull toward my future. Could I resist and change course? Was it a predetermined place with no space for my input?

I remembered a passage in Psalms: "Who is this man who fears the Lord? He will guide him on the road that he chooses" (25:12) This "fear" of God was the deepest reverence a human heart can hold—there is a solemnity we must have at times, and this helped me develop and maintain a gravitas toward my potential.

And with the twists and turns on the roads I had chosen, I believe my higher power wished me to follow my mind's judgment, and to see me lead myself through life as a good father would proudly watch his son succeed. Finding my inner spirit and personal leadership was when I went from a child of God to a man. *All is foreseen, and permission for freedom of choice is granted.*

Just as I had questioned myself months ago while stepping up those studio stairs to first meet Yiftach, I had a similar experience when I met another trainer at the gym, Amir Srouji. I instantly sensed someone who had experienced a development of personal leadership himself. While seeing him around the Cross Training Box, I had gotten to know him as many would know me while we collectively crushed our training challenges.

Amir had a career in dentistry with the full support and eager expectations of his family. But in his spirit, his compass had always been pointing in another direction. This led him to a crossroads where he could either pursue his passion for fitness and the body or follow a path planned for him by others. He was educated in anatomy and was more fascinated by how the body worked than training itself. There was something I felt I could learn from him. He understood the powerful connection of the mind over one's physical limitations.

Training others was never just a hobby to Amir. Instead of fate leading him, he chose to walk the path of his passion. It was a risk his family nearly fainted over, and for him, it was an incredibly difficult decision. He learned that you don't let others determine your path and to not let fear keep you from leaving something behind.

I took one good look inside, as if my compass was in the palm of my hand, and saw its needle pointed straight at him. There was something I could achieve with Amir. He was a leader.

After a handful of training sessions with Amir, I came to wonder if Yiftach had gone easy on me. I went from struggling to walk without a cane to using a barbell.

"Eeki, two more." Amir's brawny voice was composed—he was not the excitable type. Yet his gravitas was highly contagious and instilled a sense of mission in me with every workout. This time, I was deadlifting and thought I would need to be carried out on a stretcher.

"Two?!" I was finishing what I thought was my last one. The first rep, I could feel my grip struggling from the pain in my hands.

"Last one!"

I felt as if my feet were going to burst through the floor. Sweat was hanging on the edge of my eyelids. I tried to speak but was too winded. But still I did two more reps.

"Well done. Take it easy with group training tomorrow—in fact, take a rest day."

"I can rest when I am in the grave."

He puffed a breath that must've been a laugh. "Tell me how you feel when you wake up tomorrow."

Dreadful. I thought of getting back my wheelchair for the day. I contemplated where I was a year prior, wobbling on a cane to box jumping and performing snatch deadlifts, which may have been lighter compared to my years before cancer, but were still impressive for someone in my condition. It felt like I literally grew new legs after the loss of my old pair. Though, they might fall off if I didn't listen to Amir.

Even still, there was an important trip I had planned to make.

I had just visited this store in Kaffa Karma where my father and I had picked up some of his favorite cheese—and it was his favorite for good reason: the villagers all immigrated from Russia two centuries ago and kept to their Russian culinary tradition. The handmade cheese they produced was just like the one my dad remembered from his time in Russia after the second World War. He had barely been able to keep his food down, and his weight continued to drop week after week. I had hoped the calories would help fill him up, but his body wouldn't cooperate. As much as I considered how my mind over matter approach to life had helped me reach this very day, there was a sharp edge of reality that cut deeply. Though he never spoke it, I knew his mind was made up—he had lost the love of his life and yearned to see her. After helping my father clean himself up after the meal, I left him with Bracha who had been struggling with her own despair. She was doing everything she could to keep our father comfortable. I let them both know I was going to visit Mom.

It was a quiet drive, and my mind was blank—a rare occasion indeed. I rolled over the curb to park my car near the burial site, which rested underneath an open spaced concrete shelter, the hot sun cooking the earth just beyond the walls' reach. Before looking for Mom's gravestone, I grabbed a watering can from my back seat and filled it with water from a nearby hose. I walked along the gravel trail between the rows of graves, some plainly marked, some with photo images engraved on the headstones, until I came upon my mother's and cast my eyes to the plot next to it, which may soon be filled.

Dust smothered her black gravestone. I poured the water, and it carried the blanket of dirt away. After wiping it down with a towel, I sat on the edge and gazed upon the stone. A picture frame of her rested against the vertical slab.

Mom had shared in my journey against cancer, always reassuring me, even as I lost the use of my legs for a year—*You can do this, she had said.* Despite her dementia, she could see herself in me, and my hidden inner struggle. She was one of the strongest people in the world. She had starved physically, fled Nazi persecution with her family, watched her sister starve, and years later, struggled to escape Soviet Russia to immigrate to Israel with my father and no money to speak of, leaving everything she'd ever known behind.

It was so hard for Father to overcome her loss. I sat there, reminiscing with her. "Mom, you see what I'm doing? I am doing this because of you— because you showed me how to lead myself through darkness. You always believed in me." She was a beacon of light; I knew she was there with me in that moment, and would be in each moment beyond. If she could overcome the horrors of the holocaust, and keep fighting, I would honor her by living my life at its best.

"There's something else I must tell you, Mom. You've been here alone while we have all been living our lives… it breaks my heart, but it seems you may have company soon. Dad misses you."

It only took another month before he reunited with her, his beshert, his soulmate. It was my father's time.

He had passed away just ten days after his eighty-ninth birthday, ten months after Mom had died. I came to see him then, and I could tell he was slowly departing. He recognized me of course but could hardly speak. His eyes were distant. We all sat around him in the living room and tried to communicate with him and to cheer him up. At one point he looked at me, and with faint, garbled words showed me that he wanted to go to bed. I lifted him from his wheelchair, as he could not walk anymore, and laid him down. I covered him with a blanket and once I saw he was comfortable and sinking into slumber, I laid next to him and put my hand around him. I knew his time was coming. I spoke in his ear and told him that I love him, and I thanked him for everything that he sacrificed for me. I then kissed him on his forehead and left the room. Bracha was sitting on the sofa. I swallowed hard. "You ought to go and say goodbye." She looked at me, astonished. I gave her a long hug hanging on for what life was within my arms. "He won't be with us in the morning."

And so, it was.

During the burial, I felt like I was hemorrhaging hope. It is a terrible sorrow to lose one parent, but to lose another, especially so soon, was another blow that made me doubt I could still persevere. I felt hollow, and as much as I wished the graves before me would have remained empty, I knew that it was their time to go. There was no need to war with death because they had lived their lives.

But I prayed in this moment, I shouted in my mind over the despair that I would not die while I still drew breath and had so much to yet achieve. All was not lost. As much as I wanted to ditch my tools, my compass, I grasped onto them for dear life. *Dear Lord, help guide me ahead.*

My parents were together again, and they would watch me in the days ahead as I raced toward my goals. As heavy as the pain was, I was enlivened by my challenges—I needed to show them all I had been fighting for. I kept training, in need of goals, in need of something to fight for other than the past.

◆ ◆ ◆

A few long, empty months passed until July 2021 arrived. It was the fourth anniversary of my trip to Iceland, and I thought I would commemorate it by going again—this time to climb out of the pit of despair that gnashed at my feet.

Yiftach would join me amongst a few other close friends from the gym. I had a promise to fulfill. The King of the Mountain had patiently waited for my return.

I was as excited to touch ground in Iceland as the first time. We had our fair share of shenanigans and sightseeing, but the day of our climb, I would meet yet another disappointment. A brutal storm originating from the

North Pole swept through the country, and even before the moment we had met with the travel guide, I knew my opportunity to face the mountain would be blown away with it. We would have to return home without the triumph I had imagined. This was my second failed attempt to get a chance to climb Snæfellsjökull.

Maybe I should've dragged Amnon despite his protests. He had blamed his overwhelming busy-body life for not coming. I would send a teasing text blaming him. Luck is a fickle thing, though I came to believe it doesn't exist.

Yiftach could see my frustration. "We'll come back. Like last time, it is all this means. Third time's the charm, they say, right?"

"It will be—you'll see for yourself when we surmount it together next year."

He gave me a fist on the shoulder. The smile on his face brightened even the gloomiest days.

Disappointment can feel like a sledgehammer to the heart, but determination can deflect its brutal force. This was another rope to climb, a double dare. I still had an emptiness to fill, the hollow space left by my mother's death, but I had a goal, a life of my own to focus on, and I would return, ready to conquer the mountain.

That August, soon after the trip, I began to incubate the idea of a competition. I knew there was a world-wide, ranked one, called the Open Games. Amir was pretty clear he wasn't into the idea for me. I had looked more into it and found that the competition had a division for my age bracket, but despite this, Amir had noted this was for individuals who hadn't the physical issues I'd had, and perhaps the adaptive category would be more appropriate. We tabled the talk, but I didn't want to wait to raise the stakes for myself.

I had grown rather fond of another trainee at the gym. Zachi, a shy and soft-spoken long-distance runner and avid photographer, was a bit of an enigmatic character to me. There was such an unassuming nature to him; he was the top in his field in tech, one of Israel's largest industries, and could run at least fifty miles a week with a couple of ultra-marathons notched on his belt. He would come to many gatherings I hosted with my gym friends and would rarely mingle—but this man had such courage and determination.

I met with him shortly after my second trip to Iceland. After telling him all about it while he listened to me passionately spout about the place and the disappointing storm, a curious look furrowed on his face.

"You know Eeki, there is an ultra-marathon they are having there next year. I saw all your posts and pictures from there and decided that I am going to do it."

"Wow, an ultra-marathon? Really? I can't even run a half a mile—you know, during our gym trainings? That's really all I can do."

My legs still felt terrible, though they had pushed beyond every limit previously pressed upon them.

Zachi seemed to intently watch my expression. I recalled when I was a bright-eyed seventeen-year-old and had Olympic dreams running track in school. It seemed a little silly compared to Iceland, but there was still passion still there. But now, I can't even run a mile, and my age had little to do with it.

"Eeki, you can run." I looked at him—it was a quiet yet certain statement. "I know you. You can overcome any problem."

I hefted a small laugh, but quickly collected myself because his look was quite sincere. Despite how far I had come in my rehab, I didn't believe I'd be able to effectively run again. But sometimes when we hear such things, there is some substance beyond words, a magic in the maker of them—I absorbed his claim as a truth. Later, I went online considering whether or not it was worth it to try. That's how I found an ad for a race night in Haifa scheduled for November 5, three months away. It also happened to be the same date as my birthday. It's like it was meant to be. I called Zachi.

"Let's do it," I said. "This is the best present I can give to myself. Is there enough time to prepare?"

"Don't worry. I'm coming tomorrow and we'll do the first exercise."

It wasn't a competitive race, yet I felt like I was competing against myself. I thought how there were so many hurts and struggles behind me and I didn't want to be dragged down by them. The difference now was that I wasn't running from the past anymore, instead I was catching up to my future potential.

THE RACE IS ON

Zachi met me outside the Haifa soccer stadium that next morning before the summer heat would make an already dreadful exercise into a deadly one. There was a one half-mile loop around the stadium I had often seen joggers circuiting.

Zachi was geared up, certainly looking the part. He grinned. "Eeki, are your laces tied?"

"You have an unfair advantage with that shaved head of yours."

"We can wait for you to bald or get started."

We began a light jog. The only recent running I had done were short warmups at the gym prior to lifting. My legs felt like creaky chair legs clacking against the ground, but they soon warmed up. We were what felt like inches into the run, matched in pace, before I became aware of how taxed my lungs already were. I wondered if *Sunshine* had left a massive mess in what was once his home—it was time to clean house.

Perhaps the damage was irreparable. Maybe this was his middle finger to me after evicting him. That was one way to look at it. But *Sunshine* was never an enemy. He was actually a messenger, and I wouldn't riddle him with bullets of resentment. I knew God wanted me to find my way to the other side of this long, dark tunnel of my life, and now that I had emerged from this fight with cancer and mostly restored my lost legs, I would lead a new life without tunnel vision through an expansive open field, with ripe possibilities all around me. I could walk in the right direction with my compass in hand. But if my mind started to retreat into the dark passage, I'd lose the light of day to travel my journey.

Zachi pulled ahead when he noticed me slowing down. He kept a steady lead, knowing I would stubbornly push myself a little harder. At three quarters of a mile, a little over one lap, I nearly tripped over myself.

He seemed to anticipate this moment.

"Well done. Next time we'll have you run a full mile."

Hands on my knees, I felt like punching them. At least we made it around the stadium once. To our right was the Mediterranean, the golden sun throwing glittery confetti over it as if to celebrate something so pathetic. And as infectious as Zachi's smile was, I couldn't bring myself to make one too. We walked back to his car, though for me it felt more like hobbling. "I know this race is for anyone—noncompetitive—but I don't want to crawl across the finish line when everyone has already gone home and fallen asleep."

"Sometimes you've got to really chase your goals." He paused a moment as if to accentuate his next point. "And sometimes, you just have to keep pace and run the course. You think impatience will help me run that ultra-marathon?"

I imagined 50 miles of this. "You are crazier than I am." I laughed with whatever breath was left in me and shared a smile.

"Let's meet again tomorrow?"

"Race you there."

I juggled Amir and Zachi and the group trainings while the ILI still hibernated. Normally, I would be preparing for the first round of interviews as the program was circulating its advertisements. Some days I was grateful for the opportunity to focus on my health, but part of me remained restless about how I didn't know when the workshops would recommence. Some days I wondered if they ever would. Had I regained my bodily strength only to lose something else? I decided to see it as a dormant volcano. It would erupt at its proper time.

Time was another variable that troubled me. I hadn't been so concerned with it for most of my life. But now, it was my most precious resource—its value unmatched. In the metaphorical meeting room of my mind, I designed a little clock to complement the compass tool.

I envisioned this moment in time of my life as a new frontier. I was traversing rough terrain and foraging my way through uncharted territory, but with the sense that it was toward the promised land—a path *to*—and place where I would grow into my greatest potential. But barriers could still block my passage.

Having an appreciation for time, I would wait out this rainy season and this mighty river before me would weaken. I'd seize the opportunity to cross into the next chapter of my life. It was the direction I wanted to go, but I believed God wanted me to make camp here at its bank a little while longer.

It wasn't what I wanted. But it was what I needed. I believe it gave me time to heal, and to rebuild hope. Born from my sorrow would come the challenges that drew me higher. Maybe closer to my parents—surely, they would see me more clearly from their cushy, cloud couch in heaven.

Zachi and I kept training. Week after week, Zachi kept leading me farther and faster. And the Haifa night race grew closer.

The week before the race, I reached out to all my gym friends to see who may want to join me. I had printed out several t-shirts to dedicate my run to fighting cancer. I knew Zachi would run with me, and to my surprise everyone else was rallying to the cause with gusto.

It was the weekend before, and I wanted to run a full 5k before the big day—night rather.

"Zachi, please remind me to check if my shoes are untied when we are at the starting line. I'm counting on you, brother."

"Don't worry about the race just yet. This is an important training."

"And the others weren't?"

"Untie those legs of yours. Loosen up. This is going to be a good one."

As we stretched, I recalled how we had begun this past summer, the blazing sun oppressing our efforts, the salty sweat a sort of cleanse. The Dead Sea came to mind again. The lowest point on the earth, the most desolate body of water, would bring me to the highest point in my life.

We were already moving when I came back into the moment. We rounded the Haifa stadium like we were in the finals fighting for the championship. The cool late October winds felt like an invisible force trying to slow me down—but Zachi held pace with me. We lapped the gleaming silver dome again, and again, it was farther and faster than we had performed together before.

"Eeki, three miles!"

I was euphoric. "A little farther, c'mon!" I began to speed up.

Then Zachi nearly tripped me with his words. "Stop, right now!"

"What? Why?" My neck craned back as he slowed to a light jog and halted. I complied. "What's the problem?"

"Save that last little slice for the race, Eeki. I know you understand this."

He was right. Victory in the race would be that much sweeter.

The day arrived. And so had all my friends. I was grateful to have ordered too many shirts.

After losing two of the most important people in my life, having my gym family there brightened my soul. I solemnly held memories of my parents with me, but I still teased and joked while feeling all my hard work reaching its boiling point.

Zachi gave me a pat on the shoulder, and that sunny smile pronounced the beginning of the race. I imagined my parents at the end of the finish line, waiting for me. My knees felt good at first, but I realized the pain never completely left, though I was much stronger. Despite the illumination along the way, I felt the dark of night serve its symbolism like the delicately designed backdrop of a play. I was moving faster than I had during Zachi's trainings. He would probably remind me to keep an even pace, but I felt a sense of urgency—my breaths were like the ticking of a clock.

There were a great number of other participants, families, and friends. I imagined them all with their own life paths, but here, we had one destination, meaning something different to all of us. We were all part of a whole, despite how personalized this experience was. My gym mates were in my periphery, they would race ahead, and I would either fall back or I speed ahead—I didn't want them to steady their speed for my sake, but they did. We ran as a team. Each kilometer felt like it represented each of my greatest pains. Kilometer one: cancer. Kilometer 2: the loss of my ability to walk. Kilometer three: the loss of my mother. Kilometer 4: the loss of my father—what would be the fifth?

The clock kept ticking, my heart pounded as did my feet, and my friends were close behind, lined up together like birds in flight. I saw this shimmering light enshrining the finish line as it came into view. There were crowds cheering and clustering around it, but I was actually imagining the stars as my spectators, watching us all approach the end.

I took a quick sweeping glance behind me to see all my friends at my sides. It quickly became clear that the shimmering light was from my own teary eyes blurring the streetlights. We crossed the finish line, hands held up in excitement. I gazed at the sky and smiled, trying to hide my crying.

You see me, Mom and Dad?

I was ambushed by a rowdy bunch of my friends nearly knocking me over. We didn't stay too long; it was getting late, but I found myself up for quite some time that night, sitting on the balcony, my sweet cat Vicka watching me watch the night sky seemingly understanding what was going through my head.

My compass had guided me through one of the darkest times of my life, keeping me determined the whole way. As much pain as I had endured, inside and out, I kept moving forward, kept my ambitions and dreams alive, and went from crawling to running toward them—figuratively and literally. But I knew my toolbox, this arsenal to aid the rest of my journey, however much longer it would last here on this earth, was not yet complete.

The moon was set above the Mediterranean illuminating a space for my mind to explore. A cool breeze chilled my body, though the warmth and glow my friends had bestowed upon me this brilliantly bright evening was like a campfire. What helps someone through the night—the dark times in life—when you can't slumber until day—when you cannot see the finish line? Inspiration struck like an ember. With the dawn of the sun, a new day would come bringing with it another challenge—another truth and tool to live by. Another day to live.

Part IX

Tool: The Lighthouse

Alight, From One Candle to Another

As I had battled to live, life itself never became war. Nearly six years ago, the moment I chose to fight was the day I began the process of rebirth. When I got cancer, there was a noble cause to champion that became my becoming, but this sense of mission—while feeling divinely driven and mostly defined—still left me with a vague sense of thoughtlessness. There was a missing piece like when a word is on the tip of your tongue but just beyond your mind's grasp.

Like plucking the sweetest fruit after a long drought, I finally tasted what had been growing throughout these difficult times. My *mishpacha*, the family that had developed over the course of my adventures, had grown exponentially. It was one of those moments when the stars align, and you suddenly possess some wisdom—some truth in the palm of your hand.

All the tools of personal leadership had led me so far beyond what I thought were my limitations and drew out and developed the innate leader within myself. Through these inherited or chosen challenges came growth, shaped by the eight tools and lessons that led me to this point. Once my leadership burned brighter than ever, I found the world around me also glowing impossibly bright. It was near blinding—perhaps why it took some time to see—that the people surrounding me had become guiding lights for the doubtful and dark times that had relentlessly rocked my boat.

I have said the more I felt oppressed, the more determined I became. As it turned out, the more I embodied my personal leadership and refined those precious tools in my mind, the more my friends became family—there was a collective of people with personal dreads and dreams, and we all rallied to each other's causes. For once, I was *with* them rather than *for* them; we were open with each other, permitted to drive our relationships into deeper forms of understanding. That is an integral part of what family is. When you can mutually expose your vulnerability rather than hide behind a mask and falsify your image, you open yourself to countless possibilities.

I believe this second chance was a lesson God had bestowed upon me, predicated by my ability to teach and help others. Living for oneself will leave you alone, but providing inspiration, support, connection, and kindness—giving opportunities for others to demonstrate their personal leadership—endowed innumerable blessings on my life. It gave my life so much more meaning than what it would have been isolated, alone. Even so, that was only part of the equation.

I had been paying attention all along and saw many of my friends and family members also becoming beacons of light. I had long ago realized the importance of *giving and receiving, the* duality of nurturing connection between one and another. Like the sun, you can shine your light upon others. At the same time, you can reflect their light on your life as if you are the moon. I'm genuinely thrilled and emboldened when I see another person fulfilled and growing their own personal leadership. With shared success, everyone is elevated.

In a state of angst, you might find it hard to wish well for others when your own well-being is nil, but it is exactly this positive energy from the heart that the mind thrives on. When you push yourself to expose your inner leader, there is accountability not only to yourself but to others. *Be a lighthouse.* But if you are stuck in darkness, allow others to light your way.

Life is an ocean with much to explore, and stormy seas make for seasoned sailors. When you are adrift and lost, doubt has crashed upon you, or you're back on the rocks, a beacon of hope signals for you to move onward through the fog. While the compass had given me a newfound sense of direction and the ability to make active decisions based on my values, the lighthouse connected me to the greatest resource of all—the might of connection—the light of each person, each a galaxy of their own, creating an infinite universe larger than my life alone could ever be.

After the Haifa race under the stars with my new family, the ninth tool became clear as day. My lighthouse shining onto and encouraging others was my ultimate goal, and others shone their own light to help me reach that very same goal. This dynamic is like two candles burning brighter in unison versus each on their own.

2022 was a new year of new plans. I was itching for a novel challenge that would excite not only myself but the family I had grown. The loss of my mother and father left a black hole in my heart—the prior year was full of conflicting emotions and terrible highs and lows. But it still amazes me how much healing I had found through the leadership process and the precious people I now considered kin.

There was growing wisdom that spread in my body and being. In many cases during this time where I was supported by and supporting others, I came to understand and appreciate the value of a leadership persona more deeply. As a leader, you must have a calming and collected presence for the collective. It constitutes the reining in of one's emotions and being mindfully present with whatever challenge is at hand.

This keeps others focused on what is right in front of them as anxieties and doubts seek to distort and dissuade the person's perspective of their capability. You can't be the weakest link in a chain that binds you to others, and even more to the shared challenge and stakes. The standard must be set, but this responsibility can be a difficult burden for you to bear.

And understandably so. Part of it is that you don't have the license to weep and let your emotions run the show. You also can't go rogue and entirely cut out allies. As much as I had become more open with others, I also had to tame and contain my emotions when necessary. You may bolster yourself through others, but this doesn't occur through weakening or leaving them.

The most effective perspective is to focus on them as an ally, not your leader, so *a giving and receiving* may occur. The ones who support you go after you, for you, and behind you. There is something for them to obtain here too—the opportunity to do good and expand their own leadership.

And when you attend to others, even during times of great difficulty, you don't have as much time to dwell on your problems; instead, the solutions and pathways open ahead. I never wanted to make this book about what I did for this and that reason, or for this and that person, but—between these paragraphs, throughout my journey—I spent a great deal of time and resources nurturing the relationships and people around me. One of the greatest compliments someone shared with me was how inexhaustibly active I was in people's lives. Personal leadership receives a whole new dimension and greater definition when it also affects others. The goals were great—each challenging rope to climb was a thrill and chance to grow—but this cultivated garden of *mishpacha* made them glorious.

And so, there is a time and place for letting out raw emotion and the pressure that builds inside you. True to life, there is a time and place for everything. This burden of responsibility for your emotions and way of comporting yourself may come as a pain, even a pressure, but with personal leadership, you might find it most healing when you show its persona to others as it can inspire and encourage others to rise to the occasion. They will struggle with you not for you, and they will be as a brigade, so others can also be leaders. Set alight the candles of others and see how your flames burn ever brighter than being alone.

As with all things that happen to us, my guiding belief is that *everything is for the good*, and sometimes these things are too obvious to overlook. The international Cross Training Open Games would begin only a couple of months after the Haifa race. I had already been back to rigorous training with Amir. I felt strong despite the growing 24/7 pain I felt in my hands. They seemed to have a mind of their own. I could visualize them writhing and wringing, imploring me to notice them and how much they wanted to quit. The pain was random and almost whimsical. I would send back a vision of strong hands like when my father held my little ones, making me feel as if nothing could hurt me. Those were the hands I wanted.

Thinking of my father brought me joy, but also real pain. My parents were both gone. Some days I felt utterly broken.

I quickly learned how imperative it was to know the difference between venting and channeling. It was so much easier when I never shared anything about my struggles, preferring to deflect with humor or reverse roles completely, convincing my friends and family to talk about themselves instead. I never needed anyone or anything. Now that I was allowing people to get close to me, I sometimes didn't know when to stop kvetching. *Kvetching* is one of those amazing Yiddish words for chronic complaining. It is closely akin to venting because it is a self-absorbed way to release negative and self-pitying thoughts when they become too much to handle. Venting can feel cathartic. It's a helpful form of expression that can easily turn toxic.

Everything in moderation. Good friends, close relatives, or significant others can take some venting or even kvetching if you don't overdo it. However, the second lesson we learned about the second tool of accountability—wearing your uniform of personal leadership—ensures you don't toxify yourself to the point of having an internal-thought mutiny that turns you into a victim and alienates everyone else who is trying to help you. Be careful not to fall into victimhood and spew toxicity upon what you have carefully sewn. You are to become a lighthouse—not a black hole.

To channel is to focus and redirect your energies—this means composure. I met my sorrows with solutions. Anguishing days shrunk and turned to hours turned to minutes—the kind of moments I might wince or wish to weep at my sorrows. There were times I had to grieve, but these were secluded and selective moments that didn't overflow into my trainings or the various social spheres and responsibilities in my life. Instead, I tended to arrive ready to take a stand against the challenges at hand.

As I drove to my training with Amir, ready to request his support to join the international Cross Training Open Games, I recalled how after my mother's passing and a few months of the group's trainings at the Box, I was awarded trainee of the month. It was a precious honor that may have been the match that lit a fuse which burned and led me to the ninth tool. They awarded it to me during a painful time in the scope of this saga. They gave me a framed certificate that read:

A year ago, he got up out of a wheelchair, joined us after just a few months of rehab still healing from cancer, and just lost his mother, and he doesn't give up on training... a light for all of us.

Now I knew there was something in my journey that inspired others. I had been regularly posting highlights and milestones from my battle with cancer on social media, and what began as a humorous habit became a commitment. I wasn't just fighting for myself—I was fighting for the lessons, the buried truths found in hardship, for the sake of others who might make their lives more manageable and meaningful to themselves.

I saw Amir setting up the equipment as I had arrived a little early to warm up. While he had a great smile, it was seldom seen in full bloom—he had a serious game face while at the gym. It may have been because it was the most common place that I would see him, and most of his pictures on social media were of him there. I had been to his wedding, which certainly proved this suspicion: Amir celebrated this special day with such joy I had never seen on him before. I never saw him dance, but he did with his guests for hours. The smile on his face and shine in his eyes were a window to his heart. It was a privilege that day to see him with his insides out.

I was geared up and ready to go.

"Eeki, I'm going to go a little easier today on your hands."

"It's okay, they're feeling good right now."

"You didn't sound so sure earlier this week."

"All good, doc. You'll see."

His eyebrows seemed to smirk. I didn't know how he did it.

"Before we begin, I want to run something by you that I was thinking of doing," I asked.

"You're getting bored, are you?"

"Huh, you're a psychic now? I saw the games had a grouping for ages 55-59 for the competition. I want in."

Amir had gotten to know me so well that he anticipated me bringing this idea to him. He seemed to have already thought it through and was ready with an answer. Only it was not the one I wanted to hear.

"I don't think it is a good idea at all. Not to say you can't do it, but with your hands' condition lately, it is an injury risk—"

"I appreciate where you're coming from, but we've worked through worse."

"This wouldn't just be training though. It'll drive you crazy—I know you. Your fury and focus would be on breaking every boundary of your body. The only way I can explain it to you is it would be like driving a car with your brake lines cut. You don't need this. You're doing so well already."

It was a thoughtful take, and I didn't want to be thoughtless about this. But I would also be competing against people who also didn't have disabilities.

"I'll sleep on it," I conceded. "But if you know me—I'll be back with a vengeance on the subject."

"And I will be here, you can count on it."

It was awesome training that day, but with a few lifts I had to work around shooting pain in my hands—and Amir surely witnessed these. I wanted to be relentless but not reckless.

Later that day Yiftach came over, so I could consult him too. He was developing his rapidly growing studio in Kiryat Shmona and would come stay with me on weekends here in Haifa. Our brotherly antics were on full display during these stays—it was challenging to make sure he kept up with his chores. Certainly, a work in progress to keep the place clean.

We were eating dinner when I brought up my intentions. "Listen—"

"Listen? I'm not deaf, sometimes I just need to tune you out."

"Well, tune in right now. I got something very important I want your perspective on."

He put his fork down, exaggeratedly making eye-contact until he realized I was serious.

"I want to attend my age bracket in the international open games, but Amir doesn't think it is a good idea."

"I can appreciate where he is coming from, but—"

"Yes, I said the same thing—"

"Who doesn't listen?!" he jibed at my interruption.

I laughed. My little brother-by-bond had a reasonable point too. "Amir is totally against it, as I have said, so what do you think?"

"Yes, yes. I'm saying yes to doing it. I think you absolutely should."

"I appreciate the support," I said enthusiastically. "I have been training with him for a whole year, but you were also there for me when I was so much worse."

"You proved me wrong. See, when you challenged yourself, Eeki, the group came around to you; you were still focused on rehab the first two weeks with them and were worried you'd be left behind. But you struggled your way out, and it made you one of the leaders in the group. If you want this, your body will follow you—keep listening, wait—most importantly, you're an example to others. 2022 will be the year you show everybody if you can do it, they can do it. I believe you give people powers, strength, by showing people you can conquer challenges."

"Thank you. I love what you're saying here, and I certainly *will listen* to this, bro. Now, finish what is on your plate—I don't have any more room in my fridge."

I had followed up with Amir the next training. He seemed to be expecting some kind of speech from me. "Look, Amir, you can either take the fact you have disabilities and settle for this—letting it keep you from your goals, or you can fight it, bypass, and take control. I won't let this stop me."

His bravado shaped into a shy smile as if saying I know who you are—I know you can do this. He didn't have to say a word. "If you're going to go through with this, I'll support you.

I didn't want to let him down, let alone hear an *I told you so,* although I don't think he'd ever actually say that.

I knew I would need to be as disciplined as possible. I would honor my parents, family, friends, and all who might be able to source some inspiration from my efforts. With the right people, I could persevere. *The Soviets…*who better than them to understand me? I spoke that evening to each of my closest fellow trainees at the Cross Training studio and told them about my decision, asking what they thought of it. Well, one by one: Costa, Max, and Emanuel, all told me: *Yes. You can do this!*

Yet, a training partner of mine, Karina, might have been the most significant voice at this time. She had been on my side since day one when I joined Cross Training. I remembered how she approached me, the struggling newbie who was still rebuilding his strength, and offered to join me in the trainings. I hadn't completely realized it then, but she was a lighthouse that supported my voyage during those tidal times of ebbing and flowing difficulties. When she shared how excited she was for me to compete, it was a bolt of inspiration to succeed.

I did question what I was getting myself into the next day. I wanted to be cautious, not crazy, and the tension tore me at times in the few days leading up to our first training at the beginning of the following week. This was my next challenge, the compass pointed straight at it, it matched my plan, and I was fortified and gliding toward my goals—I chose this new fight and dared myself to do it while proudly wearing my leadership persona. I would be a lighthouse.

But there was a moment of necessary reflection. I flipped through the mental yearbook of 2021—that trialing and turbulent year—and a powerful perspective molded from my memories.

Zachi.

I had just seen him for New Years for a little gathering I threw together. One of the most unassuming individuals I know, I reflected about his leadership during our training for the Haifa race. Memories such as these can help serve as guide lights for staying on course toward your goals.

Thinking about the Haifa race was a spur in my *tuchus* as there wasn't much time before the first of three weeks of the Cross Training Open Games. Each week had its main exercises to compare to others internationally with judges to validate them. For each, you'd be allowed only one do-over, but that would be that—results locked and sealed. At this point, I had no idea how successful I'd be. I would perform the exercises at the Box, with a certified judge who would report the results that I reached: how many pull ups, how much weight I lifted on the barbell, and how many Burpees I performed. Obviously, not knowing what the other competitors did could be frustrating, like shooting in the dark, but I needed to focus on what I could do.

There was something special about the fact that I would never see anyone who shared space with me on the ranking charts. It allowed me to bring in my deepest mental and spiritual powers to control my body: I was competing against others, but in the purest way it would be between me and myself to know I could more than excel over my limitations. I could reach my aspirations and fulfill my commitments. I wondered, what stories were behind these names with no faces? My competitors may never come to know me, but I could say the same of my doubts—*the true opposition*—and that they were as unfamiliar with who I was becoming: a lighthouse.

It was only a couple of weeks until the first competition date arrived, but during this time there was quite a stir at the Box. There were upwards of 400 members total, and as close a community as it was—it still seemed there was always a new face to meet. The news seemed to spread about my entry into the games, where less familiar gym-goers would ask to share sessions. It was an explosive expansion of this social sphere, as if extended relatives were meeting for some great gathering.

I gleaned another truth as I discovered that my mission was a crucial part of my leadership. As much as I might've been a popular figure at the Box, it wasn't about me—it was about my cause and how my personal leadership was fighting for it. I fully had the intention to present myself to others with authenticity and accessibility—as a resource of encouragement and motivation, and as a source of inspiration and dedication. So, I could be what I needed in the darkest times of my life.

It was the day before the first ranked competition of three, and I decided to visit my parents' graves. Heavy gray clouds crowded the sun. It had been days since it last rained, and it looked like the sky would soon burst with tears. Before I got out of the car, I spent some time reflecting on my past.

As my life brightened, I did not forget how small my world once was. In my darkest times, I knew no light. I had to learn to see it within myself. The world could be so cruel; I often felt the trauma of my past was branded upon me, but it would not be my identity. It is a major part of why I sought to better the earth after I left it.

Naming my cancer *Sunshine*, this ironic personification of a deathly disease, was the catalyst for my personal salvation. The questions of believers and non-believers alike had plagued my mind—*what is this all for?* I had long wrestled with God's part in my life, but the circumstances we are given are meant to lead us to a deeper, ethereal essence of character—to self-creation.

In the darkest of experiences comes the greatest light. *Everything is for the good.* It was so hard to believe, and I often wondered how I might find this light in my own traumas—amongst the three men that had threatened to snuff my candle out when I was so very young. What positive purpose could this have had? I sought to solve this ridiculous riddle. The traumas of the past can cast long shadows into the future, but the brighter you burn, the smaller their reach.

Some call life a lottery, but it is a garden. What conditions, soil, and seeds are sewn are beyond our control, but the unique mission bestowed upon us—and the way our lives are nurtured—grows the greatest gifts. I was not a victim of circumstance. I was much more than a survivor. The inciting incident of my life that violated my youth—what would be the thread that tied it to its resolution all these years later?

When I finally left the car to visit my parents' graves, I looked up to the sky again and felt a sense of certainty. I wanted to share this feeling with them.

"Mama, Dad." I put my watering can down and watched the remaining dust wash off the dark, speckled gravestones. The eventual rain wouldn't reach here under their concrete canopy. "I came to ask for your blessing."

It was almost a year after each of their deaths. In Judaism, each anniversary of a person's passing is called a *yarzheit,* a special time to help elevate their souls even higher with the deeds we do. In the spirit of this, I dedicated my participation in the Cross Training Open Games in their honor.

"I know this is what you would expect of me… to fight for my life, but I know now, it is also to reach a promising future. It is not enough to survive. I was given my own hell to be forged in, and I hope, you see what a light I have become."

I felt together with them again. A light rain cleansed the dusty ground beyond the open wall. This downpour was straight from the heavens.

Warmth coated me like the golden light from my memories of our Shabbat mornings. I missed them so much. I wished I could crawl into this space in my mind like it was a magic portal, just so I could sit down with them once again on the old couch, or eat together without the keen awareness of how little time we have on this earth. "However much more time I have here, I plan to make the most of it. One day, when I see you both again, we'll have to share all our stories like we used to. And in case you were wondering, Bracha and I are mostly getting along." I cried a little while smiling. "I hope you are watching me tomorrow."

To see the light, and the inherent good in anything, the clouds must be parted to reveal the sun that is always there on even the darkest days. It requires we let go of sorrow to grab hold of serenity and the sense of hope that each difficulty will be redeemed by its realized purpose—however long it might take.

REMEMBER YOUR STRENGTH

The first ranked exercises arrived. Amir was ready for me; his most stoic face was a sight to see. I felt like I had involuntarily puffed my chest out as I approached the equipment setup.

There were 15 minutes on the clock. The more repetitions during this time, the higher the score. Every set included: three wall walks, 12 dumbbell snatches, and 15 box jump-overs. I stopped counting after the fifth set but kept on until I finished the seventh round and felt like I was going to faint. There were maybe 25 seconds left. Holding the dumbbells was like gripping molten metal.

"One more, Eeki!"

I felt like my brain was going to explode or my hands would crumble to dust—whichever came first.

"One more, Eeki!" Was I hearing double? I was lightheaded and felt like I was floating. The next thing I knew, I was being slapped on the back and crowded by not only Amir, but a bunch of fellow trainees, including The Soviets and many others, who were there specially to cheer me on. It was surreal. Memories flickered over my vision—the bodily decay while I was on chemo, my descent into a wheelchair, the loss of my parents, and the ILI shuttered due to Covid. It was a complex cluster of some of my most difficult years, which came together to lead me to this majestic moment. I pushed myself and did a few more reps!

Still, I was not quite as impressed as I thought I would be. There were two more challenges left, two more weeks to get ready, and I would need to prepare myself.

I checked the charts to see my current ranking. There were thousands of international competitors in my age group bracket of 55-59—so many people I was up against. My eyes widened seeing the rank by region category. In Asia, I was among the top ten. I checked the other profiles. As far as I could tell, these people were all bigger, stronger, and weren't sick. *I got two more rounds, two more weeks... I am going to make it to the top.*

I had taken a couple of days to rest, but I caught up with several other trainees at the next couple of training sessions. They were amazed I was even *in* the competition—never mind that I was succeeding in it. Everyone was younger and stronger than me, yet they still saw an inspiring light in my situation—my personal leadership was at work. I shared my results with my social media and came to discover more of this. It was a deep insight to see that your stories, no matter the metrics, can be impressive and meaningful—it is in your attitude and shown spirit that seemed to make the difference.

The first call I received was from Yiftach. The very same Yiftach who told me *yes, go do it.* "Eeki, you are the inspiration of my life. It is unbelievable what you can do against all odds. But one thing I want to emphasize, to make it clear, is that you will see that I was right, that you are an inspiration to others, and this is why it is worth competing—people that are younger, who have challenges, and troubles—they can have hope that there is a way through them."

"Are you calling me old?"

"Listen!"

"I *am.* I just find it unbelievable what you are saying. And take me seriously, this competition would not mean much without those that may derive this hope from me. It is a purpose that propels me. It pushes me to be better. Thank you, brother."

His words helped me feel that I was on the right path. While the compass gave me direction, it was with his affirming words that I knew the lighthouse gave me light and purpose, I would serve as a beacon to others, and this was what all the tools had led me to come to understand: *personal leadership lights and inspires others.*

The competition went on for two more weeks, and I became stronger and more motivated. Friends came to join me, doing the competition exercises alongside their own. I don't think I would have had this privilege without all the work to build a space for them in my life as a host and guest—a *giving and receiving*. It may seem too paradoxical. By following my true purpose, embedded within my soul, by following my personal leadership, I could give more to others, and receive as much from them. There is a personal path and journey to partake in—and it has been through the tools that brought me my purpose.

The second week, I improved my position on the chart, but I wasn't satisfied—there would be one more chance to max out.

I walked into the third challenge with a face more solemn than Amir's.

Amir wasn't sure I read the last challenge's details before I came (which of course I did!) since the third challenge was the toughest of all. It was the same concept: get as many sets and reps as possible, repeating them again and again. It would include dozens of bar pull-ups and jump-roping, and each round concluded with dozens of thrusters (rising from a bending, squat position to a full stand while pushing a loaded barbel in one movement from the shoulders above your head). I had 12 minutes this time. It truly deserved the name competitors called it: "an exercise from hell." Amir was there to push me a little more and remind me of how much further I could go—he could see the reps left in me when I could not. It was like a spotlight he shined in my mind—*it was there.*

And I realized it myself. There was more effort that hadn't been unleashed. He immediately saw I wasn't thrilled with my performance and kept his excitement subdued. There was another chance to score higher by repeating the challenge after three days, but only one more try.

I also saw it as an opportunity to unite my friends. I invited a couple dozen to support me. This time, it felt like I was producing a monsoon of sweat, particularly with the bar pullups, but I knew my mind was better prepared for the most difficult exercise this go-around—the thruster. The pain in my hands is a constant presence, but that day it was really wanting to take center stage. I was in agony—it was terrible—but I could not unsee the potential Amir showed me on my first attempt just a few days earlier. This was my chance to unleash it.

With my last rep, I nearly collapsed. The numbers were jumbled in my head—all effort was focused on engaging my body and willing it to do what I wanted. There were a few blurry moments of catching my breath. The judge told me my numbers, and I could hardly believe it. I managed to do 205 reps altogether out of a maximum of 216!

I fought against any excuses for myself when it came to the challenges that stood in my way to compete, still I appreciated what these numbers meant to me, knowing I had broken my own boundaries. My friends were cheering, and I felt stunned knowing that I competed against all odds. I knew I would place well on the charts—I knew I would make my parents proud—but I hoped the most that this would touch the hearts of those around me.

The results would come within the next few days, but during this time I knew that there would soon be an emotional void as I reflected on what I would do after this. It wasn't a sad or scary feeling, but I would need to have something in place—something next—something more. This wasn't it. This wasn't the big *the end*.

The ILI had been dormant for two years now due to the Covid. It wasn't dead and it wasn't on life support, but it still needed a revival. As much as I had personally evolved, there was still something more for the organization to become. When I considered the impact, I wished to leave behind, I now deeply understood it was to be able to show people life is not only about survival, but that there is a path for you to follow, and it is *only you* who sees where it leads. Who you are meant to become, and whoever is meant to be there, will be.

Paths of Change would be the name of my new workshop. The seed of this creation had been planted as I awaited the results. A few days later, I was flailing a cat toy around Vicka when the results came in. I placed fourth on the chart in Asia and ranked 180 globally. This was an amazing personal victory for me. It was a blissful moment, like when I had reached the summit of Solheimajokull, the glacier in Iceland. I shouted and bounced in my seat while Vicka watched me wide-eyed and seemingly annoyed. If I could have given her a high five, I would have, but instead, I chose wiser and immediately began reaching out to share the news.

The first person I called was none other than Dr. Amir Onn.

"...Dr. Onn, would you have ever believed I would compete and do so well in such a thing?"

"Of course. You know I did from the beginning. Remember one thing I had said, when you set goals, you will always beat cancer—it won't come back. Even more, you have outgrown so many limitations with the mentality you have. Look. I am a man of science, but there is much we still don't understand—and I do know your mind has so much control over the limits we set and choices we make. The moment you believe you can't is the moment you really can't."

I took a moment to absorb his words. We spoke for a few minutes accounting for the trials and tribulations that led me here. He was always there to help me steer my ship through the most terrifying storms. Before the end of the call, Dr. Onn had a request.

"Eeki, would you be willing to meet a few doctors from the States that are doing their residency here? I am leading their program as they are training to become oncologists. I would love them to hear your story about—"

"You seriously have to ask? I will absolutely do it. You got it."

He laughed. "Well, I was never the kind of doctor to just *tell* you what to do. Thank you.

You never know how far your inspiration might reach."

The words echoed into the few weeks ahead. I began to work on the new ILI workshop based on the lessons and tools I had learned so far. There was a tank full of inspiration, but I knew what Dr. Onn meant. We really don't know the impact we may have on others if we don't expose ourselves to them. Maybe my story would intrigue those doctors. Maybe there would be a patient whose life might be better lit if hope was infused into them.

And this brings me to one of the most fundamental points of personal leadership.

Whether you may have considered it or not by now, hope has not been an incredibly prominent theme and concept in the process and journey of my life. It was not nonexistent, but it certainly was not at the forefront of my mind.

Hope is much like the sun. It can brighten even the darkest of places in our lives. It can sustain us beyond our limits, into territories we typically may not survive. When atomic bombs are detonated and flatten our lives, hope can be the difference between life and death. I had certainly hoped I would have the chance to live beyond the doctor's death sentences—four of them, remember? But hope didn't cure my past trauma, but it did alter my attitude toward life. Hoping to live another day was not a way to live. It is not enough to just survive this world, but I still led a meaningful and moderately successful life despite this deeply rooted mentality. Still, there was much I hoped to become and to give.

Who would ever hope to have cancer—a big slap in the face that would become a battle for redemption—for the promise to reach my full potential? I learned to love the person I was growing into and not miss the one I grew away from. It was the ugliest packaging to the most beautiful gift. The essence of this life lesson was smothered in dirt and darkness, and it was up to me to reveal it. I looked forward to the future, not back to my past fearing how far I'd fall. I saw how much farther there was to climb up the ladder. I knew each day must be a rung to something more and higher.

So, there is a warning about hope. You can imagine an outcome, a future, a desire, and hope can give you the strength to get there. But there is also false hope.

Stare too long at the sun and it can blind you.

What you hope for may keep you from your path. Instead of reaching for the sun, this hope must come from within like a candle, lit in the cavernous dark of your life. It is ever present, sustained in the moment, and not found in a light source that may be lightyears away.

The reality is that you may miss hidden pathways, you might ignore the signs, you might unsee what you don't wish to know—and as hope drives you further and further toward the longing of your hearts, the object of your mind's eye—your soul may suffer the consequences. As much as you focus on the relationship and function of the mind and heart, they are merely tools of your soul—your higher self—whatever you may label this natural, core essence to your being. Sometimes the less palatable tastes of life are more nurturing to your spirit.

Hope can overcome our greatest fears, but it is important to shine light on those fears and make sure they are not the things you need.

Maybe your business is meant to sink and open a new path. Maybe your marriage has already met its end, but you still linger while the road ahead awaits. Maybe there is something else meant for you—we have free will to fight, but the universe, God, or whoever you might consider your source, often bestows lessons for our souls' development—the packaging may surprise or repulse us. These lessons are a gift, perhaps unwanted, but needed.

Let hope brighten and guide your way, but never let false hope blind you. The lighthouse tool insists that hope is wielded toward not what you want, but what you need, and what is one of the most powerful forces in the universe can very well be what destroys you.

Shine as a Sun
and Become like a Moon

While I was working away on *Paths of Change*, I was still working out and feeling the healthiest in my life despite the persistent pain in my hands. I kept my grip on the rope, pulling myself higher and closer to my goals. I had begun circulating calls about programming, setting up a new headquarters in the city of Ashkelon, and even an opportunity to expand our programs in Vietnam had come onto my radar. I was excited to be recruiting students again soon. All of these were hopes, but tempered by determination, and I knew God was proudly watching me take strides into my future.

It was only a few weeks after the competition that I faced another challenge, but this one was not planned, and would knock the wind out of me. I was returning home from an exhausting workout, planning to see my close friends Roi and Adi that evening. While in my apartment working on *Paths of Change* and entertaining Vicka, I felt especially fatigued and began coughing. She gazed at me with what I thought was a peculiar look—then, a morbid thought shouted in my mind like someone yelling fire in a movie theater. *Is it the cancer?* It was a ridiculous, intrusive thought, but I resisted giving it any credence. The Soviets and I had been planning to meet that weekend, but something told me I might need to reschedule—certainly with Roi and Adi that night.

I had texted Roi about postponing our dinner that night, but he called me instead. It was futile to hold back my coughs.

"Eeki, are you sick?" It was like an echo from that past. I nearly checked the phone to see if it was Judah who had called me like a flashback. Would Garik come barging into my apartment to ship me off to the doctor? I sure missed seeing them more often.

"No, not sick. Just pushed myself a little too hard at the Box, and my hands are bothering me." I could hear Adi in the background—it sounded like worry—and I worried this would spread like its own anxious infection. "Tell Dr. Adi (she was a dentist after all) that I am fine. Say hello to the kids, Uncle Eeki will visit soon enough."

"Of course, but don't hesitate to call if you need anything."

Was I slipping into old behaviors? *Quit it!* Doubts had become more like mindless traffic that I zipped around when the thoughts arrived, yet sometimes a simple question would make them yield to me. *Are you racing to conclusions?*

But after 24 hours of coughing, the next day the question of whether something was really wrong could not be avoided.

I was sick. That's okay. People get sick. Just because I had cancer didn't mean I needed to freak out whenever my immune system had a mood swing.

I group texted the Soviets to let them know we'd have to reschedule our gathering. The cough had worsened, and so did my worries. Had the ghost of *Sunshine* come to possess me?

Costa called not even a few moments later. "What's the problem, Eeki?"

"Got a cough and a mild fever. Just a cold."

"But it is April!" We both paused. "Have you taken a Covid test?"

It hadn't really occurred to me yet. "Not yet, but I don't want to go out and get anyone sick in case I'm carrying the virus. I am staying in anyway."

"I'll drop one off and come check on you."

"No, what are you a doctor now, Costa? Kidding… it would be a big help, but just leave it by the door. I don't want to get you sick."

It wasn't long before Costa knocked. I had let Emanuel and Max know he was helping me. There was a great spike of suspense as I considered the possibility of having Covid. Fear grew like cancer. Despite my greater health, my lungs were still working hard to recover.

"I'll see you later, Costa, thank you! Don't wait for the results. I'll text you." I heard a muffled reply behind the door. I'd have to get him something special to drink for our next gathering. What a friend.

Positive. Well, maybe it wouldn't be that bad. After all, I was vaccinated so maybe it'll make it an easy journey? I texted Costa the news.

What meds can I get you?

All good, I really appreciate it. We'll see how it develops.

It's okay, I am still waiting down here in my car.

What? Go home. It's okay! Don't you have other plans?

We quipped back and forth, and my dear friend brought a little care package.

A few hours later, my voice sounded like shoveling gravel as my cough worsened. Roi and Adi called me again. I knew if they heard me speak, they'd be over concerning themselves with what wasn't much of an issue— we could be a little pushy with each other if you hadn't noticed already, and sometimes it became almost a little game.

"Eeki? Hello?"

I had a coughing fit before I could greet him on the phone.

"You sound terrible. This doesn't seem like a little cold."

"Tested positive for Covid. It wasn't this bad a few hours ago."

I could hear Roi speaking to Adi on the other end of the phone. "Do you have a ventilator?" She took over the call. "Eeki, I have a ventilator from my clinic you can use. Roi can bring it by tomorrow. Do you know how to use one?

"I believe so."

"I can walk you through if you need. Just try and get some rest, and he'll drop it off."

I struggled to stay asleep for more than an hour at a time. My cough kept me up most of the night. It was around eight o'clock in the morning when I finally got up—later than usual. I saw a couple of missed calls from a couple of hours earlier. Roi had tried reaching me.

He also sent a text telling me to look outside my door. I was surprised he came so early, which must've been before getting his kids to school and then to work.

My body felt very weak. I found the ventilator on my doormat. I called Adi to see how to work it, and for the next 24 hours, I would be mostly bed ridden breathing through it.

The next morning, I felt like my chest was shrinking and stuck. At this point, my fears overtook me. I noticed as well that I was afraid to tell my friends—it was almost as if it would make this threat to my life even more real. At last, I connected the dots to this long thread of lessons. I needed to face this. After all I had been through, I felt the urge to believe there would be less adversity as if I had gotten some bad bank of karma bankrupt and out of my system. My friends were already there for me. It was time for me to show up. It felt like a storm loomed ahead.

By this point, everyone was telling me to go to the hospital, but I refused. I didn't want to, believing there could be a better way to treat the virus without having to lie in a bed and not being in charge of its course. I also wanted to fight it with my own strength, knowing that it is my immune system that needs to answer to this challenge, and I've already proven that I can strengthen it with more than simply medications, but by the power of my will—my mental determination.

I called Dr. Onn to get his opinion.

"This is crazy! Why are you only telling me this now? Why are you taking this responsibility? You are not a doctor."

"Because I didn't think it would get this bad. A lot of people were saying the first few hours are the worst."

"This is quite the opposite. It *is* getting worse. We'll get you to the hospital in Haifa."

We argued a bit over me going. Eventually, Dr. Onn relented. His tone changed. "I will try my best to get you some medicine due to your history with cancer, but if I can't get the request approved, you're going to the hospital."

"Agreed."

He called the Ministry of Health and submitted a request for a lifesaving medication. It wasn't easy to get—they typically didn't give the medication to just anyone because it was one of those medications that makes one feel like a storm has swept through one's body. We had to schedule a virtual meeting with a committee to get the order approved. Dr. Onn was fighting for this—for me—which was a beacon of light on a very dark night. My condition had kept steady through a sea of symptoms, but it was my thoughts that kept me afloat. There was some hidden light in the situation for me to reveal…

In the middle of the night, I got up and went to my balcony. There was a mellow lunar glow that sifted its way through the dark blanket of clouds in the sky. Still, it cast itself along the Mediterranean, reminding me of the moments with my father in Cyprus—the moment I shared the news about my diagnosis. I had finally told him the news when I was ready, believing he might never be. I was protecting him from it, and as much as I tried to hide it from my mother, of course she knew it too.

While I think it is more common that people are willing to share their challenges, there is a balance between this and not sharing anything at all. As much as I worked on not hiding my sorrows and fears, I would still show resolve and not let it flood the lives of my friends and family. The lighthouse tool is about guiding and inspiring others, but it is also to keep each other from crashing into the rocks. It may be subtle, but there is a mighty difference when your light is out. It is an unwelcoming aura and can even disorient those around you.

Throughout all these trials, I kept my ability to smile. While it may have felt like a façade at times, I knew there was a strength in it. I began to see that the best of both worlds could be achieved. To see everyone's leadership illuminate each other created what was as beautiful as a starry night over a shining sea.

A representative from the Ministry of Health called me early the next morning, approving my prescription for the medicine.

"Where do I get it?"

"You don't get it. We'll send it to you."

I had considered a little snark might be necessary, but I gave a simple "thank you."

Because it was Shabbat, a lot of places were closed, and everything seemed to move more slowly. I worried this would impact the time it would take for me to actually take it. My condition had not improved, and I was still struggling to breathe.

By noon, a cab came to drop it off.

I went to sleep that night knowing tomorrow would be better. I was absolutely relieved—both physically and mentally. I was still coughing and weakened, so I decided to spend the week recovering. My friends insisted on bringing me so much food. I was afraid I would lose all my progress with fitness. If I ever were to go hungry, maybe I'd fake sick to get fed. It was a blessing baked into the character and culture of us. I think it was a relief for everyone to see me well again despite the distance of the door standing between us while I quarantined. Especially for Roi and Adi as well as the Soviets contacting me every two hours asking *what's going on?*

Following my week of recovery, I returned to the studio, and my gym mates and I made an impromptu gathering. We celebrated, toasting to this, that, and whatever we could raise a glass to for each other. What a way to raise our spirits!

The next day, Dr. Onn called.

"Eeki, have you made a full recovery?"

"Amir," I seldom used his first name. "I have been recovering for six years now, but I think the better word is discovering."

"I understand. So, would you be willing to share your findings with those doctors I had mentioned? They are here and wondering when they might have the chance to speak with you."

"I can be there tomorrow or any time this week. You tell me."

He laughed. "Be here at ten sharp."

"Yes, sir!"

The next morning, I was spending the drive wondering what I might say to them. What might my story mean, what insights might it offer? I would be but one person who had cancer they met, and they would surely be meeting many in their futures. I rehearsed in my head a few key sentences, wondering what questions they might have, and pondered what my story might mean to the lives of their patients.

Dr. Onn was chatting with a couple of doctors, all in their white coats. I could see he was excited about overseeing their rotation. Maybe he saw himself as a teacher too. And I would come to learn just this—Amir would become a professor. I think there was something we learned from each other on this journey; he had to serve as a lighthouse himself, someone seasoned in what many or their loved ones have tragically faced in their lives.

I gave him a hug and was immediately introduced to the doctors. There wasn't enough room in Dr. Onn's office, so we found the lounge and shuffled ourselves around in a circle.

I told them who I was and about the ILI. I explained how getting cancer was a wakeup call to take charge of my life and lead it in the most fulfilling and purposeful way. I got a few raised eyebrows when I mentioned the four doctors telling me the same prognosis, of course noting the fourth at least had the idea of pursuing my childhood dream of hiking a glacier in Iceland and climbing a mountain—which still lingered in my heart.

These doctors were listening beat for beat, hearing how I used the power of my mind, my attitude, and my developed tools—personal leadership—to overcome my battle with cancer, and the successive challenges I created and was given. It was important they understood that these mental tools and the associated lessons were the very things that led me beyond six months and into six years—still running into my future with aspirations and an ever-evolving version of myself.

They wouldn't let me leave without a barrage of questions. I spent more time answering questions than sharing the story itself. I insisted that Dr. Onn and I focused on my mentality at the core of the war, and in each battle used whatever means we had available. The medications, the treatments—these were all useless without the attitude, directions, and decisions that I had to take on this tumultuous journey.

I was accustomed to speaking engagements, but I found myself a little winded by this one. My passion was unleashed, and I believe that there was a gift I could give them, to pass on, that might help someone somewhere choose to fight for their life.

On the drive home, I was struck by an idea like a lightning bolt. There was someone I had to call that was there at the very beginning.

"Eyal, hey, how are you?"

"I am breathing, and the sun is shining. All is good, my dear friend. Where are you?"

"Just came out the hospital."

"Something happen?"

"No, in fact, I got good news for you. I just had a visit with a bunch of oncologists, sharing my experiences, and how I overcame cancer, amongst everything else—"

"That's great, I think you should share your experiences."

"No, that is not it. This is about ILI—look, this was what was going through my head while I was talking to them—that there was a phone call which needed to be made. Six years ago, after the four doctors told me I was going to die, I called you, remember?"

"Of course, I do."

"Now, *I was telling them* that I was living, so I am calling you again."

"Yes, this is why I knew you were going to be victorious from the get-go. I came to respect and have known your mental prowess and the fight within you." He paused. "So, what now? I suspect there is something you're building up to."

"The ILI is coming back. I have a new workshop, and we got the old ones. Let's get it back up and running. And yes, you know me—I have one more challenge… I am going to finally climb the mountain. I am not going to get four noes from Snæfellsjökull!"

"Eeki, you lead, and everything else will follow."

"That's just it, though—this is an analogy you gave me yourself—a leader is a lighthouse. I lead, so others may too find their way. *This…* is the way."

Part X

Tool: The Mirror

A PROMISE FULFILLED

E ven under layers and doubled-up socks, I shivered in the cabin while I sat on my bed gazing out the window through a thick, foreboding fog. A colossal shape pointed toward the heavens in the distance. There was no sunshine, and an all-encompassing rain sought to drown out the sound from eight other travelers that had accompanied me to this small fishing village with a population of about thirty. *It is going to be a big day.*

At what felt like the edge of the earth on an Icelandic peninsula, Arnarstapi was having a bit of a cold snap, but only according to me. Israelis are desert people not totally accustomed to such a chill. The view of the road from my left window led to a harbor with boats bobbing in the deep blue waters. I was in awe. The Icelanders here came about 1,000 years ago to a stormy, cold, yet majestic place. Hardy and resilient, you couldn't help but be inspired. It was a land without comforts, but they made it comfortable. I felt it wrong to consider them survivalists. Some part of me felt like I could be one of them, one of those brave, courageous Icelanders going out to sea and working hard to reestablish and live their lives.

The harbor looked as if it had two hands cradling its boats. It was deceptively peaceful in this remote village. But I knew it was the bearer of extremes. This serene place must have had a history of struggle to have warranted what looked like God's reward.

A few years ago, I was supposed to be here, but I wasn't strong enough. I thought about how disappointed I was and concerned that I would never regain my strength. I was physically ready during my second trip a year ago, but the forces of nature had other plans; our guide canceled the hike due to the weather. *Life happens.* But I chose to believe something greater would come of this.

I wondered: *How did I get here?* It was a question I had asked myself after my diagnosis and every year since then, but there was a different answer this time, and it would be found at the top of Snæfellsjökull.

When one challenge is not met, it doesn't mean you won't be successful in the next one. This was a tough lesson for me to learn. It is important to understand that whether it's a failed business, a marriage's demise, a loss, or a dead dream, you've obtained an opportunity to show that your life is about growth—a greater purpose. What wisdom you've learned are life's greatest treasures.

Since beating cancer, there has been ceaseless trouble in my nerves. I like to think that, despite the writhing pain that burns within my hands, my grip on life has never wavered. Before conceding that my challenges would always be replaced with more, I needed to examine the big picture to make sense of my struggle. I concluded that life's ups and downs balance each other, and the momentum from these challenges elevate you higher than where you have been. When you've plateaued, it often may take a descent to begin the next climb. As long as you are alive, there will always be an option to improve, to find a new challenge. It is always a choice—a choice to *live* your life.

What is the purpose of my life? How do I make the most of it? These were difficult thoughts to ponder. You must lead your way toward your purpose and potential to receive a fulfilled, accomplished life despite your doubts and despair. The weight you carry in your heart can be the flaming forge to form the tools of your mind that refines and guides your soul to growth. Perhaps, calling my cancer, *Sunshine*, was symbolic of my will to grow toward the sun—to fight against nature's forces and demonstrate my tenacity.

And so, when the volcano of your life erupts, meaning any unexpected challenge that you perceive to be beyond your ability to cope, you might feel devastated. Feeling overwhelmed and thinking that a situation is permanent is very human. You often can't think beyond the feelings, but no feeling lasts forever because you are always moving forward with new challenges and experiences. When you find yourself in a devastating situation, you can reframe it by using your creativity and painting a new perspective—a new reality. You may find that this temporary, awful situation has provided the most fertile soil to grow.

With these thoughts running through my mind, I stood and remembered my personal declaration to fight for my life back in Sderot, where it all began. That was the first step toward this very day; this very *me*.

◆ ◆ ◆

"Guys! It's time for breakfast!" My voice was so loud that I could imagine the neighbors in the adjacent house confused and running to their table.

I felt a rush in my chest. I was so energized and anxious rallying my friends to get ready.

After all, this was going to be one of the most important days of my life.

I was ready for the ultimate challenge. It was Summer of 2022, just three years after I was wheelchair-bound—and here I was taking on the King of the Mountains.

Everybody rushed to the table, still in their sleepwear. Yiftach's eyes surveyed the delicious spread I had helped prepare for everyone. "Eeki, I swear I thought the volcano erupted. You must've woken the whole village!"

"That was for you! Everyone else was already awake."

These seven strong and motivated men and one woman, who was determined to match their strength, crowded the table like a bunch of hungry Vikings. They were soon to become—or already were—my closest friends.

I looked at each one of them as they were chatting around the table, trying to determine their roles for this day. Their words and the sounds of utensils served as a bit of a drum beat as my philosophical thoughts intensified. Breakfast would be our only actual "meal" for the day before embarking on our journey to mount the ruthless ice-and-snow-covered volcano.

Yiftach would be my "bodyguard," willing to give his life to save us all if anything dangerous threatened our journey.

Belihun: he'd take charge of documenting the great moments of the climb. Yes, he could read my emotions so intuitively.

Yan: he'd be there to offer a strong hand whenever it got tough.

Zachi: he would help me keep pace.

As for Ira, being the only female among a bunch of tough men, she was tough as stone for sure. She consulted with me before taking the journey with us: Despite my concerns, I encouraged her to face the difficulties because this was an opportunity for her to grow personal leadership. She would serve as an inspiration for us today, overcoming all doubts troubling her mind.

And then there was the "Trio," beginning with Avishai whom I felt like an older brother to (It might've been nice to be the younger brother for a change, but I was too old for that!). His shy smile and compassion would be a boon to the team.

Also, Oded, who was always too tough on himself, and I struggled to persuade him to cut himself some slack. When he did, his beautiful character would burst out like steam spouting from a hot tea kettle.

Finally, there was Iko. Go ahead and imagine a group going on an exciting journey where there was Eeki and Iko—the banter born from this would drive us all nuts.

Eeki!

What?!

No, I meant Iko! Hilarious. Iko was strong-minded and fit for challenges. I knew this magical climb would strengthen him no less than it would to me.

Watching this fine group of warriors surrounding me was like living in a dream. How did I gather such a wonderful, incredible team who all trusted me in taking them for what could be a once-in-a-lifetime trip? And how challenging would be it for me, the old guy.

Geez, I'm older than all of them by at least twenty years. What was I thinking?

But I knew that I was not going to disappoint any of them. I would be as strong as they were on our climb of Snæfellsjökull. After all, I knew that it was all in my head: *When my mind says go, the body follows.*

With all these metaphorical "uniforms" laid out for the team, I needed to make sure I properly donned mine. I dragged them all here for this crazy climb, so I would need to project leadership for them. I couldn't passively participate, and I would need to push myself more than ever. All the values I had adopted and developed would need to be demonstrated. Finally, I would be fully accountable for all of this.

After finishing breakfast, we were all in a good mood, except that electrical anxiety still coursed through my veins. We had about four to five hours until our climb.

We had gotten geared up to leave. Belihun was readying his camera as we would have some time to sightsee. As we gathered in the foyer, everyone seemed anxious. Zachi finished tying his boots. "Did you guys see the mountain this morning? It was covered in fog."

Yan peeked out the window. "The king knows we're coming to take his throne!"

Ira laughed. "Get ready to accept your new queen."

Zachi smiled along with Avishai.

Iko, Yiftach, and Belihun were discussing what they wanted to see before the climb. We hadn't gotten to tour the village, so I knew there would be time for everyone to get their heads together. Perhaps these few hours would be a sort of warmup. I wanted to watch the waterfalls which Iceland is rich with; the result of the melting ice on Snæfellsjökull. I thought it would provide a connection to the mountain to drink from its waters before hiking and climbing it.

As we came out of the house, I noticed the fog was slowly dissipating with spots of sun poking its fingers through. It was like an ebb and flow of what seemed like certainty versus doubt, like a dramatic dance above the rippling waters of the vast Atlantic Ocean surrounding the island. With the sun's blue-hued rays on its waves, it warmed its freezing temperatures and my heart. It was a fantastic contrast to the mountain behind us and the hardened rocky landscape between.

The village was cold and quaint, perhaps even cozy, except this feeling was surely tempered by the hard work it must have taken to keep it that way. Being so small, there wasn't too much to see, so after about a half hour, we took a ride to visit some waterfalls and the rock arcs that folded and reached into the ocean. It felt like the edge of the earth.

After a short visit to the village, we drove to our first destination. Rocks crunched under the car as we stopped at a small valley in between a few waterfalls. None of them were notably high, but the way the water fell from the top of the hills to the ground was like music refreshing our souls. Deep in my heart I knew the task ahead would require me to be at my best, and the visit to the waterfalls would provide me with the tranquility I needed. Everyone took a taste, laughing as the ice-cold water soaked our faces and even hair. I imagined myself like one of the first inhabitants of Iceland, drinking what he thought would be holy water while praying for his mythical gods to help him and bless his coming conquests of the island. *God be with me.*

There was another spot of waterfalls at our third and final stop before we readied for our climb. Everyone hopped out of the cars, but I told them I would catch up soon. My mind began to drift as I watched the group from a distance: my friends who had already spent seven days in this magical land of ice and fire. We had hiked almost every day, in tough terrain with windy conditions, but this... this would be the grand finale and ultimate goal: to summit Snæfellsjökull.

The sky was a majestic backdrop. *Look at yourself. You're 58 and your life could have ended six years ago from cancer. Within all those years, there was always a struggle—a test for if you wanted to stay alive or not.*

Memories flooded in like overstuffed bookshelves in a library. *How did I make it this far?*

I looked back at all the challenges and realized how often I forgot how many times I "won." Struggles and successes in high school, when I got wounded in the military, the abuse... I managed to pull out distant memories that reminded me how resourceful and resilient I could be for any and all challenges in my life.

While everyone was enjoying the waterfall, I was looking at the smokey-blue horizon and seeing all those memories like a movie of my life projected against it. The expression recurred: *everything is for the good*—all my defeats-turned-victories, my triumphs, the personal growth throughout it all—prepared me for today.

I was now in a different section of my mental library. It was all too easy to forget your wins and how many times things worked out in the end, but even more was how I made this so. Maybe things didn't quite resolve as I thought they would, but still I prevailed.

But even after all this, I couldn't help but wonder, *where is my life taking me?* In the fog, I saw my future was about lighting up others. I would continue to develop my own personal leadership and provide others with the opportunities and tools to do the same.

My daydream burst like a bubble. "Wow, why did you stay in the car? You didn't want to see the waterfalls!?" Avishai exclaimed. Everyone else's expression seemed to reflect the question as they climbed into their seats.

"It's okay. I just rowed down the river of my life."

"Really got lost in thought, didn't you, Eeki?" Zachi said as he buckled in.

"Was just meditating before our big climb. Belihun must've taken some pictures that I could see later. It's all good. Everything is for the good—even the bad."

"Come back to earth, Eeki." Ira said.

I laughed. "We need to get back to the house. We have only two hours before we need to leave in the afternoon for our 'Midnight Hike.' Remember, I chose this special option from the different offers the hiking company had because we'll get to see the sun when we reach the summit. Anyway, we'll have some sandwiches and protein bars—nothing too heavy. We'll all take a short rest and then get ready." I could see the humor quickly clouded like vapor in a mirror as everyone seemed to appreciate how soon we would be taking our first steps at the foot of the mountain. Yiftach quickly lightened the mood, and the ride back was as noisy as one can imagine. Loud banter, laughter, excitement in the air—we all needed it.

Back at the house, we gathered ourselves and performed our final preparations for the climb. It was more about mental readiness than anything else, though Yiftach was fooling around with Belihun—taking too long to get their things ready—but this aside, we had an eight-hour journey, a midnight mountain mission to see the sun, Iceland's famous "polar day" with the greatest possible view. I firmly reminded everyone to get a light nap...

...and in the blink of an eye it was almost 3:00 p.m. When I woke up everybody, I told them to get dressed and be ready as we needed to be at the hiker's hut where the two guides were waiting for us. It was just a short walk, and to my misery, the fog came rolling back even thicker than the morning. *Very soon we're not even going to see the peak of the mountain...*

I wondered if my expectations were higher than the mountain itself. I wasn't going to change my mind about the importance of this, but worried the weather would. It worsened throughout the day, and I wasn't so sure it would improve, but this time we weren't going to be denied the chance to climb Snæfellsjökull. Not again.

I realized there were a lot of doubts piling on like layers of snow, slowly burying and bleaching out the colorful excitement that carried throughout the day. I knew I needed to ground myself into a more concrete perspective for myself to remain focused, but as much as for my friends. In all my morning introspection, I had begun to feel disoriented just by high noon, wondering what I had dragged this rowdy bunch into. Perhaps, I was imagining what would go wrong, borrowing trouble from the future that would collect anxious interest as my worries grew. I needed a *blueprint* to create a solid foundation for the challenge ahead.

I took an accounting of who was with me, my allies, and considered their strengths again. I would need to stop doubting myself and my motivations. I had made it this far, and there was no sense creating questions that sought to make nonsense. I knew what attitude to take, I knew this was something I had dreamed of all my life, and that it would be one of my crowning personal achievements. It occurred to me how special it was to have this opportunity later in life as a means to show me how capable I was despite my age and condition.

The truth is, the pain in my knees and hands never went away. It is a constant in my life, like a fierce force to press against. In some ways, it keeps me activated. I wish I could will it away, but I know I can only twist it to my advantage until some treatment is found for it, maybe in my lifetime. The battle plan for this climb was built on every single day back to my diagnosis. This was another rung to the ladder, except I felt like it would peak and then plateau—I would need to find something else to climb, something higher after this. My mind stopped wavering and wandering when I surveyed all the values, allies, and tools at my disposal. The blueprint for success was as concrete as it could be.

One of the powerful purposes of the battle blueprint is establishing and directing *intention* toward your goal and purpose. It affords you flexibility when the unexpected happens, yet you remain rallied with those on your team, and sturdy with your convictions.

❖ ❖ ❖

As we entered the hut, I considered how the wear and tear of constant pressure can erode the will of even the strongest minds. I knew this would be a long hike, and that it wouldn't just end when we reached the top. There would be trouble and times I would feel like giving up, but I saw this as an opportunity to demonstrate how rooted in my personal leadership I had become.

Will my knees buckle under the pressure? Surely, but I'd get back up. I planned to have falls and failures, but like I had come to realize in my battle with cancer, they were never reasons to give up, and only insisted there was more of a need for a mental fortress to house this battle blueprint that would effectively ward out the doubts and despair of adversity. Because once you can rid yourself of self-doubt and despair, adversities can then be seen as opportunities for growth.

We entered the hut, and the two guides were waiting for us there. I immediately recognized George, although it had been four years since we had met and hiked the glacier—when he and his associate also told me that I couldn't climb the mountain because I was in the middle of my struggle with chemotherapy treatments and my body was totally worn down. It was the same George who just a year ago had to cancel the climb on the mountain because of a North Pole storm that took over the island.

My eyes screened him. He looked like the same Scandinavian Viking from the old era, very tall with red, long hair and a very determined look on his face: one of a Viking warrior. He welcomed us with a hearty smile. We gave each other a brotherly hug. Accompanying George was another guide from Spain, quite far from home as you can imagine, who would soon prove himself a natural leader, guiding us through unbelievable challenges on the way to the peak.

We sat in a circle on metal folding chairs as the two men explained in detail what to expect. It wasn't long before they began loading the equipment on each of us. We were told the glacier was surrounding the mountain for about half of the way up its nearly mile-high peak of 4,800 feet. The rest of it lay under heavy snow, which he insisted was going to be very difficult and demanding to walk through. He described how we would walk tied to each other with a rope to ensure that no one fell and disappeared into one of those big rifts in the ice, some that could easily swallow an elephant.

I could see everybody intently listening, anxiety spackled on their faces, but deep in their eyes was the flame of excitement. My thoughts wandered as I considered how I was the one who "dragged" them on this once-in-a-lifetime adventure—although, at the same time, I knew they'd all jump at the offer to stand by my side! I mentally put together a string of beaded moments during the trip, recognizing that they all knew how important this was for me. My biggest test since cancer, and they're taking part in this climatic part of my life's story...

Tears were forming in my eyes. I was sentenced to death six years ago and here I was with friends about to embark on what was once merely a childhood dream. Instead, it became a vision, a representation of the day I chose to fight for my life.

I had zoned out during the guides' orientation for a few seconds, that is, until Belihun approached me and gave me a strong hug. I hadn't realized he may have been watching me—as incredible a photographer as he was, he must've captured the emotion in those moments and understood their magnitude. "Don't you ever worry. I'm behind you all the way and will guard your back."

I felt strengthened by his loyalty. My mind continued to wander as I considered my home and my ancestors, the ancient Israelites, and their arch nemesis, *Amalek*.

The Amalekites and their nation's founder, Amalek, had sneak-attacked the Israelites not long after they'd escaped by splitting the red sea. Amalek is considered the spiritual incarnation of doubt and despair—these forces may ambush you just when you feel you have escaped your pains and struggles, just when you feel a sense of success. The Amalekites did just this during the Israelites' exodus.

How can you overcome such forces? There is a shining example: It was Joshua, one of the greatest leaders and military commanders, who would conquer them. Perhaps one of the prime paragons of personal leadership, Joshua led the defense against not only the Amalekites but also doubt and despair—and prevailed. The battle lasted until dusk. For fear that the battle's tide would turn under the dark concealment of night, Moses, to whom Joshua was his protégé, raised his staff, so God would still the sun until the battle was won.

Regardless of belief, it is a remarkable story that reflected my own experience. I thought of *Sunshine*, and considered how cancer lit my battlefield until I was able to prevail, not just with my life, but with the true ability to *live my life*. Even Joshua needed encouragement. So, God said to him, "Be strong and courageous. Do not be frightened, and do not be dismayed, for the Lord your God is with you wherever you go…"

You might say your purpose is with you wherever you go. Your adversities are not meaningless and there is something for you to take from them. *Be strong and have courage.* Trust you can find what it is that you need to learn from them to move forward.

So, when it comes to personal leadership, you must be strong, brave, and have faith in your abilities to face the forces of doubt and despair. It was only when the Israelites doubted and despaired over their challenges, and when they lost their sense of self, that they stumbled.

As I have previously shown you, it was important to establish a mobile stronghold within myself to overcome the challenge ahead. It would contain a place where my mental trophy room would remind me of my achievements and capabilities, and there was a special spot on the shelf for this one. The fortress would protect all I had fought so hard for.

REACHING THE SUMMIT

It was awe inspiring to feel so small at the bottom of the mountain. Have you ever stood at the foot of a skyscraper and looked all the way to its top? At the slopes of Snæfellsjökull, it felt nearly like that, and as if I was trying to set my eyes on the precise point of the peak of achievement. But the significant difference between the two is the whole of the mountain was covered with heavy fog. For a person who likes to prepare himself for challenges, this was more than a hindrance. I couldn't even imagine what the way up looked like. *Where's the damn summit?*

It took a few minutes to divide into two groups as all of us were tied to a rope through belts we wore, and thus began the journey. As the warrior-philosopher Lao Tzu once said, "a journey of a thousand miles begins with a single step," and I felt the echo of standing on my feet to take this first step to fight cancer six years ago, which now felt like thousands of miles behind me. Just before we picked up the pace, Yiftach rushed toward me and gripped my shoulder. "Remember, you have been our spiritual leader all the way to Iceland, to this very moment, and we are here to support you. So don't be afraid of showing us when it's too much for you."

"I am the big brother, and it feels like you taught and watched me learning how to walk."

"And you showed me how the mind can be strengthened more than any muscle. The mind moves and the body follows." His words were the backwind that pushed me forward.

And the more I focused on my friends, the greater sense of reward was felt from climbing this rope—the determined sense of challenge was near intoxicating and fueled the fires of ambition.

From the first dozens of feet, I noticed the surreal swirl of mist and fog shrouding our surroundings, where you could hardly see the person in front of you. We followed the constant instruction of our guides, who not only directed us, but also warned us of the rifts in the ice sheets.

It was a tough start. I had to get used to walking with heavy boots, crampons crunching into the ice, freezing wind blowing in my face, heavy layers of clothing to protect me, and a heavy bag of equipment on my back, but the toughest of all was walking tied to a rope to the person in front of me and behind me. Each time one of us slipped and fell on the ice, we all had to stop and reorganize. And guess who fell more than the others? This was my rope tool, which I had visualized during my fight against cancer, come to life.

Ambition is a key feature for utilizing the rope tool, but it seemed now to show that as you actively lead yourself with a fierce grip on life, there is a security of doing it with others, and no one wants to feel like dead weight. We were all there for each other, and it increased accountability—there were increased stakes—and we would stake our flag at the mountaintop together. Nearly four hours later, we made it to the middle section of the climb.

This is where the ice gradually turned into very deep snow. If we thought it was going to get easier because we weren't walking on ice anymore, we really knew nothing.

Every time you took a step, your leg would get stuck in 12 to 20 inches of snow, and the challenge of pulling it out to take the next step was like a never-ending exercise at the gym. It reminded me of my goofy marches with Yiftach when I could barely walk.

The fog was getting heavier and thicker if that was even possible, and while the grip on the ground in snow felt better than when walking on ice, this was a bigger burden on my knees. I tried as much as I could to ignore the fact that the nerves in my knees were still disabled by 20%, but the pain became unbearable.

We were halfway to the top, and I already felt as if I lost most of my bodily energy. My mental radar picked up some dread lurking in the fog. Could I make it to the top? *It hurts so badly. I don't know if I can go on like this for much longer.* I wanted to stop. Maybe just a little break, but some part of me knew that as soon as I did stop, I would be ambushed by a sense of despair.

Then I remembered Belihun, Yiftach, Yan, Zachi, Ira, Iko, Avishai, and Oded—the shared commitment we all had. Watching their determination drew mine out. It was like a challenge in and of itself. I pushed myself even harder, and I wouldn't be cutting anyone any slack.

Yiftach and Zachi had been the dynamic duo pulling their weight. Zachi, with all his experience running, seemed to be leveraging his own strengths for the sake of us all. The silent leader was now a shining example for us all, along with the determined and optimistic Yiftach—they were two candles blazing brighter together than on their own.

We trekked on for what felt like an eternity. George called out that we had less than 800 feet to the summit, and an electric shock seemed to course through the rope. It was in that very moment, when I was feeling that I might not be able to make it to the summit, that something shocked and powered my mental systems back online.

Ira suddenly stumbled and fell. Obviously, when one of us falls all the others must stop since we are tied by a rope. She could get to her feet, but her face was covered in frustration, and I felt what must've been the same inclination to just give up and roll down the mountain in those moments.

George called out to her, "Do you need to rest?! It's okay, we can stop here before we climb the last part of the peak."

All I needed was to see another person struggling, in need of support and encouragement, to forget that just a few seconds ago I felt like stopping altogether too.

I turned to her. "Ira, look at me, you are younger than me by almost 20 years. Now if I can do this, you can also! Just look at me, Ira—maybe I don't have many wrinkles, but my body is weak, I have terrible pain in my knees, but it's still up to my mind and soul to tell my body what to do."

I continued: "Tell your body that it needs to serve the goal that you've put ahead of it. Now, look around you and see your friends who are also struggling. They may not show it, but if you ask them—one by one—they'll tell you that the challenge is terribly tough for them, just as it is for you."

She looked around her and the others nodded their heads in agreement.

"We're in this together!" Yan shouted.

Ira looked at me, still struggling to mentally uplift herself. "How can you just ignore what your body is telling you?"

I freed my grip on the rope and approached her. "I did not ignore what my body was telling me. It is not like running a horse to death. Instead, it is my body that reminds me I need to keep on leading it to the goal—it's nearly in your grasp. So, whenever you feel you're about to lose your grip on the reins, reconnect with your sense of leadership—the ownership over your body and attitude—reconnect with the reason you are doing this. Then, your body will follow."

Ira gave me a hug. "Keep up, old man. Let's see you put your money where your mouth is!" I noticed George looked pleased as she stepped back in line. "I'm okay! Let's move on!"

Ira was reenergized. It was now clear to me; the rope tool could be used to pull up others as much as oneself.

It took another hour climbing Snæfellsjökull until our guides announced that the summit was right around the next bend. I felt my heart skip a beat, my eyes darting around the thick fog, looking for any evidence of this. I couldn't tell if we were at the beginning or the end. The guides could have walked us in circles, and we wouldn't have known any better. Earlier, I was told that you know you're on the summit of the mountain when you see two razor sharp rocks, one at each side of the peak. Two pointed rocks that from a distance looked like the horns of a Viking's helmets. This was the reason local Icelanders called it the King of The Mountains.

It was the final approach. Just as it was with fighting cancer, recovering my ability to walk, the Haifa Night Race, the International Open Games competition, reigniting the ILI, and everything in between—the final stretch showed me yet again that there is a source of energy deep in one's soul that turns the rope into wings.

My senses heightened, anticipating one of the most beautiful moments in my entire life. I felt tears but couldn't tell if they were from pain or pure joy. The fog blanketed our surroundings, but as if God's hands fanned it away, golden sunshine burst through, refracting against the snow like diamond dust. We all could clearly see we were standing between the two rocks, the king's crown, looking down at the slopes as if they were some silky snow raiment. The midnight sun presented the most incredible light in what was the darkest part of the night. *Thank you, Sunshine.*

The sun had hidden its face on my first glacier hike of Sólheimajökull, five years ago. It was as if the ultimate good that came from my cancer was still concealed from me at the time. And now, the truth was in full bloom. I would never have reached this height if I had not fallen so low into the abyss. I would not be in such a position where I could shine my light on others—I considered all the opportunities that lay ahead of me at this very moment.

A passage from the Torah echoed inside my mind: "May the Lord bless you and keep you; the Lord make his face shine on you and be gracious to you; the Lord turn his face toward you and give you peace" (Numbers 6:24-26). I was in a daze while everyone hugged, shouted, and took pictures—I wondered if we'd caused an avalanche with all the ruckuses! I needed a moment to process what we had just achieved, so I stepped off to the side and opened my hands wide, my eyes closed, and I whispered to God.

"Thank you, God! You gave me another chance to live. To live and help my parents return to you, I know they're here with me now, Mama, Dad—you've given me the chance to help others find their way—to find themselves."

Words failed; It was difficult to express something I had never felt before.

My body shook. As I stood in silence, I felt a strong hug, opened my eyes, and there was Belihun. "I can't even explain to you how my heart melted when I heard you speaking to God, thanking him."

I continued to cry. "We did it, Belihun! We did it!" Everyone else had crowded around, nearly knocking each other over with all the excitement. Somehow, we must've forgotten how exhausted we were. I tried to cling onto this moment as long as I could before we were prompted by our guides to make our descent. It was strange. This moment was so small in the grand scheme of things that I wondered what could possibly be any more exciting thereafter. It is a time someone might say, "This is the happiest moment of my life," but with a bitter aftertaste, as if what follows would never reach such heights again. This is perhaps only if you live for happiness. Instead, if you live for a meaningful purpose, there is not enough time on earth to exhaust it. Joy will follow.

As we began our first steps down, our mood declined along with our energy. The fog had quickly returned. Descending was much more painful on my knees than going up, which oddly distracted me from the pain in my hands. It was a rapid shift from metaphorically climbing the rope to trying to keep myself from falling over flat on my face. I imagined myself cranking the cord on a faulty parachute. A great deal was at stake since I was tied to other people who were also struggling.

My first fall turned heads and I quickly fought to my feet before my friends could offer a hand. I knew there was a deeper concern for me because of my medical history. It was a critical time to show myself and others that I could keep pace, and if all else failed, I knew they'd come to my aid.

It was clear to me that there was no choice, I couldn't stop, yet the thoughts that I should and would were unrelenting. I should have known the descent would have been exponentially more difficult for me. *If you keep falling, you're going to pull everyone down with you.* This concern was as much about my mentality as collapsing on my rear end.

It reminded me that even when you've just experienced some miraculous moment—something that reminds you everything is more than okay—you can easily just slip into an attitude of defeat and despair, as if it never happened at all. With that old attitude of *every day is an island unto itself,* it made me more susceptible to this forgetfulness. But now that I viewed life as a constant path of renewal and growth, I could look below me as if on a ladder and see the mighty roots I had grown into my innermost self. I was grounded in my personal leadership. Each day was a rung on the ladder to something more.

I was wavering but not in a mental freefall. Many times, during my battle with cancer and renewing my body, mind, and spirit, I certainly felt I would plummet into the middle of the earth. As I fell down a few more times while we were descending, I noticed a stronger sense of determination and control. This wasn't an isolated event. I had my literal backpack of supplies and equipment, but another one I wore on my mind. In this one, was all the growth and mental tools I had honed and sharpened throughout my entire life. I didn't feel like I was falling. It felt more like I was using a paraglider now, directing myself with a newfound focus—there was a conscious choice in where I would land. *What am I learning from this? Where do I need to land to best see this lesson?* These thoughts helped steer me toward a softer landing. I was transcending the pain and fighting disorientation by grounding myself into the moment.

Whenever you feel you're falling, seek a graceful landing. Sometimes you can treat new challenges and unknowns as if it requires a whole new skillset, but the tools of personal leadership are meant for any job. As soon as you get back up from any fall, you'll need to keep moving forward into the next chapter of your life and not spend several pages writing around the key lessons. Don't worry… we're getting closer to the last and final tool!

◆ ◆ ◆

What goes up must come down. This contrast between the highs and lows of life boggled me as we all continued to struggle down the snowy slopes of the mountain. It may seem like the constant gravity of life can try and keep you from prospering and feeling joy, but you could say that it is because of this resistance that there is meaning and joy at all. The farther we went down the mountain, the further my mind drifted into the future, but all I could see was a veil of fog. That pinnacle moment of light with the sun celebrating our triumph was useless against the mists and twists and turns ahead of us.

This was a whole separate challenge that required the compass.

There was such a contrast between how I felt ascending and summiting Snæfellsjökull and the hardship and vision going down. The pain remained but I felt every step was like God turned the earth's gravity dial up several notches. I wasn't the only one who struggled going down from the mountain; it's a really a tough experience no matter what age you are and what shape you're in. I noticed the severity on everyone's faces. You could see the struggle was more in the mind for each one of us. I wondered what they were thinking, what Yiftach and Belihun were wondering about what's next in their lives, what Ira was seeing in her own future, what Iko and Yan, and Oded were imagining. Zachi and Avishai… the greatest difference between ascending and descending was that without another mountain peak in sight, ambition could sizzle out. It was a different kind of battle.

Everyone had their fair share of slips. As we advanced downward, the fog was slowly disappearing. My eyes were searching like little spotlights seeking the little village we left more than twelve hours ago, and where sweet and warm beds awaited us. I knew we would not see the village for a long while yet, but I knew that there's a compass that would lead us in life and that it was leading us home now. We could trust it. And more importantly, even if a surprising new hardship would follow this victory, it could be a challenge that would bring us to even greater heights. I learned to accept that the unknown is sometimes better left as such. I'd rather believe in the mystery of opportunity than think that nothing might be there.

This is how it goes. I said to myself. If one wishes to aspire to greatness in life, to overcome significant problems that seem to be the greatest challenges ever, one must know that while there are victorious days, they may be followed by bad ones. It's a cycle and needs to be completed, just as the sun and moon share the sky.

A few hours later, the end was in sight. It was a mild moment, and nothing in comparison to what we felt at the top. We were back at the cars, taking off all our equipment. I felt like the excitement and adrenaline would soon wear off and the reality we were up for several hours beyond our bedtimes would come crashing down on us like an avalanche.

We were all driving back to the house. Everybody was silent, digesting the adventure. There was a short stop at the climber's hut, and then we headed home. It was almost 4 o'clock in the morning, and I was sure that everybody would dive immediately into their beds. "Goodnight, everyone! I am not setting my alarm, so don't take its place in the morning—or afternoon." I made a beeline for my room, but just as I reached for the door, Yiftach said, "I'm not going to sleep now! We have this huge jacuzzi outside, and that is where we should be right now, Eeki."

I looked at him like he was crazy. Had he lost his mind on the mountain? He grabbed my arm, and everyone followed his lead. "What are you all thinking? Did you just climb that mountain with me or not?"

"It is time to celebrate!" Yan pumped a fist. Even Zachi didn't hesitate to go, and I then knew I couldn't say no. I brought this rowdy bunch here, having poured excitement and encouragement from the beginning, but when I wasn't shining so bright like a sun, I soon reflected their energies like a moon. It seemed the roles had reversed, and now they were inspiring me. It was a lighthouse moment. Going down the mountain felt like the sun setting for me, what was next in life? My compass had led me through this mental fog of uncertainty, but now these friends around me were lighting my way forward. Something stirred within me. My brain started putting the pieces together. Something was in store for me back home.

The jacuzzi was so big outside that we could easily enjoy enough space and the jet streams. It was surreal. There we were, lying in hot water of about 100 degrees Fahrenheit while outside it was freezing cold (well, it's

Iceland, isn't it?) at 4 a.m. and the sun was already up. It was a reminder to always look for the lighthouses in life, those around you that are exuding their personal leadership.

What I had shown from the beginning came full circle when my friends shared their light and leadership. It was in the conversations that followed which solidified this for me. I felt a great sense of pride hearing them laughing, chatting, and planning what they would do next when they got back home. They seemed so excited about life when typically, the dread of a vacation's end would bring down the mood. Looking around at these young leaders that followed my call to go to Iceland and allowed me to lead them through this trip I had carefully planned and scheduled for nine days—and most of all—to fulfill my dream of conquering the mountain, made me melt into a mushy sentimental mess.

A short two days later, I waved farewell to the snow-covered peaks of Iceland from the window of the airplane. Heading back home after this epic journey allowed so many thoughts and ideas for the future to flood my brain. My friends had reignited my ambition when my tank was nearly drained.

As I looked upon the clouds, I realized one thing was clear: After I stood up to this challenge, five years after I first hoped to climb Snæfellsjökull and three years after I rose from the wheelchair—nothing was going to be the same again.

I'm returning to Israel, to my daily life, equipped with so much energy and confidence, and with so much wisdom to share, that I'm going to break all barriers and fulfill my mission of training people to grow their personal leadership. I had taught and trained leadership, but God knew I wasn't walking my own path. There were old wounds and ways of living that were killing me, but now I had renewed myself and understood my purpose had come full circle.

It wasn't only me being reborn. Not even a week later, I was on my way to meet my students at the first ILI workshop in more than three years. All along, it had felt like I was estranged from what I imagined were my own children.

I wasn't expecting what awaited me. My training partners and students all stood and clapped when I walked into the classroom. There was a huge bouquet of flowers and a colorful sign hanging from the ceiling: "Welcome

Back, Hero." I couldn't resist the tears pouring from my eyes. I hugged them like they were each a long-lost love.

I asked them to sit, thanked them, and promised to talk about my trip during our break in two hours. The workshop was about "decision-making" and we needed to dive into it immediately.

Well, I decided to do something else. As I was looking at each one of their faces, beginning to talk about personal leadership and the core role of decision-making, I felt I needed to ditch the plan on the syllabus. There was another story I needed to tell, not my usual opener.

"Change of plans, everyone." I surveyed the room seeing so many intrigued faces. "I have been imagining how this class would be in my head for a few years, but this image quickly changed after my recent trip to Iceland. So, I am going to share with you a story how I developed ten mental tools that renewed my life as I created and led myself on my path of personal leadership."

LOVE LETTER TO YOU

Dearest Reader,

I know you have patiently waited to see what this tenth tool could possibly be.

I needed to show you the prior nine beforehand because the mirror is the most important, yet it's dependent on each one before it. I want you to see something I am envisioning right now as I write these words to you: I am seeing a leader, someone who can brave the wilds of their life and replace the fear with the strength and courage that has always existed within them. I see someone who has been freed and continues to liberate themselves from all the doubts and despairs of life that seek to destroy it.

There were so many times I wanted to give up. I would diminish the importance and meaning of my life's path. I would weep and feel my grip slipping, my knees buckling, but the constant pain became the greatest reminder that I was not where I needed to be. Four different doctors told me I had six months to live, and I've now been alive for more than seven.

I would have died without realizing that these leadership tools applied to me. They helped me grow and showed me how to live. I give my life as a gift to you. I ask you to take a private moment and find a mirror. You can do it now—there is no need to wait.

And as you look at your reflection, find your eyes and focus on them. If you cannot see, envision this in your mind's eye.

Whatever you do, do not stray and look away. Eye contact is often difficult with other people as it is so intimate. Now is the time to become comfortable with your reflection and to see the galaxy behind your eyes. There is a leader inside you. There is life that is precious and has purpose. You are someone with the greatest gift to give to others, but only if you see the value in yourself. Keep looking. Push past the histories, hurts, and judgments, and express your love and gratitude for the person you see before you. Continue searching. What you know of this person represents only one planet in a galaxy of growth and potential.

As you feel the connection of your eyes weakening, don't retreat. Instead, push yourself to see your inner strength, which will reveal itself. Everything you need to overcome your struggles is inside you. You are looking at the co-author of your life.

My story is a reflection of what you can achieve in life. My victory is representative of what you will find—even when all looks lost and broken—if only you allow yourself to expose and unleash what's inside you. Use the tool of the mirror and learn to love what you see with compassion, understanding, and hope for your future.

One of the greatest insights I learned from my cancer was that I had not fully lived my life. I was held down by traumas, doubts, and the unwillingness to take a deep look into my soul and nurture it. I wasn't achieving my full potential, but once I chose to fight for my life, I would need to remind myself who I was fighting for—the person in the mirror and all the people that would be inspired and uplifted by this journey.

The mirror is the most accessible tool. It is a reflection that all the others already exist inside you, but simply need to be practiced. I used to be afraid to look inside myself, but it has become so much easier to see the blessing I am, and what I have been blessed with. I knew God expected more from me, but it did not matter if I did not. When you suffer, when you hurt, when you are angry, you care, it is a sign of strength, it is a reminder you are not where you should be.

Liberate yourself by looking in the mirror and seeing the blessing before you. The tools are there. Just imagine what I had found was good enough to beat cancer and live to tell the tale to you. I fought for this story, so I could see yours brighten. Now, go look into yourself and see what I see—the beginning of a struggle for your accomplished life. Take the reins. I'm here with you.

Lead the way.

Tool Manual

This section of the book serves as a brief overview and beginners guide to your toolbox. Reading the chapters of this book is necessary to make use of its tools, and to become an expert, you must practice them for your own purposes. True to the principles of personal leadership, there is no one other than yourself that can sculpt your destiny. Record your responses to each prompt and revisit them as needed to forge your brighter future.

THE TOOLS:

Tool 1:   Take the Reins
Tool 2:   The Uniform
Tool 3:   The Library
Tool 4:   The Blueprint
Tool 5:   The Fortress
Tool 6:   The Rope
Tool 7:   The Parachute
Tool 8:   The Compass
Tool 9:   The Lighthouse
Tool 10: The Mirror

Tool 1: Take the Reins

The golden rule for taking the reins is to declare that you are going to fight for your life.

Call to action:
Your mission is to remind yourself what is worth fighting for in your life. Create a comprehensive list and elaborate on each item's importance.

Tool 2: The Uniform

Wear the uniform to identify as leader by modeling your personal leadership.

Call to action:
You want to model your leadership? Count all your capabilities and match them to current challenges and goals that you have.

Tool 3: The Library

Taking a journey through the chapters of your life without regrets will bring a better understanding of what lessons you learned and earned, so that you more clearly see the path ahead of you. Your life's library contains the books of knowledge you need.

Call to action:
Identify what you consider to be the major hardships and mistakes of your past, and explain what choices led to and from there and what other options were present at the given time. For each, derive and describe the wisdom earned.

Tool 4: The Blueprint

Your whole being is an inventory. It contains all the personal assets in your life including the non-material; the values that drive you; strengths and areas of growth; your allies you've made; and your goals and desires.

Call to action:
Inventory and design the protocols for managing your expectations and actions. Create a visual display of this. Then, list the choices of what is worth abstaining, maintaining, and obtaining in your life.

Tool 5: The Fortress

Burying the victimhood and survivalist mentality and stepping out of your mental walls is vital to expanding your life beyond your perceived limitations.

Call to action:

Make a list of the following: your areas of needed growth, your maladaptive behaviors, your vulnerabilities, and your personal and interpersonal barriers and boundaries. Then create a separate list that revises and reworks them into your desired improvements.

This will become your personal constitution to be housed in a place where others can't damage it.

Tool 6: The Rope

Use the rope to pull yourself toward desired and beneficial thoughts away from hopelessness, defeatism, and despair. Push doubts, negativity, and distractions out of the way. Think of this as a physical effort in your brain just like climbing a rope.

Call to action:

What new challenges can you dare yourself to take on? Accept and commit to achieving them. Sequence their fulfillment. Explain why you chose them and what growth you can derive from the created experiences?

Tool 7: The Parachute

As temporary downturns occur during your passage toward personal leadership, create "wind resistance" for negative thoughts by using your leadership persona to narrate your thoughts, so that you may better mentally and emotionally regulate. Also, don't restlessly wait and hope for resolutions, instead develop the resolve to find them by guiding your descents into higher ascents.

Call to action:
Speak to yourself as a guide, mentor, and confident leader. Create an inner monologue that turns the parachute into a paraglider that will secure a softer landing. Write down the words that create your new self-language.

Tool 8: The Compass

When the future seems clouded, you still have your compass to help you find your way around using your innate sense of direction. The indecision and divisiveness formed between your heart and mind is united and clarified by the compass, so that you may move toward your true north.

Call to action:
Identify cases in your life where your heart told you to do something great and your mind opposed by mispresenting your capabilities to achieve those desired goals. This will be the key to reading your compass.

Tool 9: The Lighthouse

In a state of angst, you might find it hard to have concern and act for the better of the ones who support you, go after you, care for you, and are for and beside you. However, being a lighthouse through developing a thrill for supporting other's successes and encouraging them as a leader will allow both you and others to light the way ahead.

Call to action:

Make a list of what you can give and how you can support your significant friends and allies. Commit yourself to giving as a leader but also graciously receiving and allowing them to follow you and expand their own leadership.

Tool 10: The Mirror

Remind yourself every day of your victories and what strengths led to them. Look deep through the root of your development and how certain challenges nurture your core traits and competencies.

Call to action:
Recognize that each tool presented to you during our mutual journey already exists within you and your mental toolbox. They are simply skills to develop. Describe how they will strengthen you and reveal your leadership now that you accept that they are yours and are to be used by you.

EEKI ELNER is regarded as Israel's pioneer in leadership training in the business and social world. After a career of twenty years of serving in corporate development, strategy, and marketing planning, then as an advisor to two Israeli cabinet members— Elner founded in 2008 The Israel Leadership Institute, a non-profit educational organization offering the most unique leadership training approach in Israel and the world.

When doctors gave Eeki only six months to live and diagnosed stage four lung cancer, they advised him to wrap up his affairs. But he wasn't ready to give up and stop living. After training leaders for many years, he knew he must implement his own leadership philosophy, realizing that he had to "walk his talk" to save his life. So, with the help of co-author Joshua Adams, Eeki created a narrative that presents the personal-leadership principles he had been teaching that allowed him to grow into his full potential and beat the odds.

"There is no substitute for learning more about yourself, acquiring knowledge and wisdom, practicing new skills, and developing your potential for greatness. Building leadership awareness is critical to professional progress and personal success—essential to long-term achievements and satisfaction." — Eeki Elner

EekiElner.com

Co-author **JOSHUA ADAMS** is a licensed social worker, psychotherapist, editor, and writer. He received his MSW from The Ohio State University, where he also was juried into a creative writing program as an undergraduate.

"Creativity has helped shape my life's journey through pleasures and pains while opening my eyes to discover God's meaning in them. I believe the best help you can get is your willingness to get help.

The day I met Eeki Elner was the day I helped myself to his tutelage and tools of personal leadership to renew my own path after a life of many challenges. There's something for everyone to learn from his story as there's perhaps nothing more universal in the human experience as dying to live."

Adams has taken this journey with Eeki Elner to share the remarkable story and mental tools that helped spare Elner's life. He is a co-presenter with Eeki in leadership workshops stemming from the book.